OBLOMOV *and his Creator*

Studies of the Russian Institute
Columbia University

OBLOMOV
AND HIS CREATOR

The Life and Art of
Ivan Goncharov

By Milton Ehre

PRINCETON UNIVERSITY PRESS
PRINCETON, NEW JERSEY

Copyright © 1973
by Princeton University Press
All Rights Reserved
LCC: 72-5378
ISBN: 0-691-06245-5

Library of Congress Cataloging in Publication
data will be found on the last printed page
of this book.

This book has been composed in Linotype Caslon Old Face

Printed in the United States of America
by Princeton University Press,
Princeton, New Jersey

The Russian Institute of Columbia University
sponsors the *Studies of the Russian Institute*
in the belief that their publication contributes
to scholarly research and public understanding.
In this way the Institute, while not necessarily
endorsing their conclusions, is pleased to make
available the results of some of the research
conducted under its auspices. A list of the
Studies of the Russian Institute appears at the
back of the book.

To my wife

PREFACE

AN AMERICAN comedian says that he uses the title *Oblomov* as a test of intellectual pretension—to see whether his interlocutor will respond "Goncharov"; a distinguished member of the Royal Society of Literature of the United Kingdom confesses that for a long time he could not remember whether Goncharov wrote *Oblomov* or Oblomov wrote Goncharov. Clearly we do not know the writer or his work well enough. Russians may know him too well. His novels— *A Common Story*, *Oblomov*, and *The Ravine*[1]—and a volume of travel sketches entitled *The Frigate Pallas* have remained popular ever since their publication, and his masterpiece *Oblomov* has become standard reading fare in Russian schools. Mention it to a Russian and it is very likely that he will respond with "Oblomovism"—a term from the novel that has entered the language to indicate, in the translation from Smirnitsky's dictionary, "sluggishness, apathy, inertness." It has also become a critical catchword for the condition of the Russian gentry, Russian backwardness, and even the Russian soul.

The purpose of this book is twofold: to make a major Russian novelist of the nineteenth century more familiar to those who know him only through *Oblomov*, and to reach beyond the standard clichés of Goncharov criticism to a contemporary reading of his art. The best of modern literary criticism proceeds from the assumption that the meanings of art are intimately related to their forms, and the assumption guides this book. Goncharov's works are discussed with close attention to style, structure, and distinctions of genre, not as ends in themselves, but to penetrate to their implications for an understanding

[1] *Obryv*, the title of Goncharov's final novel, properly means "a precipice," but I have chosen to follow André Mazon's lead and call it *The Ravine*, which better approximates the place described in the work.

of his themes and his view of experience. An introductory chapter provides a historical and biographical context for the scrutiny of individual works which follows. This introductory chapter summarizes some of the traditional arguments of Goncharov criticism—which are by no means all wrong—and states the major themes of this book. It makes use of material accumulated by energetic Soviet scholars in recent years, which were unknown to Goncharov's previous biographers, and offers several new interpretations of aspects of his complex personality. It also suggests connections between the novelist's life and his art, a subject that is resumed in a later summary of his trilogy of novels. I have chosen to keep art and life apart, because, though I believed that a historical and biographical context would explain much, I did not wish to lose sight of those qualities which make Goncharov, like any writer who survives, our contemporary.

Translations of quotations are my own unless specified otherwise. Transliterations follow a modified version of the British Standard System intended for the convenience of the general reader. Important adaptions are: indications of soft signs are omitted from names of persons in the text but are retained in footnote and bibliographical references; "y" is used for "ĭ," and for "yĭ" and "ĭĭ" at the ends of names (Dostoevsky, not Dostoevskiĭ; "ë" is rendered as "e" in surnames and "yo/o" elsewhere. Where a conventional English spelling exists, it is usually given preference.

I am fortunate in having colleagues in the study of Russian literature who are gracious in sharing their considerable knowledge and insights, and I am grateful to all who taught, advised, and encouraged me. I would be remiss, however, if I did not mention for thanks Professors Robert Belknap, Fruma Gottschalk, Richard Gregg, William Harkins, Hugh McLean, Rufus Mathewson, Ralph Matlaw, and Edward Wasiolek, who read the manuscript at various stages and made valuable suggestions. Thanks are also due to Mr. Vaclav Laska, the Slavic bibliographer at the University of Chicago, who took pains to acquire materials I needed, and Professor Richard Wortman, who advised me upon the historical background. Grants from the American Philosophical Society and the National Endowment for the Humanities assisted me through two summers of research and writing, and a grant from the American Council of Learned Societies permitted me to make substantial progress in my labors through six months free from academic duties. I appreciate their generosity and interest. I thank Mrs. Juanita Denson, Miss Jean Hall, and Miss Karen Summers for typing the final manuscript. Finally, I must express my gratitude to a friend, Gerd Fenchel, and to my wife for much.

Chapter two originally appeared in a slightly different version under the title, "Ivan Goncharov on Art, Literature, and the Novel," in the *Slavic Review*, XXIX, No. 2 (June 1970), 203-218; chapter four, also in a slightly different version entitled, "Goncharov's Early Prose Fiction," in the *Slavonic and East European Review*, L, No. 120 (July 1972), 359-371, published by the Cambridge University Press. A quotation from Samuel Beckett's *Waiting for Godot* is reprinted by permission of Grove Press, Inc., copyright 1954 by Grove Press, Inc.; a quotation from T. S. Eliot's "Burnt Norton," in *Four Quartets*, copyright 1943 by T. S. Eliot, is reprinted by permission of Harcourt Brace Jovanovich, Inc.

Contents

OBLOMOV *and his Creator*

CHAPTER I

A Portrait of the Artist

A gentleman . . . with the soul of a bureaucrat, without ideas and with the eyes of a boiled fish, upon whom God, as if for a joke, has bestowed brilliant talent.

Fyodor Dostoevsky[1]

He had his unpleasant sides which were caused by proud seclusion, and he was a profoundly unhappy man in his domestic surroundings to which he clung with hands grown numb from terror of loneliness. But when he was in high spirits . . . he was interesting, and instructive in manner, and touching in the mute plaints of his heart begging for love.

Anatoly Koni[2]

Nature gave me delicate and sensitive nerves—hence that terrible impressionability and feverishness of my entire character; no one ever understood this—. . . they [could] not decide what I am!—a dissembler, an actor, or a madman, or whether it is only the power of imagination, intelligence, and feeling that, sparkling diversely, struggles out of me and plays, while crying out . . . for a form. . . .

Ivan Goncharov[3]

GONCHAR[4] is the Russian word for "a potter," and in the distant past the Goncharovs may have been artisans. At least since the early part of the eighteenth century they lived by trade, mostly of grain, in the

---

[1] Letter to A. E. Vrangel', November 9, 1856, *Pis'ma*, ed. A. S. Dolinin (Moscow-Leningrad, 1928-1959), I, 199.

[2] Letter to E. P. Letkovaya-Sultanovaya, June 11, 1898, *Russkaya literatura*, No. 1 (1969), p. 170.

[3] Letter to M. M. Stasyulevich, June 13, 1868, *M. M. Stasyulevich i ego sovremenniki v ikh perepiske*, ed. M. K. Lemke (St. Petersburg, 1911-1913), IV, 22.

[4] Dates throughout, unless cited otherwise, are according to A. D. Alekseev, *Letopis' zhizni i tvorchestva I. A. Goncharova* (Moscow-Leningrad, 1960),

middle Volga town of Simbirsk (now Ulyanovsk). They were fairly successful at it, but either not venturesome or not lucky enough to accumulate significant capital. A massive stone house in the middle of a town where most homes were still of wood provided the most tangible sign of their prosperity. Simbirsk, though a provincial center, still had the look of a village while Ivan Goncharov was growing up, and the Goncharov home possessed many of the trappings of the rural estates of the gentry surrounding the town—barns, stables, huts for the domestic serfs, orchards, a garden. What it lacked were large expanses of land and the numerous field serfs found in the country.[5] Later the novelist showed little interest in nature or the life of the peasantry.

In addition to owning a home that somewhat resembled an estate of the gentry, the Goncharovs had managed in the middle of the eighteenth century to become legal members of that class. Ivan's paternal grandfather, Ivan Ivanovich Goncharov, had served in the

---

and *Bibliografiya I. A. Goncharova* (Leningrad, 1968). They have been left in the Old Style of the Julian calendar, twelve days behind the Gregorian calendar. Two editions of Goncharov's collected works are used conjointly— more frequently, *Sobranie sochineniy*, 8 vols. (Moscow: Goslitizdat, 1952-1955), and, when necessary, *Sobranie sochineniy*, 8 vols. (Moscow: Pravda, Biblioteka Ogonyok, 1952). They will be referred to as *Sobr. soch.* with the addition of (Pravda) to distinguish the latter edition from the former. Sources for Goncharov's life and times are cited at relevant points. Though the two large biographies of Goncharov are outdated in their approaches and incomplete, they were often helpful. The more sensible and scrupulous is André Mazon's *Ivan Gontcharov: un maître du roman russe* (Paris, 1914). E. Lyatsky's *Roman i zhizn': razvitie tvorcheskoy lichnosti I. A. Goncharova* (Prague, 1925) includes much valuable material. Soviet scholars are less interested in Goncharov's psychology than in the social context of his art. A. G. Tseytlin's *I. A. Goncharov* (Moscow, 1950) presents a great deal of new information accumulated in the Soviet period.

[5] Ivan Goncharov's father was a merchant of the third guild, which meant that his capital was from one to five thousand rubles. P. S. Beysov, *Goncharov i rodnoy kray* (2d edn. rev.; Kuybyshev, 1960), p. 123. The novelist described the Simbirsk of his childhood in "Na rodine," *Sobr. soch.*, VII, 224-315. For a contemporary's description of the Goncharov home, see G. N. Potanin, "Vospominaniya ob I. A. Goncharove," in *I. A. Goncharov v vospominaniyakh sovremennikov*, ed. N. K. Piksanov (Leningrad, 1969), p. 23.

military and worked his way up through the ranks to become an infantry officer. His achievement gave him the official status of a "gentleman." It is doubtful, though, that *parvenus* like the Goncharovs had even begun to attain the cultural refinement and delicacy of manner that legend ascribes to the gentry but that in a backward country like Russia more often than not remained unrealized ideals. Despite his newly won status, Ivan Ivanovich retained legal membership in the merchant class and continued to live by trade. Russian merchants of those years little resembled the individualistic bourgeoisie of the West, who sought to dominate politics and culture as well as business. Living in a semi-feudal society, they usually shared the traditional customs and beliefs of the peasantry about them, especially in a sleepy backwater town like Simbirsk. As late as the middle of the nineteenth century the critic Nikolay Dobrolyubov's appellation "dark kingdom" for the society of backward and superstitious provincial merchants depicted in Ostrovsky's plays struck a chord in Russian readers. The Goncharovs may also have been Old Believers,[6] as many merchants were, and Old Believers, among the most tradition-minded of Russian Christians, tended to be deeply suspicious of anything resembling secular culture.

Undoubtedly the grandfather was above the run-of-the-mill—he was literate and ambitious enough to have wanted to improve his family's situation. Also Ivan Ivanovich began a family chronicle—one of the very few sources of information about the Goncharov family—in which he displayed a modicum of interest in the world beyond his granaries and barnyards. Alongside the expected announcements of births, weddings, and deaths are quotations from religious texts, occasional notations of exceptional natural phenomena, and mention of outstanding historical events such as the Pugachev rebellion, which reached the outskirts of Simbirsk. However, the mechanical manner in which events are recorded in the chronicle, its dry matter-of-fact tone and lack of any embellishment, suggest a man whose vital concerns did not extend far beyond family and business. This may be the nature of a family chronicle. Nevertheless, the impression remains

[6] M. Superansky, "Ivan Aleksandrovich Goncharov i novye materialy dlya ego biografii," *Vestnik Evropy*, No. 11 (November 1908), p. 24.

5

that language in the home of the future novelist, in its written form, was largely a tool for practical ends—whether to make inventories of sacks of grain or to keep track of the doings of the family.[7]

Ivan Goncharov's father, Alexander Ivanovich, continued the family grain trade, also owned a candle factory, and was several times elected to serve as mayor (*gorodskoy golova*) of Simbirsk.[8] Though his election would suggest that he was a fairly capable and ambitious man, we can assume that his intellectual and cultural horizons had not expanded significantly beyond those of the grandfather. Such posts in Tsarist Russia offered limited responsibilities and required little education. Ivan was only seven when his father died in 1819 at the age of sixty-five, and he seems to have forgotten him.

The novelist's mother, who was nineteen when she married the fifty-year-old Alexander (it was his second marriage), was also of the merchant class, but in Mazon's phrase *plus peuple que bourgeoise*.[9] Her responsibilities in managing a large household of servants and children (four survived out of six) did not permit Avdotya Matveevna to supplement her meager education with that modicum of knowledge of the affairs of the world the Goncharov men had been able to achieve. Nevertheless, Ivan adored his mother—"*there is nothing and no one about whom my thoughts are so bright, my memories so sacred, as of her*" (italics in original) he wrote his sister Alexandra on the occasion of her death.[10] The ways in which he remembered her and the terms in which he stated his adoration are important and revealing. It was not, of course, for any qualities of mind or imagination that the writer admired her, though he considered her intelligent; nor was it an unusual capacity for maternal warmth and tenderness that stirred him. Instead, whenever Goncharov went beyond a vague expression of affection to particulars, it was always her talents for

---

[7] The "Letopisets" has been published in part by Superansky, *ibid.*, No. 2 (February 1907), pp. 574-577, and Beysov, pp. 121-124.

[8] *Vestnik Evropy*, No. 11 (November 1908), p. 24. *Goncharov v vospominaniyakh*, p. 23.

[9] Mazon, p. 6.

[10] To A. A. Kirmalova, May 5, 1851, *Vestnik Evropy*, No. 2 (February 1907), p. 587.

housekeeping that he commended. His mother was "an excellent, experienced, and strict housekeeper," he recalled in his reminiscences; ". . . her work was so strictly executed," he exclaimed in eulogizing her to Alexandra. The frequency of the modifier "strict" or "severe" is striking. She loved her children, but with "strict justice." Faced with breaches of discipline, she was "severe" and could be "implacable."[11] Did a certain reproach hide behind the epithets "strict" and "severe"? Was Avdotya Matveevna, for all her managerial talents, deficient in her ability to convey maternal warmth? The product of her upbringing points to such a conclusion, since for much of his life Ivan Goncharov behaved like a man who had received too little love as a child. Once he admitted as much, ironically in the same letter to Alexandra where he had declared the sanctity of his mother's memory, though he denied any feeling of grievance—"She loved you more than the rest of us, . . . but who of us can complain that you were singled out and we were neglected."

Mothers or maternal figures play an important role in the lives of the heroes of Goncharov's three novels. Alexander Aduev's mother in *A Common Story* (*Obyknovennaya istoriya*), Boris Raysky's great-aunt (affectionately called "grandmother") of *The Ravine* (*Obryv*), and Oblomov's housekeeper differ from their obvious prototype in a number of ways. What they have in common is an undeniable talent for maintaining an orderly and comfortable home—a virtue that in the fiction is always praiseworthy and even idealized. In the case of Oblomov's housekeeper—her name, Agafya Matveevna, points straight to the novelist's mother—the mother-substitute suffers from an almost total inability to express whatever feelings she may have. Instead, the very act of housekeeping—feeding, cleaning, caring for Oblomov—becomes her means of self-expression. When we come to the novel, we shall discover that this total absence of passion in Goncharov's most famous maternal figure, instead of being viewed as a

---

[11] *Sobr. soch.*, VII, 234. A niece of the wife of Ivan's brother Nikolay described her as "rather coarse with despotic tendencies." Nikolay's son called her "cruel." Her neighbors, however, respected her. See V. M. Chegodaeva, "Vospominaniya ob I. A. Goncharove," *Goncharov v vospominaniyakh*, p. 107, and Superansky, *Vestnik Evropy*, No. 11 (November 1908), pp. 25-26.

fault, has also been turned into a virtue, though a highly ambiguous one.

If Avdotya Matveevna was somewhat cold, it may have been because she was "suspicious" or "mistrustful," as her son Ivan once described her. Her "suspiciousness" was apparently something more acute than a mere provincial mistrust of the outside world or the traditional caution of merchants, for Goncharov goes on to call suspiciousness his "innate and inherited illness."[12] According to the novelist's nephew and Avdotya's grandson, Alexander Nikolaevich Goncharov, suspiciousness or "fear of people," as well as a susceptibility to melancholy, inertia, and apathy ran deep in the Goncharov family. Alexander felt he belonged to "a psychically sick and unstable family." He was born too late to recall his grandmother or to have known his grandfather, but family accounts told that Ivan Goncharov's father "was an abnormal man, a melancholic who often spoke incoherently and was very pious. . . ." Alexander remembered his own father, the novelist's brother Nikolay, as prone to bouts of extreme melancholy and an absentmindedness approaching total abstraction. Nikolay avoided people, behaved obsequiously before his superiors, whom he secretly resented, and was capable of "amazing suspiciousness." He would return home from his teaching duties in the Simbirsk gymnasium, where he could not control his students, and spend hours searching through the house for something or someone—no one knew what. Fearful of authority and hesitant about asserting himself, he took out his frustrations on his children, whom he beat frequently and arbitrarily. What was said to have been the extreme piety of the novelist's father was in his brother religious fanaticism and exaggerated scrupulousness over ritual detail—a Byzantine formalism, in Alexander's description, that characterized Avdotya Matveevna's home as well as her son's. Anna, the other Goncharov sister—Alexandra seems to have escaped the family malady—underwent periods of abnormality during which she would buy up great stores of material and spend days on end sewing, while slandering and abusing anyone who dared to approach. At such moments she gave vent to "fantastic

---

[12] Letter to S. A. Nikitenko, June 4, 1869, *Sobr. soch.*, VIII, 409-410.

suspicions" which, she felt, were inherent in the Goncharov family. Otherwise Anna was bright, had a sense of humor, and was "a superb housewife."[13]

The Goncharov family was not one to produce confident and independent children. Suspicious and mistrustful people—paranoids in the jargon of our day—are unlikely to permit themselves spontaneous expressions of emotion, as Avdotya Matveevna apparently did not, and will appear arbitrary to a child who has no way of understanding the rationalizations with which they justify their fears. Men tend to repeat the habits of their parents, and it is a good bet that Nikolay, whom we know more intimately than the novelist's parents, thanks to the reminiscences of his son and his former students, typified a pattern of parental behavior learned in the Goncharov household. The death of Ivan's father, coming when the boy was only seven, surely heightened the insecurity of a child already exposed to an unstable family situation. The child was separated in age from his father by almost six decades; if those family accounts the nephew heard are correct, the melancholia and self-absorption of the father made him even more distant; now the child was irrevocably separated from the father by the fact of death. Understandably he put all his hopes on his mother and turned to her in search of the security he so desperately needed. If the mother was cold, or if she really loved his sister and neglected him, the child could still see a sign of caring in her energetic devotion to housekeeping, a token of love in her dispensing of food, strength and control in her severity. The big gap was the missing father. Fathers are as conspicuously absent from Goncharov's fiction as "mothers" are omnipresent. Alexander Aduev is fatherless, Boris Raysky is an orphan, Oblomov's father appears as a dim shadowy figure in a dream. The mature Goncharov, though he was able to feel close to a number of women, tended, sooner or later, to run into

[13] *Vestnik Evropy*, No. 11 (November 1908), pp. 5-48. A. N. Goncharov's reminiscences are often discredited because of his animosity toward his famous uncle, but he had no apparent reason to libel a family of which he was a member, or his father, for whom he expresses more pity than anger. The accounts of Nikolay's former students also describe an extremely eccentric individual. See Beysov, pp. 131-132.

difficulties with his male friends, especially when they were men of accomplishment and authority such as the editor and publisher of the *European Messenger* (*Vestnik Evropy*), Mikhail Stasyulevich, or in the most famous instance of all, Ivan Turgenev.

Fortunately for Ivan Goncharov and for Russian literature, a man the novelist called his substitute-father stepped into the breach created by his father's death. The Goncharovs kept a boarder who had become very close to the family and was the godfather of all four Goncharov children. With the death of the father, Nikolay Tregubov moved from the separate building where he had resided into the great stone house and assumed responsibility for the upbringing and education of the children. Tregubov had many of the things the Goncharovs lacked—considerable wealth, education, and experience of the larger world beyond Simbirsk. He had graduated from the Russian Naval Academy and served as an officer with the Russian fleet. Ivan Goncharov remembered him as a man who was an aristocrat in manner as well as lineage; Tregubov was "everything that is well expressed by the English word 'gentleman'; . . . he was an unalloyed original of honesty, honor, and nobility. . . ."[14]

As Tregubov presented to the young Ivan an image of aristocratic refinement unknown in his own family, he was also able to introduce him to the finer aspects of the culture of the gentry. Simbirsk was something of a joke in the early nineteenth century for its provincial tedium and inactivity—"Sleep and idleness have taken complete hold of Simbirsk," Lermontov complained in "Sashka"—and the line catches Goncharov's feelings about the place. Nevertheless, many of the gentry of the area kept homes in town, and a small minority had attained to that high level of culture that permitted the gentry to set the tone of Russian civilization well into the nineteenth century. Alongside the usual run of balls and parties, those who had entrance to the salons of the local aristocracy could attend theatrical perform-ances and concerts, visit picture galleries, and meet men and women interested in art and ideas. A striking number of Russian writers—Nikolay Karamzin, the poets Ivan Dmitriev and Nikolay Yazykov,

---

[14] "Na rodine," *Sobr. soch.*, VII, 233-242. Tregubov is here called Yakubov.

Pavel Annenkov, Dmitry Grigorovich, the talented families of the Freemason Ivan Petrovich Turgenev and the novelist Sergey Aksakov—came from the Simbirsk area or had lived there.[15] Tregubov was himself something of an intellectual, though his interests turned to the physical sciences, history, and not imaginative literature. He moved in a circle of men interested in books and ideas, specifically the ideas of the French Enlightenment. One of their circle, a Prince Mikhail Barataev—from all accounts a remarkable man—had organized a local Masonic lodge called the Key to Virtue, and several members, including Tregubov, had contact with the Decembrists of the 1825 revolt. Tregubov and his friends seem to have been representative figures of the liberal segment of the gentry of the age of Catherine and Alexander I. They were cultured aristocrats, ardent disciples of Voltaire and the French Encyclopedists, men dedicated to enlightenment and the rational reform of society, who at the same time showed few scruples about owning other human beings as serfs. For the most part their liberalism proved quite ephemeral before the wave of reaction following the ascension of Nicholas to the throne.[16] It was such men, and especially Tregubov, who gave Ivan Goncharov his first important contact with liberal and humanistic ideals, as well as a glimpse of a broader and more subtle way of life than that found in a narrow, tradition-rooted merchant family.

However, Goncharov's remembrances of Tregubov are not unequivocally favorable. He recalled with fondness his godfather's indulgence and protectiveness of the Goncharov children, which "softened the strict system of maternal control over us." It was Tregubov who first cultivated the child's sensibility, for, as Goncharov ruminated in his reminiscences, indulgence, when it is not excessive, "gives birth . . . to tender feelings in the hearts of children." Yet this softness of Tregubov is also the butt of Goncharov's irony. Ultimately Tregubov and his friends are seen as congenial and charming

---

[15] See Beysov, pp. 6-20, and N. A. Derzhavin, "Na rodine I. A. Goncharova," *Istoricheskiy vestnik,* cxxviii (April-June 1912), 869-877.

[16] Beysov, pp. 22-23. M. Superansky, "Vospitanie I. A. Goncharova," *Russkaya shkola,* Nos. 5-6 (May-June 1912), pp. 14-15. Barataev appears in "Na rodine" as Bravin.

11

eccentrics, men of intelligence, culture, and generosity of spirit, who are incapable of turning their fine sentiments into constructive activity. Perhaps more important for Goncharov, they were men totally ignorant of the practical side of life. Tregubov had not the slightest idea of what was going on in his estate and left all the details of management to Avdotya Matveevna. Goncharov said that in Tregubov and his friends he had his first impression of "Oblomovism"—the term he employed in *Oblomov* for the lassitude of his "gentleman" hero.[17] If so, it is only part of the story, for the provenance of Oblomov is more complicated than the reminiscences indicate. As we shall see shortly, there was a good deal of Oblomov in Goncharov himself. Also, works of literature grow out of other works of literature as much as from life, and a comic tradition of grotesque indolence left its impress on Goncharov's creation. Oblomov undoubtedly has more in common with some of Gogol's incorrigible idlers, and Oblomovka with the landscapes of "Old World Landowners," than they have with Tregubov or Avdotya Matveevna's establishment in Simbirsk.[18] All the same, the heroes of Goncharov's fiction belong to the gentry and are, like Tregubov and his friends, men of noble sentiments and expansive natures who lack a capacity for action and a sense of the practical.

Goncharov's early biographers—Lyatsky, Mazon, Superansky—saw two distinct social worlds coinciding to shape the novelist: the traditional and narrowly practical society of the old merchant class and the milieu of the enlightened cultivated segment of the gentry—the worlds of Avdotya Matveevna and Tregubov respectively.[19] Their descriptions are still valid and important, though the effects of these diverse influences upon Goncharov were more complicated than has been supposed. He never fully reconciled the two aspects of his upbringing. On the surface he made himself into the model of a gentleman in the Tregubov mold. He received a broad humanistic education, assimilated vague ideals of enlightenment and reason,

[17] *Sobr. soch.*, VII, 235-242.

[18] See Mazon, pp. 158-163, and Tseytlin, p. 153.

[19] Lyatsky, p. 12; Mazon, pp. 12-13; Superansky, *Russkaya shkola*, Nos. 5-6 (May-June 1912), pp. 12, 16.

learned to speak French with fluency and to write a Russian that is a model of smoothness and polish. Contemporaries remembered him as a man who in society was immaculately dressed, careful in manner and speech, ironic, and reserved. As a young man he was even a bit of a dandy.[20] As the novelist became a public figure and a high official in the Tsarist bureaucracy he learned to move in the circles of the upper aristocracy, was received at court, and even served a stint as tutor to the heir apparent to the throne of the Empire. An inkstand from Alexander III in honor of his literary achievement filled him with pride.[21] Nevertheless, Goncharov always remained a bit of an outsider in the world of the Russian aristocracy, painfully conscious of his different origins and upbringing. The melancholy image of what he remembered as the "narrowness and suffocating atmosphere" of his youth with its "lack of freedom, of fresh air, of a purer and more decent society, of human beings, ideas, feelings" never deserted him. He was not above resentment toward those who had the good fortune to have been born into wealth and high social standing. Turgenev, who played such a curious part in his life, became, among other things, a surrogate for all the "well-bred" writers who, Goncharov felt, had it easier than he did, for Turgenev had "intelligence, and education, and talent, and an income of ten thousand, and freedom, and earthly paradise beside a beloved woman [Pauline Viardot]!"[22]

A measure of alienation, though painful in life, can be an advantage for an artist. Goncharov's position—close enough to the world of the Russian gentry to feel sympathy for its ideals and values and yet distant enough to develop critical detachment—enabled him to become one of the great chroniclers of that class. The confrontation of the differing value systems he encountered in his childhood became a major theme of his fiction, though in a much transmuted form, so

---

[20] See *Goncharov v vospominaniyakh, passim.*

[21] His pupil was Nikolay Alexandrovich, son of Alexander II, who died in 1865 and never came to the throne. See Mazon, pp. 339-341, and also E. A. Goncharova, "Vospominaniya ob I. A. Goncharove," *Goncharov v vospominaniyakh,* pp. 178-179.

[22] Letter to S. A. Nikitenko, July 3, 1866, *Sobr. soch.* (Pravda), VIII, 351-352.

that his estates of the gentry often resemble the modest small-town establishment of Avdotya Matveevna and some of his bourgeois entrepreneurs are indistinguishable in manners from their aristocratic brethren. What Goncharov seems to have distilled from the experience of his childhood are, on the one hand, the "bourgeois" practicality of the Goncharovs, the kind of hard knowledge that comes from a life in business, and, on the other, the idealism of Tregubov and his friends. Practicality versus idealism provides, in differing manifestations, the central opposition of his fiction.

Ivan and his brother Nikolay were the first of the Goncharovs to receive formal education. Tregubov taught Ivan to read and write and, when the boy was eight, his mother sent him to a boarding school maintained by a priest and his German wife, a converted Lutheran, for children of the local gentry. Fyodor Troitsky was an exceptional provincial priest in that he was well educated and had a large library of secular literature. It was here that Ivan was introduced to imaginative literature other than the Russian fairy tales he heard at home. The priest's wife, who knew French as well as her native German, began his training in foreign languages.[23] Apparently Avdotya Matveevna was not pleased with the education her son was receiving. After a brief two years she took him out of Troitsky's school and shipped him off, at the tender age of ten, to the Moscow Commercial School, where, she must have felt, he would receive the sort of training that would open opportunities for a boy from the merchant class. The curriculum of the school, however, except for a few required commercial subjects, emphasized the broad range of liberal arts and sciences taught in schools for the gentry. The caliber of teaching was inferior and the treatment of students brutal. The authorities were more concerned about order than knowledge, and the students suffered accordingly. Goncharov omitted mention of the Commercial School in his reminiscences and autobiography—it was his practice to omit what was painful in his past from material intended for publication—but in his private correspondence he recalled the place with special bitterness. The official reports of the school indicate that, though he eventually turned out to be a model student, he ini-

[23] See Goncharov's "Avtobiografii," *Sobr. soch.*, VIII, 221, 225.

tially did poorly and was even mischievous.[24] The adult who tried so hard to conform had felt, it seems, a spark of rebellion as a child.

Bitterness did not sound the only note in Goncharov's memories of his youth. Raised in a home marked by suspiciousness and mistrust and under the aegis of a severe mother, deprived of whatever love his aging father had to give, sent away from home at the age of ten to be abused by narrow-minded and stupid teachers, Goncharov still managed to idealize the condition of childhood. Perhaps it should come as no surprise. When we love those responsible for our misfortunes we may choose to hide our anger by turning it into its opposite. The deprived cling desperately to the memories of those moments when childhood, whatever its horrors, offered the nourishment, warmth, and maternal protection lost in the competitive adult world. Goncharov came to feel that the purpose of life may be to recapture something found only in childhood and youth, that, in the words of an acquaintance to whom he confided his thoughts, ". . . youth is freely given that toward which science and art strive as a final end. . . ."[25] Childhood remained the golden age, but Ivan had experienced too keenly the essential limitation of the child—his powerlessness before the whims of adults—not to retain a skepticism as to how golden it really was.

If the adult could ward off painful memories by idealizing the past, the child was able to escape through literature. Goncharov later described the reading-matter of his youth as "an unimaginable mixture," read without guidance or order, which "could not help influencing the intense development of an imagination already by its nature too lively." Like many Russians of the early years of the nineteenth century, he read from a grab-bag of diverse elements—standard neoclassical authors such as Racine, Fénélon, Voltaire; among the Russians, Lomonosov, Fonvizin, Derzhavin, and Kheraskov; forerunners of the new sensibility like Karamzin, Rousseau, and Sterne; and

[24] Superansky, *Russkaya shkola*, Nos. 5-6 (May-June 1912), pp. 14-22. See Goncharov's letter to his brother Nikolay, December 29, 1867, *Sobr. soch.* (Pravda), VIII, 362-363.

[25] Reminiscences of A. Ya. Kolodkina, in F. A. Kudrinsky, "K biografii I. A. Goncharova," *Goncharov v vospominaniyakh*, pp. 92-93.

romantic writers then in fashion. The latter particularly attracted the young Goncharov, who had acquired a taste for the heroic, fantastical, and melodramatic. While still at home he listened avidly to fairy tales narrated by the servants and his nanny, and read heroic legends from the Russian past; the ex-naval officer Tregubov had stimulated a continuing interest in accounts of the exploits of voyagers and explorers that later provoked Goncharov to undertake a journey around the world and write a travel book of his own. While he was a schoolboy his reading turned to works like Tasso's colorful epic *Jerusalem Delivered*, Mrs. Radcliffe's gothic horror stories, the melodramas of passion of Mme. Cottin, the flamboyant adventure tales of Walter Scott and the Russian romantic novelist Alexander Bestuzhev (Marlinsky), and the more extravagant adventure fiction of Eugène Sue.[26] Such a stew of mixed merit would hardly deserve mention—what cramped adolescent has not sought escape in the like?—except that Goncharov's fiction often treats ironically, not so much the specific items of his youthful reading, though there is some direct parody, as what we may call the "romance sensibility." The kind of mind that lives in imaginings of heroic deeds and ideal circumstances or expresses itself in a language divorced from the constraints of actuality continued to fascinate the novelist through his literary career.

Ivan failed to receive his degree from the Commercial School. Once again Avdotya took her son out of a school, this time on financial grounds. The Goncharov business had run into difficulties, and she decided to enroll her son at Moscow University.[27] The university had for some time offered young men of the lower social ranks (excluding serfs) one of the few opportunities existing in Russia to climb the social ladder. Though quotas for the several social classes existed, the place had a more democratic cast than other Russian institutions, as sons of the aristocracy competed with the offspring of the

---

[26] *Sobr. soch.*, VIII, 221-223, 228. Goncharov's first published work, which appeared in the *Teleskop*, X, No. 15 (1832), pp. 298-322, while he was still a student at Moscow University, was a translation of several chapters from Sue's *Atargull*. In the novels he gave similar reading lists to his protagonists.

[27] Superansky, *Russkaya shkola*, Nos. 5-6 (May-June 1912), pp. 22-23.

poorer gentry, schoolteachers, village priests, and provincial merchants like the Goncharovs. If the failure of the family enterprise made a career in business unfeasible, a university education would allow Avdotya's son to rise to a high position in the civil service.

Though the government wanted it so, Moscow University of the thirties was not at all an institution to turn out complacent and unquestioning bureaucrats. Ivan Goncharov had unknowingly come to the university (he attended from 1831 to 1834) at a critical moment in the life of the institution and a turning-point in the history of Russian thought. After the debacle of the 1825 revolt, intellectually curious and ambitious sons of the aristocracy, who might formerly have pursued a career in the army, turned to the university, where they began to seek alternative values to those of official institutions. Well into the forties the government interfered little, and the university was an island of relative freedom in the otherwise bleak landscape of the Russia of Nicholas I. It was also the scene of exciting intellectual ferment. The quality of instruction had been improving since 1825 to meet the requirements of a more serious generation of students, and the addition of a number of professors under the sway of ideas spreading from the great German universities (and of some who had received their training in Germany) turned Moscow University into a hotbed for the cultivation of German romantic idealism. Several of the faculty, including Goncharov's influential professor of fine arts, Nikolay Nadezhdin, drew the bulk of their ideas from the German philosophers and especially from Friedrich Schelling. The glory of Moscow University in the thirties, however, was its students. Among Goncharov's classmates were, besides the poet Lermontov, several remarkable young men who were to help shape the thought of their age—Vissarion Belinsky, Alexander Herzen, Nikolay Stankevich, and Konstantin Aksakov, among others. They formed now-famous philosophical circles for the study of German idealism—first Schelling and later Hegel—which continued to thrive and attract the leading minds of the age after their university days (the Herzen circle, unlike that surrounding Stankevich, was also interested in utopian theories of socialism coming from France). When the students of the thirties came to prominence in the following decade—they are called "the

men of the forties"—they abandoned formal metaphysical speculation to turn their attention to the problems of Russian life and soon
found themselves in rival camps of "liberal" Westerners and "conservative" Slavophiles. The shared style of thought, however,
remained romantic and idealistic at least through the thirties, and few,
if any, members of that exceptional generation managed to sever all
ties with the ideologies of their formative years.[28]

Romantic idealism temporarily satisfied many needs of gifted and
high-minded young men trapped in a repressive social system. Not
least among these were the exalted importance that idealism, especially
in Schelling's formulation, attached to the individual self for men living in a society that valued the individual all too little, and the supreme
significance it bestowed upon artistic creation—an activity not as
stringently constricted as other intellectual pursuits in the Russia of
Nicholas. In Schelling's metaphysics, which need concern us little here,
the self is of paramount importance, for it contains in microcosm the
harmony of the unfolding reality of the universe; poetic intuition and
the artistic process provide the shortest road to self-realization in
knowledge of the Absolute. The idealized heroes and heroines of
Schiller's plays, who proclaim the absolute worth of personality,
friendship, and love in the face of a world of cynical power and crass
philistinism, furnished a literary counterpart to the yearnings of philosophical idealism for the generation of the thirties. Many young men
and women of the period, initiating what was to become a Russian
tradition of living out the implications of thought and literature,
endeavored to turn their lives into, in the words of one of them, "a

---

[28] On Moscow University of the period, see M. N. Tikhomirov (ed.),
Istoriya Moskovskogo universiteta (Moscow, 1955), I, 77-240, and R. A.
Kovnator (ed.), *Moskovskiy universitet v vospominaniyakh sovremennikov*
(Moscow, 1956). For an excellent and brief summary in English, see Martin
Malia, *Alexander Herzen and the Birth of Russian Socialism: 1812-1855*
(Cambridge, Mass., 1961), pp. 57-61. Goncharov's reminiscences of his stu-
dent days are in "V universitete," *Sobr. soch.*, VII, 193-223. Samples of
Nadezhdin's lectures may be found in N. K. Kozmin, *Nikolay Ivanovich
Nadezhdin: zhizn' i nauchno-literaturnaya deyatel'nost', 1804-1836* (St. Peters-
burg, 1912), pp. 265-347.

work of art."[29] They resolved, often with determination and unquestionable sincerity, to realize fully the potentialities of their personalities, so that they might serve as living exemplars of the ideal friendship and love of Schiller's "beautiful souls" and the ideal harmony of Schelling's intuitions or Hegel's spirit of reason. Paradoxically, and the paradox is at the heart of romantic thought, the individualism of this generation, its urgent demand for complete self-expression and self-realization, coexisted with a yearning to identify with larger, embracing totalities, whether the Absolute, the world-mind or -spirit, the organic oneness of nature, or the more durable collectivities of nation, people, and the march of history.[30]

The first reflex of the scholar is to dismiss any influence of this romantic generation upon Ivan Goncharov. There was nothing in his background or education to prepare him for flights of metaphysical speculation. In later years the son of Simbirsk merchants proved to be anything but an enthusiast. Instead he carefully cultivated a public image of caution and sobriety. Goncharov recalled participating in student circles at Moscow University to discuss the lectures of his professors, but these were not the important Stankevich or Herzen groups. (Later, in 1846, he did, however, take part in discussions at Belinsky's home in Petersburg.)[31] He shared some of the literary interests of the age and even translated from Schiller and Goethe

---

[29] Nikolay Ogarev quoted in Malia, p. 51.

[30] On the period, see Malia, *Alexander Herzen*; Isaiah Berlin, "A Marvellous Decade: 1838-1848," *Encounter*, IV, No. 6 (June 1955), 27-39; V, No. 5 (November 1955), 21-29; V, No. 6 (December 1955), 22-43; VI, No. 5 (May 1956), 20-34; E. H. Carr, *The Romantic Exiles* (London, 1933); Edward J. Brown, *Stankevich and his Moscow Circle: 1830-1840* (Stanford, Calif., 1966); and D. I. Chizhevsky, *Gegel' v Rossii* (Paris, 1939). Famous contemporary accounts are Herzen's, in A. I. Gertsen, *Byloe i dumy*, ed. I. S. Novich and S. Ya. Shtraykh (Leningrad, 1947), pp. 40-350, and Pavel Annenkov's "Zamechatel'noe desyatiletie," *Literaturnye vospominaniya*, ed. B. M. Eykhenbaum (Leningrad, 1928), pp. 161-601.

[31] *Sobr. soch.*, VIII, 61. "Neobyknovennaya istoriya," *Neizdannaya rukopis'* I. A. Goncharova, *Sbornik Rossiyskoy Publichnoy biblioteki*, II, No. 1: *Materialy i issledovaniya* (Petrograd, 1924), pp. 7-8 (henceforth referred to as *Sbornik*).

19

(who was also read at the time as a romantic), but his greatest excitement was reserved for Johann Winckelmann, Nikolay Karamzin, and Alexander Pushkin.[32]

Goncharov's enthusiasm for the distinguished German art historian was part of a new passion for the art of Greece and Rome aroused by his Moscow University professors, Nadezhdin and Shevyrev.[33] Winckelmann's estheticism also may have appealed to the youthful Goncharov. His unabashed idolatry of Pushkin tells us little—what Russian has not adored the greatest of Russian poets? Goncharov said that it was through Pushkin that he and his generation "sobered up from the affectation and sentimentality of the French school . . . ," by which he probably meant those romantic melodramas of his boyhood reading.[34] Given the character of Goncharov's early literary enthusiasms it may well be that Pushkin provided a first important illustration that literature could reflect, besides fantasy and emotional self-expression, the purposeful designs of the critical intelligence. It is unlikely, though, that he took from the poet much more than inspiration. Critics sometimes designate Goncharov's avoidance of exaggerated pathos and the ironic restraint of his fiction as Pushkinian, but little resemblance exists between the tersely brilliant and classically spare prose of Pushkin and Goncharov's slow, deliberate, and introspective manner. The choice of Karamzin is more telling. Goncharov's "youthful heart . . . gave itself to Karamzin" not as a historian nor even as a writer, but "as the most humane of writers" and a "moral influence."[35]

Nikolay Karamzin (1766-1826) is labelled a "sentimentalist" or "pre-romantic," and, though he more than anyone was responsible for introducing the cult of feeling into Russia, he also retained from his intellectual origins in the eighteenth century a good deal of the

---

[32] *Sobr. soch.*, VIII, 222-223. A. F. Koni, "Ivan Aleksandrovich Goncharov," in *Goncharov v vospominaniyakh*, pp. 255-256. Goncharov destroyed these early translations.

[33] *Sobr. soch.*, VIII, 225.   [34] *Ibid.*, p. 471.

[35] *Ibid.*, pp. 222, 471. See also Goncharov's "Zametka po povodu yubileya Karamzina," first published in the newspaper *Golos*, November 23, 1866, in *Sobr. soch.*, VIII, 138-140.

clearheadedness of the Enlightenment and its appreciation of analytic reason. His Rousseauism is never pushed to extremes; it is tempered, in Mirsky's description, by "an elegant moderation and a cultured urbanity [that] are the constant characteristics of his writings." It could live at ease with a political conservatism that accepted the hierarchical authoritarianism of Russian institutions, since salvation for Karamzin lies not in the political sphere but in the individual sensibility: ". . . everyone can love, love his relatives, his family, his friends—this is true happiness, which unites all people, which allows the Tsar and the farmer to feel that they are brothers, children of one Father, born with the same hearts. . . ."[36] Goncharov failed to specify what drew him so strongly to Karamzin, but "elegant moderation and cultured urbanity" undoubtedly explain much of his appeal (as well as that of Pushkin) for a man who regularly avoided intellectual and moral extremes. Also, as we shall shortly see, Goncharov, like Karamzin, locates his morality in the impulses of the individual sentient "heart," while at the same time maintaining a civilized respect for enlightenment and reason and seldom allowing his moral sensibilities to be offended by the inequities of the Russian social system or the injustices of Russian autocratic rule.

It is a long leap from Karamzin's sentimentalism with its admixture of eighteenth-century rationalism to the romantic exaltations of the thirties, though both tendencies served to draw men into themselves and away from political or social criticism. Goncharov, from what we know of his background and future career, seems an unlikely candidate to have made the jump. Nevertheless, few men ever find it possible to live totally untouched by the intellectual and moral climate of their age. In the succeeding chapter we shall discover how certain concepts that came to prominence with the rise of romanticism colored Goncharov's view of art. Also, as a young man Goncharov may have been something of a romantic in the colloquial sense of the term. According to Gavriil Potanin, who knew the Goncharov family and

---

[36] D. S. Mirsky, *A History of Russian Literature: From its Beginnings to 1900*, rev. edn., ed. Francis J. Whitfield (New York, 1949), p. 61. Karamzin, "O lyubvi k otechestvu i narodnoy gordosti," *Sochineniya* (St. Petersburg, 1848), III, 494.

left one of the earliest accounts we have of the novelist, "Goncharov in his youth was the same sort of ecstatic dreamer that young people of the thirties and forties were. . . ."[37] As late as 1860 the novelist was still able to describe himself as an "incurable romantic, an idealist" who had waged "a thirty-year Don Quixote struggle with life"—i.e., ever since the *thirties*. He called himself a "romantic" because he could not be reconciled to life as it was. Man requires some ideal, he writes, an "ideal of perfection," of "the beautiful," of "the common good," that will transcend the bare and ugly facts of existence. The ideal may prove unrealizable; its realization may even be undesirable, for nothing would remain to strive for, but without it life is impossible.[38] At times the ideal took the form of a belief in the inevitability of human progress and the existence of "a single common purpose" toward which all forms of thought—science, art, religion—tend. It always expressed itself through a faith in the supreme moral significance of art.[39] Goncharov's lofty conception of the artist's calling reflects the spirit of Russia's romantic age. The seeds of his abiding faith in human progress may have been first implanted by Tregubov and his friends, though he remembered them in their post-1825 mood of defeat. More likely, the tone of high optimism about human destiny and possibility that often intrudes into his writings also dates from the thirties and forties. It was his professors, he recalled, who produced "a moral influence in presenting ideals of the good, of truth, beauty, perfection, progress. . . ."[40] Also, for the remainder of his life Goncharov continued to identify with the men of the thirties and forties—an identification that made him extremely hostile to the materialistic and positivistic views that came to dominate much of Russian thought in the following decades.[41]

Goncharov, as we shall see shortly, had his moments of doubt. Also, there was another side to the coin of his idealism, an aspect of his

---

[37] *Goncharov v vospominaniyakh*, p. 30.

[38] Letter to S. A. Nikitenko, June 8, 1860, *Sobr. soch.*, VIII, 331-335.

[39] *Ibid.*, pp. 154-157. For Goncharov's views on art, see below, chap. two.

[40] *Ibid.*, p. 229.

[41] See e.g. a letter to Ekaterina Maykova, April 1869, and "Predislovie k romanu *Obryv*," *ibid.*, pp. 400-402, 148-151.

psychology that is strikingly similar to that of his predecessor and the great Russian prose writer of the thirties and forties, Nikolay Gogol. As for Gogol, the ideal for Goncharov was an elusive shadow always in danger of being swallowed up by the dirt, filth, and triviality of life: "... if you knew," he wrote to a friend, Ivan Lkhovsky, in 1853,

> through what dirt, through what depravity, trivia, coarseness of ideas, mind, and motions of the heart and soul I went through from the cradle and what it cost my poor nature to pass through a phalanx of all sorts of moral and material filth and error in order to pull through to that path on which you saw me, still coarse, impure, awkward and still yearning after that bright and beautiful human image of which I often dream and which, I feel, I shall always pursue as vainly as a shadow pursues a man.

Though the abyss of filth in man is bottomless, he continues in a later letter to Lkhovsky, the sources of good may run deeper. One must go to a perhaps nonexistent extreme before saying "... everything is over; ... man has lost his way and will not return."[42] Oblomov, another "man of the forties," says much the same to the writer and social satirist Penkin, who would use literature to scourge society of vice: "Man, give me man! ... love him. ... Cast him out of society? ... That is to forget that a higher principle existed in this unfit vessel; if he is a corrupted man, he is yet a man, that is, he is you yourself. Cast him off? But how can you cast him from the sphere of humanity, from the lap of nature, from God's mercy? ..."[43]

As Goncharov was touched by the moral pathos of Russia's roman-

---

[42] *Ibid.*, p. 258, and pp. 276-277 (June 13, 1857).

[43] *Ibid.*, IV, 30. The protagonists of Goncharov's three novels—Alexander Aduev, Ilya Oblomov, and Boris Raysky—all belong to the generation of the thirties and forties. The action of *A Common Story* (*Obyknovennaya istoriya*) extends approximately from 1830 to 1843, of *Oblomov* from 1843 to 1851 (excluding the epilogue and backflashes). For computations, see Tseytlin, pp. 64-65, 163-164. Because of anachronisms in the text it is impossible to date the action of *The Ravine* (*Obryv*), but Goncharov claimed to have intended Raysky as a representative figure of his generation (*Sobr. soch.*, VIII, 400-401). Goncharov compared his own ideals to Oblomov's in a letter to A. G. Troynitsky, June 25, 1867, *Vestnik Evropy*, No. 12 (December 1908), p. 453.

tic period, he also at the time shared its estheticism. The opening
section of an essay written in the early forties entitled "Is It Good or
Bad to Live in the World?" ("Khorosho ili durno zhit' na svete?")
divides human experience into two disparate and incompatible categories—the practical and the ideal or esthetic. In characteristically
romantic fashion Goncharov declares his preference for dwelling in
the ideal, though he modifies it from a metaphysical entity into one
"half" of life.

> Is it good or bad to live in the world? Both one and the other. Life
> consists of two distinct halves: one is the practical; the other is the
> ideal. In the former we are slaves of labor and anxiety; this half
> is poisoned by material necessities: each person, like a bee, is daily
> obligated to bear *a drop of his honey for the common good* into
> the bottomless hive of the world. The intellect is the autocratic
> sovereign in this life. Man brings many sacrifices to this despot.
> He gives up many of his best moments and joys in exchange for
> griefs, dry labors, and endeavors which are alien to the soul. As
> much as one might like to, how boring it is to live for others! . . .
> The other half is not like that. There is no antlike bustling or
> *mouselike scurrying about* for the common good in it. There you
> cease to live for all and live for yourself, not with your head alone,
> but with the soul and the heart and the mind together. That half
> is the esthetic: there is expanse for the heart in it, which is opened
> to tender impressions, expanse for sweet thoughts, for disquieting
> sensations and tempests, which are also not intellectual and politi-
> cal, but tempests of the soul that freshen the burden of a dull exist-
> ence. Here are ideal joys and sorrows. . . . The moments of that
> life are filled with the play of mind and feeling, of flowering, liv-
> ing pleasure in all that is wonderful in the world. . . . Some sort of
> lightness and freedom rules in existence, and man does not bend
> his head under the burden of constant thoughts of duty, labor, and
> obligations.[44]

[44] The essay was first published by Lyatsky, in *Roman i zhizn'*, pp. 119-125.
It is cited here according to Tseytlin, pp. 445-449.

This division of life into two distinct "halves"—in *Oblomov* Goncharov and his characters will again speak of life's differing halves—is of tremendous importance for his fiction. Similar divisions dominate his three novels and sometimes dictate their formal structures. The novels tell the stories of men who live in the "esthetic half" and prefer the play of their imaginations to facing the practical exigencies of life. Each novel proceeds through a series of contrasts between the antagonistic realms of the practical and the ideal, though in Goncharov's final novel, *The Ravine*, the pattern is less consistent. An imagination that perceives life as a manifestation of diametrically opposed moral categories can easily tend toward allegory, and we shall discover allegorical urges appearing at the edges of Goncharov's fictional world. The dominant mode, though, is ironic. In his fiction he reversed his evaluation of the two halves of life so that the "ideal" became the butt of his irony, and the fancies and rhetoric of his "esthetic" heroes the object of parody. In doing so, he followed a major tendency of the realistic novel, which, as it broke away from the romantic climate of its origins, engaged in a continuing polemic against the romantic imagination.

However, irony and parody are among the most complex of literary modes. An ironic statement meant to blame can easily turn into its opposite by a slight shift in intonation or context. Parody of necessity incorporates and preserves the parodied object. It is a central thesis of this book, and one especially relevant for *Oblomov*, that Goncharov, while making high comedy out of the illusions of his heroes and subjecting their dreams of ideal possibilities to relentless irony, never gave up his search for an ideal he could affirm and a "bright human image" he could believe in. His fiction often surprises us by its unexpected leaps from an ironic undermining of ideal visions to an affirmation, if not always of the substance of his heroes' dreams, then of the ideal-making imagination. Indeed, the quest for the ideal provides some of the richest as well as, unfortunately, some of the most banal moments of his art.

Not all the novelist's life was taken up with yearning for an ideal or despair at his inability to find one, though in later years the accent of despondency came to dominate. For one, Goncharov had to work for a living. In 1834, the year of his graduation from Moscow University, he began a career in the Russian bureaucracy that almost paralleled his literary career. The bureaucrat finally retired from the service in 1867 after steadily rising through its ranks, and the writer completed his final novel a year later. Goncharov complained bitterly that the need to earn a living forced him to spend his energies and time at tasks he disliked and kept him from his literary interests.[45] His responsibilities in the service turned him into a part-time writer, working mostly during his summer vacations and spending many years on a relatively small corpus. They may have had some beneficial aspects besides the obvious boon of financial security. An extremely nervous man, given to morbid introspection, he probably derived a measure of security from the fixed routines a bureaucracy imposes and the official identity it bestows upon its members. Also, if he was as a young man the "ecstatic dreamer" Potanin described, a life of prosaic labor within the elaborate hierarchy of the Russian bureaucracy, where every decision was subject to the review and censure of superiors, surely contributed to the sense of human limitation that characterizes his fiction.

There was a playful and light side to Goncharov that also kept him from complete abandonment to the exaggerated enthusiasms and high seriousness of some of his contemporaries and that for many years balanced the morbid strain in his nature. He enjoyed good company, good food, and as a young man even cut a fine figure on the dance floor. His early associations were with people who looked to art not only or primarily for significance but for pleasure and enjoyment as well.[46] Foremost among these were Nikolay Apollonovich and Evgeniya Petrovna Maykov and habitués of their popular salon in the Petersburg of the 1830s and '40s.

The Maykovs were an old aristocratic family who had long distinguished themselves in Russian cultural life. Nikolay was a well-known painter of the period; Evgeniya wrote poetry and short stories;

---

[45] See, e.g., a letter to A. A. Tolstaya, April 14, 1874, *Sobr. soch.* (Pravda), VIII, 441.

[46] See Mazon, pp. 33-36.

two of their sons, whom Goncharov tutored for a while, were to achieve distinction in nineteenth-century letters, Apollon as a poet, Valerian, before his untimely death, as a critic. The style of the Maykov salon is often called "romantic" or one of "art for art's sake," but it is unlikely that Nikolay and Evgeniya employed such literary slogans to account for their personal inclinations. The Maykovs, unlike the intense young men of the philosophical circles of the thirties, maintained a relatively casual approach to art. They were secure aristocrats, whose "romanticism" did not go beyond a fashionable *Weltschmerz* and for whom "art for art's sake" was an ingrained habit instead of an esthetic credo. Art in the Maykov home often took the form of a family pastime and social entertainment. Evgeniya and Nikolay conducted literary readings whose subjects were the activities of family members and friends, arranged parlor games that allowed the assembled guests to display their verbal wit, and from 1836 to 1838 produced a handwritten literary magazine and in 1839 an almanac, patterned after the family albums popular among the gentry.[47]

It was in these family manuscripts that Goncharov's first original literary efforts appeared. The four poems he wrote for the 1836 issues of *Snowdrop* (*Podsnezhnik*), as the family magazine was called, are amateurish and undistinguished. Their mood is one of melancholy, either over a lost love, the indifference of nature, or in one poem, "Lost Peace" ("Utrachennyy pokoy"), a lost paradise where the poet was one with nature—the first appearance of a central theme of Goncharov's fiction. Stock romantic clichés—"fateful secret," "pale brow," "evil demon," "the magical moment of love"—dot almost every line; the style is discursive and rhetorical and the reader searches

---

[47] See the reminiscences of A. V. Starchevsky and A. M. Skabichevsky, in *Goncharov v vospominaniyakh*, pp. 51-55, 70-72. Also D. V. Grigorovich, *Literaturnye vospominaniya* (Leningrad, 1928), pp. 191-192. For a description of the contents of the magazine and almanac, see Semevsky, "*Podsnezhnik i Lunnye nochi*, izdavavshiesya v semeynom krugu Maykovykh," in *Apollon Nikolaevich Maykov: ego zhizn' i sochineniya*, ed. V. Pokrovsky (2d edn. rev.; Moscow, 1911), pp. 3-5. Lyatsky, *Roman i zhizn'*, pp. 110-140, includes much first-hand material and several poems of Evgeniya Petrovna (pp. 112-113).

in vain for a genuinely lyrical line. A brief example from "Melancholy and Joy" ("Toska i radost' ") should suffice:

> Zachem vdrug sumrachnym nenast'em
> Padyot na dushu tyazhkiy son?
> Kakim nevedomym neschast'em
> Eyo smutit vnezapno on?[48]

(Why does a distressing dream suddenly fall upon the soul like gloomy foul weather? With what mysterious misfortune does it of a sudden disturb the soul?)

The problem, of course, is that Goncharov was not a poet, but the poems also reflect his literary situation. Though romantic thought left powerful traces in Russia, literary romanticism failed to mature into a full-blown movement, and its brief episode was already on the wane when Goncharov began writing. Except for the work of several isolated talents like Lermontov and Tyutchev, the romantic manner had grown tired and hackneyed by the end of the thirties. The stories Goncharov wrote for *Snowdrop* and the 1839 almanac *Moonlit Nights* (*Lunnye nochi*) will be discussed in a separate chapter. They are dominated by what has come to be called "romantic irony"—a lighthearted banter that takes neither character nor situation seriously. The fashionable melancholy and insouciant playfulness we find in Goncharov's first literary attempts from all accounts characterized the "romanticism" of the Maykov salon. It was a romanticism lacking in conviction or creative force and could not exert a lasting influence. It could, however, as it did in Goncharov's hands, provide an easy target for parody.

Nevertheless, a measure of playfulness can be helpful to an artist, especially when beginning his career. After the grand eloquence and portentous generalizations of Professor Nadezhdin, Goncharov discovered among the Maykovs an artistic environment in which he

---

[48] The four poems—the other two are "A Fragment" ("Otryvok") and "A Romance" ("Romans")—are in *Zvezda*, No. 5 (1938), pp. 243-246. For some comments, see Vladimir Markov, "The Poetry of Russian Prose Writers," *California Slavic Studies*, I (1960), 82-84.

could relax and experiment or "play" at writing without undue worry as to its ultimate significance. He also found a sympathetic audience for his first, hesitant literary efforts and several of the never numerous intimate friends he could call his own. If a residue of Simbirsk provincialism had survived his education at Moscow University, it became indiscernible after his encounter with the sophisticated Maykov milieu. Henceforth Goncharov moved easily in similar circles. His friends tended to be, like the Maykovs, cultivated and urbane men and women, often of aristocratic lineage or highly placed in the Tsarist government, who, in contrast to the young intellectuals of Moscow University, did not feel alienated from the values and manners of the gentry. In short, of his two backgrounds—of the Goncharovs and of Tregubov—the novelist chose to identify himself with a style of life resembling that of his godfather. And as with Tregubov, when Goncharov came to write about the Maykovs in an early short story called "A Cruel Illness" ("Likhaya bolest'"), it was, we shall discover, with the same ambiguous mixture of affection and irony that characterizes all his descriptions of the Russian gentry.

A later chapter will treat the complicated history of Goncharov's trilogy, but the curious circumstance that all three novels, though written over a twenty-five-year span, were conceived at about the same time—from 1844 to 1849—requires comment at this point in his biography. As Goncharov worked intermittently on *Oblomov* and *The Ravine*—*A Common Story* was written all of a piece in the forties—he occasionally responded in his fiction to the pressure of events. The great bulk of the experiences that found their way into his fiction, however, were already behind him when he conceived his trilogy. The impulse to create seems to have derived largely from the conflicts and yearnings of adolescence and youth. His novels tell the stories of three young men—Alexander Aduev, Ilya Oblomov, and Boris Raysky—whose paths to maturity are remarkably similar to that taken by the novelist: childhood in the remote provinces, removal to the city, the university, and a period in the government service. Two of his heroes are aspiring writers and the third, Oblomov, has the imagination, though not the vocation, of a poet. Moreover, Goncharov was in his mid-thirties when he planned his trilogy, and each novel describes a pattern of disillusionment that has run its course by the time the hero is in *his* mid-thirties.[49]

Goncharov's protagonists differ from each other and from their creator in important ways. Their disillusionment, if it is at all biographical, also reflects the historical situation of a generation coming to maturity at the moment when the inflated bubbles of romantic enthusiasm of the thirties had collapsed. Also, the loss of illusions is a central theme of the novel; in France, Stendhal, Balzac, and the Flaubert of *Madame Bovary* and *l'Éducation sentimentale* have made it at times seem its only important theme. A history of nineteenth-century literature could probably be written on the basis of changing treatments of the problem of illusion and reality: from the romantics' identification with the hero who dwells in illusion to the realists' ironic use of his plight to discredit romantic mythologies. In Russia, ever since Pushkin's *Eugene Onegin* (1823-1831), Chatsky of Griboe-dov's *Woe from Wit* (1825), and Pechorin of Lermontov's *A Hero of Our Time* (1840), the hero disillusioned in his contact with social actuality was a recognizable type, who was understood to epitomize the alienation of thinking Russians and especially those of the gentry. Turgenev's story "The Diary of A Superfluous Man" (1850) gave the epithet "superfluous" currency in Russian discussions of the type. It is sometimes difficult to tell whether such social typologies were intended by the writers or existed only in the minds of critics and readers, but in the novels of Goncharov, as in those of Turgenev, they seem intentional, as do the somewhat didactic contrasts to a more active and practical hero. Clearly then, Goncharov's protagonists echo a European and Russian literary tradition of long standing and considerable force. Nevertheless, the several close correspondences between his biography and the lives of his central characters make us wonder whether the novelist underwent some crisis during his passage from youth to maturity that led him to transmute his personal experience into the artifacts of fiction.

"Byron is right," he wrote to a close friend, Yuniya Efremova, in 1849, "in saying that a decent man should not live longer than thirty-

---

[49] See Tseytlin, pp. 64-65, 163-164. For Raysky's age, see *Sobr. soch.*, V, 7.

five years. Past thirty-five only bureaucrats live well. . . ."[50] Unfortunately, we do not know what caused Goncharov to feel that life may have come to an end in the middle of its passage. From his earliest surviving letter, written at the age of thirty, when he described himself as suffering from "the boredom and idleness of our age,"[51] his correspondence is one long and unceasing complaint of ennui, depression, and despair. Its most usual expression is the word *skuka*, which is properly translated as "boredom," but which in Goncharov's usage refers to a sense of encroaching emptiness and a nameless anxiety. His *skuka* was a profound and intangible malaise of the spirit instead of a momentary reaction to unpleasant circumstances. If those few scattered accounts depicting Goncharov in his twenties as a playful and sociable young man are correct (the playful side of his nature never disappeared entirely), something catastrophic may have occurred to plunge him into despair and a lifelong struggle to retain his sanity. Or, more likely, Goncharov despaired because *nothing* had happened. He had come to that difficult time in life, the passage from youth to middle age, when the routines and patterns of existence have become firmly established and one looks forward to more of the same or back upon the yet unrealized dreams of a fast-disappearing youth as perhaps unrealizable. This twilight period of youth may be especially difficult for a man who felt dissatisfied with his occupation and who had not yet married, though he very much desired and needed a family.

We know almost nothing about Goncharov's relations with women through the 1840's. A failure in love, however, is one of the two major causes of the crises his fictional heroes suffer. Unrequited love is of course as much a literary convention as is the disillusioned hero. Russian novelists, following the lead of Pushkin's *Eugene Onegin*, have several times presented the love of a woman as a challenge to the integrity of their idealistic and ineffectual heroes (such confrontations run through Turgenev's novels as well as Goncharov's).[52] The

---

[50] *Sobr. soch.* (Pravda), VIII, 275.

[51] To A. N. Maykov, March 2, 1843, *Sobr. soch.*, VIII, 235.

[52] In "Luchshe pozdno, chem nikogda," *ibid.*, pp. 77-78, Goncharov wrote

specific form love took in Goncharov's fiction, we shall discover shortly, also reflected his personal dilemma.

The other cause of crisis in Goncharov's fiction stems from a fear of failure in art, with the qualification that Oblomov, unlike Aduev and Raysky, has ceased even to hope to express his rich imagination through creative activity. The fear was very much Goncharov's. In 1849, while working on *Oblomov*, he wrote his editor at the time, Andrey Kraevsky, that because of "old age" (he was all of 37) he may have lost "any ability to write," and such fears seem to have accompanied each of his literary undertakings.[53] The despair his creative activity plunged him into was one of the reasons he gave for his surprising decision to accept a post in 1852 as secretary to Admiral Evfimy Putyatin on a government-sponsored expedition to inspect Russian possessions in North America, which the expedition never reached, and to seek a commercial treaty with the Japanese. To his friends who expressed astonishment at the intention of the cautious and unventuresome bureaucrat to circle the globe on a sailing vessel, Goncharov replied that since childhood he had been drawn to travel by tales of distant lands (which he first heard from the sailor Tregubov), that the trip would advance him in the service, and—probably the most compelling reason—that he feared that his imagination was drying up and hoped for renewal through the novelty of a voyage: ". . . I was dying of idleness, boredom, oppressiveness; nothing refreshed my imagination. . . . I was perishing slowly and tediously; I needed a change—it was all the same whether for something better or worse, as long as it was a change." He felt that the trip would offer an opportunity to write an easier sort of book than a novel, one that would require less of an effort of the imagination, a volume of travel sketches in which the author could simply put down, "without any literary pretension," what he saw.[54] The result was a charming book

---

that Pushkin's "ideal" Tatyana provided an archetype for Russian literature, including Olga of *Oblomov* and Vera of *The Ravine*.

[53] *Ibid.*, p. 256.

[54] Letters to E. P. and N. A. Maykov, November 20, 1852, *Literaturnoe nasledstvo*, Nos. 22-24 (1935), p. 354, and to E. A. and M. A. Yazykov, August 23, 1852, *Sobr. soch.*, VIII, 248-249.

of travel sketches entitled, after the name of the ship on which he spent almost two years of his life, *The Frigate Pallas*.

The *Pallas* was an ill-equipped and rickety ship, and the journey, first to England, then round the Cape of Good Hope and through the Indian Ocean to China and Japan, passed through many detours and hardships. The outbreak of the Crimean War further complicated matters, since the British controlled the seas, and in August of 1854 a weary world traveler was deposited on the coast of eastern Siberia to begin an arduous overland trip home. He arrived in Petersburg in February of 1855. In the fall he was in love.

Goncharov had first met Elizaveta Tolstaya in the early forties at the Maykovs, when she was still an adolescent. She was fifteen to seventeen years younger than he, and strikingly beautiful. A rival appeared on the scene—Elizaveta's cousin, Alexander Musin-Pushkin—and it soon became apparent that Goncharov was not her choice. It is in the nature of biography to reconstruct a life according to the available evidence. Elizaveta looms large in Goncharov's life story because the relation had an aura of crisis about it, but also because his correspondence to her has survived. The correspondence is so revealing, however, that our relative ignorance of his previous experiences with women need not be lamented.[55]

In many ways Goncharov acted like any other man in love. He sent Elizaveta gifts; he took her to the opera and theater; he was tender, playful, and solicitous. He also felt intensely jealous of Musin-Pushkin. A niece of Goncharov's wrote years later that Ivan Alexandrovich was able to charm women easily, loved to flirt with them— his letters to women are often playfully flirtatious—but failed to pursue his courtships to a conclusion: ". . . a caution, a mistrust of himself and others kept him from becoming intimate with a woman or marrying her. If the object of his love married, a baseless jealousy of

---

[55] The correspondence and a description by P. Sakulin is in *Golos minuvshego*, No. 11 (November 1913), pp. 45-65, 215-235; No. 12 (December 1913), pp. 222-252. Goncharov's biographers have suggested a number of other love affairs but the evidence is scanty.

his rival would blaze up in him."[56] It would seem that in his amorous dramas the male rival, whether imagined or real, played at least as important a role as the woman. If jealousy is a not uncommon lot of infatuated lovers, there were other ways in which the forty-three-year-old lover behaved strangely.

With a few momentary exceptions Goncharov scrupulously avoided a direct expression of his feelings; instead he equivocated, hinted, and, in his phrase, refused "to dot his i's." His indirection took an extremely curious form—one that bewildered Elizaveta. Often in his letters to her Goncharov avoided the first-person singular pronoun and referred to himself instead as "he," "we," "my best friend," and even "they." With one of his letters he inserted a short literary piece entitled "Pour et contre" in which the question "she loves me, she loves me not" is thrown back and forth by two characters called "I" and "he."[57] Unexpectedly, "he," the character who is placed at a distance in relation to the personal "I," turns out to be Goncharov speaking for himself.

"He" is a tormented lover—intense, passionate, suffering—who expresses himself in torrents of eloquence over his "ideal," his "angel," and feels tormented at the thought that she may love another. "I" is skeptical, commonsensical, ironic. At times "Pour et contre" approaches parody, which is of course self-parody, as "I" undermines "his" effusions by interrupting with a prosaic remark or gesture— " 'Well, pal, as I see it you've gone a bit balmy,' I remarked, puffing on a cigar"—or by pointing to a stock romantic cliché, the word "demons," in "his" self-consciously literary speech:

My angel said to me: "There is your road, you will not reach [your destination], you will come upon a swamp"; she took me by the hand, showed me the way and disappeared. I walk timidly along this road, but I am bored without her; why did she abandon me? I run after her, I scream "I am grateful," but she disappears into a crowd. "But you are not walking along the same road," I

[56] V. M. Chegodaeva, in *Goncharov v vospominaniyakh*, p. 105.
[57] *Golos minuvshego*, No. 12 (December 1913), pp. 222-230.

cry out to her: "Look out, demons walk there." "In Russian—
wood-goblins (*leshie*)," I remarked.[58]

Earlier we saw how in the essay "Is It Good or Bad to Live in
the World?" Goncharov split the world into two opposing halves—
the ideal or esthetic and the practical. "Pour et contre" at moments
like those just cited reveals what we shall discover to be an essential
trait of his fiction: the ironic juxtaposition of inflated diction and
lofty sentiments with the prosaic, humdrum, and ordinary—"wood-
goblins" not only are Russian but they lack the grandeur of "demons."
"Pour et contre" also suggests that the oppositions of Goncharov's
thought and fiction, whatever their possible intellectual and literary
sources, mirrored a division in his personality. "He" and "I" are
obviously but two aspects of the novelist's self, debating on one level
whether Elizaveta "loves me or loves me not," and on a deeper level
the self's relation to the life of the emotions—the esthetic half. "Do
you really joke like this in your solemn and sad moments?" "He"
asks in indignation at "I's" mockery, and "I" responds, "Yes, always
and everywhere: a joke never grows old; it does not betray, does
not become tedious; in torments a joke calls forth a smile. . . ." "Joking is my element," Goncharov writes, now in his own person, in a
letter to Elizaveta, "You think I joke because I am gay; and I joked
at times when terror and turmoil were in my heart. . . ."[59] Joking—
we would say irony—was Goncharov's finest defense, his way of putting pain and desire at a comfortable distance. Relations with women,
he wrote to Anatoly Koni many years later, are "cheerful, comfortable, and pleasant" only when they have "the significance of comedy.
. . . Writhing in convulsions of passion I could not help at the same
time noticing how all of it taken together was silly and comical. In a
word, tormented subjectively, I looked upon the entire course of such
dramas objectively . . . and, when I sobered up, it all ran off me like
water from a duck's back."[60]

[58] *Ibid.*, pp. 228-229.   [59] *Ibid.*, pp. 222, 234.
[60] July 11, 1888, cited in L. S. Utevsky, *Zhizn' Goncharova* (Moscow,
1931), p. 81.

The split of the self we find in "Pour et contre" and the Tolstaya correspondence was such an attempt to view a subjective drama objectively and to turn pathos into harmless comedy. Through irony and projection Goncharov dissociated himself from the burden of his emotions. Even in his letters, and not only in the literary contrivance "Pour et contre," it is not "I," but "we," "he," "my best friend" who misses Elizaveta, who longs for her, who fears she may no longer care: "You were *angry* or felt *insulted*. . . . But with whom and for what? Was it not with my sick *friend* who trustingly and carelessly entrusted to you his soul, all his doubts and the contradictions into which he continually fell (symptoms of passion: Did I not mock him much for it!)?"[61] As in "Pour et contre" the feeling half of the self is identified with the other, "my friend," and "I" becomes the property of the ironic and mocking half.

Irony and projection are strategies for self-protection, but they also carry their own dangers. If a person continually dissociates himself from his feelings because they bring him "terror and turmoil," he may simply end up empty. Since it is through feeling that men reach each other, his connection with the human world may be lost as he further and further isolates himself behind his defenses—in Goncharov's case, behind the protective mask of his irony. Threatened with the loss of Elizaveta, Goncharov began to fear that his tie with life might be severed: "Take away from me this right to speak with you and I shall lack a great deal; the very thread of life will vanish; the very living nerve that connects me with people and society will be paralyzed."[62] Such is the fear that dominates the minds of the three protagonists of Goncharov's trilogy.

It is doubtful whether it would have made much difference in Goncharov's life had he been able to continue to speak with Elizaveta. It was rather his way of handling any human relation in which passion or deep feeling was involved that was the source of his troubles. Faced with the uncertainties of the life of the emotions, his way was to "joke," to turn the emotional side of his nature into an object of parody, and finally to kill it. On December 31, 1855, when he rec-

[61] *Golos minuvshego*, No. 12 (December 1913), p. 240.
[62] *Ibid.*, p. 236.

ognized that the short-lived love affair had run its course, he pro-
nounced what amounted to an epitaph over the corpse of his feelings:
". . . 'my best friend' is already gone; he does not exist; he has perished, evaporated, crumbled into dust. Only I remain, with my apathy
or melancholy. . . . he [the "best friend"] died peacefully, as he says,
for 'inspiration, for tears, for life.' . . ."[63] "He" dies and an empty
or apathetic "I" remains. Irony, however, was still at hand to mitigate the pain. In the next to last letter of the correspondence, dated
February 20, 1856, Goncharov promised to send Elizaveta a now
famous group portrait of himself and other leading writers of the
age—Tolstoy, Turgenev, Ostrovsky, Alexander Druzhinin, Dmitry
Grigorovich—if she would but add the word *vous* to her remark "je
ne sais qu'aimer." " 'Why do you need it?' you will ask; and I myself
don't know, but it's very nice; my appetite will improve and I will
sleep better. . . ."[64] He had already turned his love and suffering,
which were real, into a joke.

The Elizaveta Tolstaya correspondence not only is extremely
revealing of Goncharov's personality; it also provides us with a key
for an understanding of the genesis of his art. Like "Pour et contre,"
his novels, and especially *A Common Story* and *Oblomov*, center
upon an opposition of two men: a protagonist disposed to extravagant
flights of imagination and rhetoric but incapable of action (Alexander
Aduev, Oblomov, Raysky), and an antagonist who is ironical, practical, and commonsensical (Pyotr Aduev) or merely a practical man
of action without a talent for irony (Stolz, and Tushin of *The
Ravine*). Like the "I" of "Pour et contre," Goncharov's narrators
incline to the party of the ironical and/or commonsensical men.
Scholars of earlier generations, who identified literary criticism with
biography, sought to determine who Goncharov was—the Oblomov
type or the Pyotr Aduev type. His contemporaries split their vote.
The writer's corpulence, slowness, and a distant look that sometimes
crept into his eyes reminded some of Oblomov; others, and these
were in the majority, thought they saw Pyotr Aduev in his elegance,
ironical reserve, occasional didacticism, and a prosaic sobriety that

[63] *Ibid.*, pp. 244-245. Goncharov is paraphrasing Pushkin.
[64] *Ibid.*, pp. 249-250.

disturbed the image of an artist held by more idealistic Russians.[65] The Tolstaya correspondence—and in a less compact form the whole of Goncharov's correspondence—would indicate that he was both Pyotr Aduev and Oblomov, that irony was a defensive mask contrived to hide a turbulent and uneasy self, while in his secret life he was, like Oblomov, imaginative, idealistic, and extremely vulnerable.

However, such neat divisions into the two Goncharovs (or the two Tolstoys or the two Dostoevskys) can be as simplistic as earlier searches for the single character of a fiction who embodies the creator. Art is not mere projection; it is a self-conscious and dynamic activity of the human mind. If Goncharov started out with projections of differing aspects of his personality, in the process of creation he turned his private dilemma into an intellectual problem that cried out for solution. As in his personal life, he tended in his fiction to compartmentalize experience into opposed categories of the practical and the esthetic, the real and the ideal, emotionalism and rationality. He did not, however, stop at simple representation but went on to trace the implications of such a split for the Russian character and ultimately, as we shall see, for human consciousness. In a letter to a friend, written while he was working on *The Ravine*, Goncharov said about Boris Raysky, with whom he otherwise identified more than any of his other protagonists, ". . . if I know what Raysky is, if I am able to create him, it means that I am his critic, it means that I cannot be Raysky. . . ."[66] The remark, which may be taken as Goncharov's statement of the biographical fallacy, pertains to all of his fictional creations. To that persistent question, who is Goncharov? I can answer only that, as in a dream, he is involved in many of the important products of his imagination—Alexander *and* Pyotr Aduev, Oblomov *and* Stolz—but, as in a work of art, he is also the creative intelligence who manipulates their destinies for purposes of artistic illumination of the human condition.

[65] See *Goncharov v vospominaniyakh, passim.* In giving advice to members of his family he sometimes sounded remarkably like the pedantic and practical uncle of *A Common Story.* See, e.g., a letter to Alexandra, December 1, 1858, *Vestnik Evropy*, No. 2 (February 1907), pp. 588-589.

[66] To S. A. Nikitenko, August 21, 1866, *Sobr. soch.*, VIII, 366.

The death sentence passed upon "my best friend" proved premature. Goncharov, so far as we know, did not fall in love again, but he had not yet died "for inspiration." Quite the contrary. Over a year later, in the summer of 1857, he experienced the most dramatic outburst of inspiration of his career—a sudden flood of creative energy that permitted him to write the bulk of *Oblomov* in six weeks. Until 1857 the novelist had not progressed past Part One, and the love plot—the Oblomov-Stolz-Olga triangle—remained to be worked out. It may very well have been that the force of his experience with Elizaveta—the sufferings he underwent and the hesitations he became aware of—furnished the emotional impetus necessary to complete his long-dormant novel.

Several of Goncharov's biographers have gone further and suggested that Elizaveta became the model for Olga.[67] The neatness of the theory is marred by the fact that Goncharov had a character called Olga in mind as early as the forties, but he may have modified his original conception after his love affair.[68] Also, though several candidates vie in Goncharov scholarship for the role of models for his important characters, I have chosen to ignore such supposed sources because I fail to see what is gained by reducing a fictional creation about whom we know a great deal to a real person about whom we know almost nothing. We see Elizaveta and many of the persons in Goncharov's life solely through his eyes—he burned most of his papers, letters, and manuscripts[69]—so that what we have before us is not Elizaveta Tolstaya but the artist's perception of her. That perception is strikingly similar to Oblomov's view of Olga. The "real" Elizaveta, like the fictional Olga, is an ideal woman, an "angel," who promises salvation through escape from isolation. Even the same metaphors of music and light employed in *Oblomov* for Olga describe

[67] The view originates with Sakulin, *Golos minuvshego*, No. 11 (November 1913), p. 56. O. M. Chemena has recently argued for Ekaterina Maykova, the wife of Vladimir, as a model for both Olga, and Vera of *The Ravine*. *Sozdanie dvukh romanov* (Moscow, 1966).

[68] See Lyatsky, *Roman i zhizn'*, pp. 324-326.

[69] For an account, see S. Shpitser, "Zabytyy klassik," *Istoricheskiy vestnik*, CXXVI (1911), 684.

Elizaveta's spirituality and redemptive powers.[70] Was Elizaveta all that perfect? It is doubtful: Goncharov was often quite critical of her shortcomings. But he also felt it necessary to see her in ideal terms. At one point in "Pour et contre," "he" (i.e. Goncharov) despairs that the object of his love is only a woman, that he cannot assure the permanence of her presence and admire her without fear of loss, as did Pygmalion gazing upon Galatea. He compares the novelist, painter, and sculptor Boris Raysky, who conceives of the women in his life as works of art, to Pygmalion, and mentions the Pygmalion myth again in *Oblomov*.[71] Pygmalion in creating Galatea crossed the boundaries that separate art from life, and it would seem that Goncharov had come to realize, if only dimly, that the angelic Elizaveta was a product of his imagination belonging more properly to art than to life. His biographers, though they differ about the models for Olga, are unanimous in postulating a straight line proceeding from experience to art. It is much more likely that Goncharov began with a mental image that colored his view of life and found form in his fiction. Seen this way, his stringent irony was not only a device for protection against emotion, but also a check against the excesses of his imagination.

At times in Goncharov's experience life imitated art—a circumstance that ceases to appear strange if we regard the sources of his fiction as certain potentialities he perceived in himself and a way of looking at the world instead of the mere data of biography. Though he began writing to the twenty-year-old Sofya Nikitenko with frequency in 1860, after the publication of *Oblomov*, she, as much as Elizaveta Tolstaya, was his Olga. Sofya was the daughter of Goncharov's close friend, the prominent bureaucrat and memoirist, Alexander Nikitenko. Mazon cites first-hand testimony of a certain "nuance 'amoureuse' " in their friendship, but such nuances crept into almost all Goncharov's relations with women, and they do not seem

[70] See *Golos minuvshego*, No. 11 (November 1913), p. 230, and No. 12 (December 1913), pp. 228-229.

[71] *Ibid.*, p. 226. *Sobr. soch.*, VI, 154-155. In *Oblomov* (IV, 243) Olga is compared to Pygmalion, Oblomov to Galatea, but, as we shall see, he also very much conceives of her as a work of art.

to have been more than good friends.[72] As Elizaveta resembled the Olga of the earlier phase of *Oblomov*—a love object transformed into an ethereal ideal—Sofya recalls the Olga of the later stages, the demanding young woman who insists upon the fulfillment of duty. Goncharov's letters convey an image of an extremely serious, high-minded, and humorless young lady. For a number of years she assisted the novelist by copying and sorting his notes and manuscripts for *The Ravine*. When work on the novel bogged down, as it often did, Sofya assumed that an Oblomov-like indolence was at fault and undertook to reform the novelist. He proved a difficult case.

Like many Russians of her age Sofya had learned to consider art a public responsibility and a form of service to the nation. When this "guardian of [his] moral side," as the distinguished novelist referred to the callow girl young enough to be his daughter, castigated him for neglecting his responsibilities to Russian literature or urged him "to steel himself in struggle *like iron in a fire*" (how little she knew her man!), he felt compelled to plead illness, fate, his difficult life, and harsh youth as reasons for not living up to her expectations.[73] It was to Sofya Nikitenko, more than anyone else, that Goncharov spoke of his lofty ideals for humanity lest she think poorly of him. He also fought back, as Oblomov seldom does, and in the process articulated another aspect of the debate that runs through his fiction.

Subsumed under the opposition of the practical and the ideal of "Is It Good or Bad to Live in the World?" was an opposition of duty and pleasure. The Elizaveta Tolstaya correspondence has taught us that the argument of that essay mirrored a debate within the self— of a "He" and an "I" who hinted at two aspects of the novelist's personality. To a degree the Sofya Nikitenko correspondence again embodies an argument of the artist with himself, for he shared her rigorous sense of duty and obligation, and her idealism. Confronted with these qualities in another and badgered by Sofya's insistent moralism, he again countered, as in "Is It Good or Bad . . . ," with a re-

---

[72] Mazon, p. 117. The published correspondence is in *Literaturnyy arkhiv*, IV (1953), 107-162, and *Sobr. soch.*, VIII, and *Sobr. soch.* (Pravda), VIII, *passim*.

[73] May 30, 1868 and May 16, 1866, *Sobr. soch.* (Pravda), VIII, 370, 352.

minder of the human need for pleasure and joy. However, it is not the rarefied pleasures of the soul or of an ideal realm that Goncharov now describes to Sofya, but the more ordinary human joys to be found in artistic creation and personal affection. Art may be a duty, he concedes, but it is "also a pleasure in itself"—even a "sensual pleasure." Her view of life is too severe and ascetic; she insists upon duty, but the efforts of our lives should be directed at being human (*byt' chelovekom*), and one becomes human through loving: our "first duty is love"; one must love "in any way possible."[74]

In arguing with Sofya about love and duty, Goncharov tried to define a middle ground between her (and his) abstract idealism and the sphere of simple animal passion—an area that would be distinctively human. Like the attitude toward the love of the "He" of "Pour et contre" from which the novelist had earlier separated himself, Sofya's view is too literary, too "Schiller-like." "Passion is always ugly" but there is nothing "alive" or "human" in the "mute adoration" we find in certain novels. A poetical love, a love based on the preconceptions of the imagination, cannot survive the first moments of a relationship. Love is not an abstraction; we cannot love an idea but only what is human, what is incarnated "in flesh." Characteristically, though, Goncharov describes love here and elsewhere as closer to friendship than what we usually conceive of as love between a man and a woman. Love is a bond of mutual sympathy from which "ugly passion" has been excluded and that promises "a quiet, peaceful, deep, and solid happiness. . . ."[75]

The search for a principle that is distinctively human to oppose to Sofya's abstract view of experience led Goncharov to cast doubt upon, or at least qualify, his belief that man requires an ideal of human perfection. ". . . Ideals and idealizations," he warns Sofya, "that is, an immoderate and . . . sterile striving toward them, have always caused people to suffer more than have real sufferings." Our nature and destiny demand an ideal but we must always take account of "the weakness of man, his fragility, his extreme imperfection." Tragic and

[74] June 21, 1860, *Sobr. soch.* (Pravda), VIII, 328; June 8 and 23, 1860, *Sobr. soch.*, VIII, 332, 339, 340.

[75] August 21, 1866, *Sobr. soch.*, VIII, 362-365.

epic poets like Homer, Sophocles, and Racine have provided us with heroic images and "lofty aspirations." However, comic writers—Aristophanes, Plautus, Cervantes, Molière (and we should not forget that Goncharov was primarily a comic writer)—furnished an alternative image in their representations of human weakness. Their motto has always been, "Do not forget yourself, man, and do not clothe yourself in God's mantle!"[76]

Though he often spoke of man's inevitable progress to a perfect future, morality for Goncharov, as stated in his letters to Sofya, did not depend, as it did for many Russian intellectuals, upon a dedication to what was to come. An abstract sense of virtue, he felt, will not necessarily lead to moral acts; nor can the operations of governments and social institutions, however worthwhile, qualify as good deeds. The true moral act is instead personal and immediate; it is the expression of "a loving and living human being" who does not place himself above his fellow men but "gives himself as a friend." We must recognize our common humanity. There exists a core of personality or a "human nature." Though we may change our manners (*nravy*), we cannot alter our nature and cross "the human boundary" in the name of "impossible human ideals. . . ." To withdraw from humanity into asceticism is immoral, even if one performs philanthropic acts out of a theoretical belief in the good: "Monks are egoists; they will not enter the kingdom of life . . . because they do not wish to mend others and are unable to save themselves together with others."[77]

The identification of the good with a selfless and personal human act that comes from the "heart," of salvation with community, and the acute awareness of human frailty we find in the correspondence to Sofya Nikitenko, did not mark a retreat from the search for "a bright and beautiful human image" or the faith that human history was marching steadily and surely to a common goal of perfection. The idealism and the personalism—a longing to transcend the human condition and a hope to love man as he is—dwelt simultaneously in Goncharov's thought and provided a major and unresolved tension of his fiction. The tension is perhaps characteristically Russian. The

[76] *Ibid.*, p. 367 (italics removed).
[77] July 24, 1869, *Sobr. soch.* (Pravda), VIII, 394-397.

constrictions and backwardness of Russian life drove men to dream of ideal solutions, but the important Russian novelists—Dostoevsky, Tolstoy, Turgenev—though they searched for values and an image of man that would transfigure contemporary reality, also possessed a keen awareness of the actualities of the human condition and the dangers implicit in treating man as an abstraction. "I am only against intellectualizing," Goncharov wrote another woman friend, "against . . . *deciding beforehand* life's questions which have not been experienced personally. . . ."[78] A reminder of the complexities of actual experience may very well be what the art of the novel, and the Russian novel in particular, is about.

In December of 1855 Goncharov accepted an important position in the government service. He became an official censor—a role that seems incompatible with that of a writer but that was not uncommon in Russia, where it was a deep-seated tradition to serve the state. The accession of Alexander II to the throne in 1855 marked the beginning of a period of political and social reforms including a short-lived liberalization of the censorship. The government wanted prominent writers in its censorship apparatus to improve relations with the literary community. Goncharov, already a civil servant, was a logical choice. He served from 1856 to 1860 with a local St. Petersburg censorship committee under the administration of the relatively liberal Ministry of Public Education. In 1863, when the censorship was reorganized and centralized under the Ministry of Internal Affairs headed by the conservative Pyotr Valuev, Goncharov became a member of a committee that acted as a supreme board of review of Russian censorship organs. He finally retired from the service in December 1867 with the rank of Actual Councilor of State—an achievement that entitled him to be called "His Excellency."

Goncharov may have agreed to enter the censorship service in order to escape his tedious bureaucratic duties and be closer to literature. If so, he was naive, and the decision was unfortunate. Censors, no matter how well-intentioned, are never loved by writers. Goncharov became, as a contemporary recalled, "an object of indignation

[78] To Ekaterina Maykova, May 16, 1866, *ibid.*, p. 348.

for the liberals. . . ." Satirical epigrams, caricatures, and direct attacks appeared in the press. He overheard disparaging comments of his friends. The onslaught came chiefly from the radical left, but even moderates like the literary historian and memoirist Pavel Annenkov or the critic Alexander Druzhinin—who was otherwise favorably disposed to Goncharov's work—felt uneasy before the spectacle of a writer turned censor.[79] It was with some justification that the novelist came to fear that "if I wrote the devil knows what, even then there would be no compassion for me, if only because of my title and position."[80] The extremely thin-skinned and retiring Goncharov, who had made it a principle of his life to avoid controversy and public exposure, suddenly found himself in the middle of the polemical storms of the Russian scene. The hostility he encountered while a censor undoubtedly contributed to his gradual withdrawal from society—a withdrawal that made him a virtual recluse in the last decades of his life.

His sense of isolation was also due in part to changing historical circumstances. In the forties and into the fifties Goncharov, though never on intimate terms with his fellow writers, was vaguely sympathetic to the more forward looking elements of the Russian intelligentsia. Along with other promising young writers of his generation, among them Dostoevsky and Turgenev, he had gravitated toward the circle of writers and intellectuals surrounding the influential critic and leader of the progressive Westerners, Vissarion Belinsky. Like

[79] E. A. Shtakenshneyder, "Iz *Dnevnika*," in *Goncharov v vospominaniyakh*, pp. 60-61. See, e.g., N. F. Shcherbina, "Molitva sovremennykh russkikh pisateley" [1858], in *Stikhotvoreniya* (Leningrad, 1937), p. 211, and A. I. Gertsen [Herzen], "Neobyknovennaya istoriya o tsenzore Gon-cha-ro iz Shi-pan-khu" [1857], in *Sobranie sochineniy* (Moscow, 1954-1965), XIII, 104. Shi-pan-khu is the Russian version of the Chinese word for Japan; Herzen implies that Goncharov is as feudal in outlook as the Japanese he had visited. In a letter to Annenkov, December 8, 1858, *Sobr. soch.*, VIII, 303-304, Goncharov complained of being publicly humiliated and ridiculed by his addressee. Druzhinin's reaction is quoted in *Sobr. soch.* (Pravda), VIII, 309.

[80] Letter to A. A. Kraevsky, July 7, 1859, *Russkaya starina*, CXLVIII, No. 10 (October 1911), 61.

Dostoevsky, Goncharov was one of Belinsky's several "discoveries."[81] His first works were published in the liberal and eventually radical *Contemporary (Sovremennik)* and he took part, with such leading Russian writers as Nekrasov, Tolstoy, and Turgenev, in the social and intellectual life surrounding that historical journal. Goncharov never shared Belinsky's radicalism or his ideological fervor. He was attracted by the critic's unquestionable sincerity, and he also identified Belinsky with what was new and vital in Russian literature.[82] For a brief moment the political left and the artistic *avant-garde* had felt a common purpose and found themselves in the same camp.

The age of Alexander II and the Reforms changed all that. The late fifties and sixties witnessed a profound split in the Russian intellectual world. The "new men"—young radicals like Nikolay Chernyshevsky and Nikolay Dobrolyubov who, like Belinsky before them, wrote for the *Contemporary*—assumed a more intransigent position than had their radical forbears of the forties, while the artists, many of whom had matured in the idealistic and theoretical climate of the preceding decades, felt outraged by the materialism of the new radicals and their utilitarian view of art. Although the writers generally applauded the reforms and the emancipation of the serfs, the radicals considered them a sham and engaged in thinly disguised calls to revolution. Class distinctions also played a role in the break, since a number of the prominent radicals of the sixties were of lower-class origin (Dobrolyubov and Chernyshevsky were sons of priests) and, like Turgenev's Bazarov, cultivated manners designed to shock the gentry and finally extinguish its dominance of Russian cultural styles. In the sixties the alliance of radical criticism and literature of the age of Belinsky, which despite ideological differences had developed out of a shared dedication to the new realistic, or as it was called in Russia,

[81] Nekrasov deserves a share of the credit. See I. I. Panaev's account in the excerpt from "Vospominanie o Belinskom," in *Goncharov v vospominaniyakh*, pp. 46-47.

[82] In the late forties he was advising his friends to read Herzen and the *Contemporary* and informing them that "we [of the literary world] expect much from Belinsky," who had become the literary critic of the journal in 1846 (letter to Yu. D. Efremova, October 25, 1847, *Sobr. soch.*, VIII, 237-238).

"natural" movement, came apart. A mass desertion from the *Contemporary* took place, in which almost every important writer of the period, including Goncharov, participated—the poets Afanasy Fet and Apollon Maykov, the dramatist and poet Alexey Tolstoy, Ostrovsky, Turgenev, Leo Tolstoy (Dostoevsky was in exile at the time). Nekrasov and Saltykov-Shchedrin alone among the major writers stayed with the radicals. However, since radical criticism in Russia wielded an influence over the reading public disproportionate to the actual number of committed revolutionaries, writers of Goncharov's generation could now anticipate a reception that was at least wary when it was not hostile. In the politically overheated atmosphere of the period, a writer's politics or "tendency" became of prime importance not only for the young radicals but for their enemies on the right as well. Confronted with a radical criticism and its social demand that literature serve the cause of progress and revolution, surrounded in the government service by conservatives and some reactionaries who exerted pressure from the opposite direction, Goncharov felt increasingly isolated: "The young do not forgive you for remaining a man of your age, epoch, upbringing, and customs. . . . The old are dissatisfied that you do not do what you are unable to do. . . ."[83]

What were Goncharov's politics? Some describe him as a conservative; others, and these are in the majority, as a liberal. Everyone agrees that he was relatively indifferent to politics. Part of the difficulty lies in the terms—one man's liberalism is another's conservatism; what is perceived as liberal in one situation may prove conservative in another. Indifference to politics, however, when it is not the result of cynicism—and Goncharov was anything but a cynic—can easily lead to political positions sometimes liberal and sometimes conservative. A man uninterested in politics because, like Goncharov, he sees salvation in personal terms—in the individual moral act or in the lonely struggle of artistic creation—is likely to be tolerant of a wide range of political views. Since his concerns lie elsewhere, does it matter what theories men propound as long as they do not infringe upon his personal world? But once they do intrude, when theory threatens

[83] Letter to N. D. Khvoshchinskaya (Zaionchkovskaya), January 23, 1872, *ibid.*, VIII, 442.

to manifest itself in violent action, or when it touches upon those institutions that provide him with the opportunity to cultivate his private gardens, then the indifferent and formerly liberal individual may turn into a staunch conservative.

Such, in broad terms, were Goncharov's politics—liberal as regards the expression of opinion and conservative in the defense of certain fundamental institutions. The dearth of political commentary in his correspondence has compelled scholars to extrapolate his views from his literary works and especially from his sole political novel, *The Ravine*—which I shall discuss separately—or to seek them in his censorship reports. Official government documents available for the perusal of supervisors hardly constitute an ideal source to ascertain what a man really thinks, but they are virtually all we have.[84] I am in basic agreement with Mazon, who found Goncharov in his censorship activity "a partisan of liberalism," though not without "a certain timidity" that made him ordinarily "the most formalistic of censors"— his colleague Nikitenko accused him of constantly straining to remain in the good grace of both the government and the radicals. Voensky described him as "an enlightened and humane censor who always tried to find means for a soft effect upon writers, did not resort to severe measures," and sometimes resembled, instead of a censor, "a well-inclined critic concerned about the purity and finished quality of a literary composition" (Goncharov could not refrain from commenting upon the style of works under his surveillance).[85] He was surprisingly indulgent of the most radical sentiments—whether it was

[84] A representative sampling of Goncharov's censorship reports and descriptions of his activity may be found in K. Voensky, "Goncharov-tsenzor," *Russkiy vestnik*, CCCV (October 1906), 571-619; Mazon, *Ivan Gontcharov*, pp. 189-209, 344-421, and "Goncharov kak tsenzor," *Russkaya starina*, No. 3 (March 1911), pp. 471-485; V. Evgen'ev (Maksimov), "K kharakteristike obshchestvennogo mirosozertsaniya I. A. Goncharova v 60-kh godakh," *Severnye zapiski*, No. 9 (September 1916), pp. 126-152, "I. A. Goncharov kak chlen Soveta Glavnogo upravleniya po delam pechati," *Golos minuvshego*, No. 11 (November 1916), pp. 117-156, No. 12 (December 1916), pp. 140-179.

[85] Mazon, *Ivan Gontcharov*, pp. 194-195, 202; Nikitenko, "Iz *Dnevnika*," in *Goncharov v vospominaniyakh*, pp. 123-127; Voensky, *Russkiy vestnik*, CCCV (October 1906), 573-574.

Dmitry Pisarev's propagandizing of socialistic communes in a review of Chernyshevsky's novel *What Is To Be Done?*, a French novel translated as *Reminiscences of a Proletarian* that sided with the French working class in the revolt of 1848, or an article by the Russian radical Pyotr Tkachev deploring unequal distribution of wealth and land—again in France, but Russian readers were accustomed to making the shoe fit at home.[86] Goncharov passed many an item whose views he personally detested. In the manner of a classical liberal he had confidence in the capacity of the marketplace of ideas to test opinion and reject what was false or harmful. As he put it in approving for the *Contemporary* an article by Maksim Antonovich, which he read correctly as socialistic and materialistic in tendency: "Extreme views show themselves to be flimsy before strict science and die away from the contact of critical analysis, as has already happened to many theories including, among others, communism in foreign writings."[87]

Goncharov, however, perceived certain limits to the exercise of freedom. Like most members of his class he feared the potential for violence of the Russian masses and was content to restrict freedom of thought to those who were more or less his social peers. Also, though the writer should be given "full freedom" to expose "common faults and social ills," he must not deviate "from the true goals of art [and] seek the dark side, instead of in human errors, in institutions themselves. . . ."[88] Goncharov is here following government policy, but he apparently agrees. It was not after all necessary to add "the true goals of art" to a definition of what was legally permissible. Goncharov reduces politics to a critique of manners. He felt that there

[86] See *Russkiy vestnik*, CCCV (October 1906), 579-583, and *Golos minuvshego*, No. 11 (November 1916), pp. 142-145. The Pisarev review was "Novyy tip"; it appeared in *Russkoe slovo*, No. 10 (1865). The novel, *Histoire d'un homme du peuple* (1865), was by Émile Erckmann and Alexandre Chatrian. Tkachev's article was "Proizvoditel'nye sily Evropy," in *Russkoe slovo*, No. 12 (1865).

[87] *Severnye zapiski*, No. 9 (September 1916), pp. 132-136. The article was "Pishcha i eyo znachenie." It was subsequently turned down by Nikitenko. See also "Predislovie k romanu *Obryv*," *Sobr. soch.*, VIII, 155-156.

[88] *Golos minuvshego*, No. 12 (December 1916), pp. 173-174; *Severnye zapiski*, No. 9 (September 1916), pp. 147, 139.

existed a central core of personality, a "human nature," that could not be changed, and he also seems to have accepted contemporary institutions as part of the nature of things, for he never seriously questioned them.

The problem is: which institutions? Serfdom was certainly not one of those he considered inviolable, though in his usual timid fashion he did not criticize it openly until after the emancipation (in *The Ravine*) when his condemnation could make no difference to anyone. When Goncharov advised against seeking error in institutions, he of course had the Russian autocracy and its agencies in mind. Mazon is correct in speaking of Goncharov's "natural submission to tradition . . . , a tradition that is autocratic and orthodox in its foundation. . . ." He is also extremely perceptive when he detects "a good share of indifference and scepticism" creeping into Goncharov's traditionalism, a scepticism that he did not dare express openly, but that suggests itself in "the impression of artifice, of effort, and boredom" we receive from his censorship reports.[89] Goncharov failed to articulate an intellectual defense of his "conservatism" because its roots were more psychological than ideological. His "natural" or "instinctive" submission to authority was a reflex born of his fear and an expression of an urgent need for stability. Though he was certainly liberal for his time in his tolerance of dissenting opinions and his hopes for gradual progress, the threat of violent change, of sudden disruption of the way of life he knew and felt comfortable with, frightened and angered him. Faced with the turbulence of a social order moving toward chaos, he reacted as he had before the turbulence of his own emotions and withdrew behind a mask of dull indifference: ". . . it's not that he doesn't understand," Dostoevsky wrote of him with penetration after vainly trying to engage this *"great mind"* (Dostoevsky's italics) in a discussion of the contemporary situation, "but that he doesn't want to understand."[90] Goncharov slipped into the role of an unquestioning

[89] *Ivan Gontcharov*, p. 203.

[90] Letter to Kh. D. Alchevskaya, April 9, 1876, *Pis'ma*, III, 206. One of the delusions of the paranoia of Goncharov's later years (see below) was that the government suspected him of disloyalty, which would account for his increasing caution.

member of the party of order, but had the form of that order changed—and we shall see in our discussion of *The Frigate Pallas* that his view of an ideal society is more bourgeois and Western than traditionally Russian—he would have, perhaps, just as easily conformed, because it was order he loved and not autocracy.

There was one institution, however, that he did defend vehemently—the family. It is characteristic of Goncharov that in his report on Pisarev's review of *What Is To Be Done?* he passes casually over indications that Pisarev sympathizes with communism and even atheism, and yet finds that "punitive measures" may be in order because Pisarev "applauds Chernyshevsky's subversion of morality and the foundations of the family."[91] Goncharov's angriest diatribes against the left, when they were not denunciations of the radicals' utilitarian theories of art, invariably centered on the so-called woman question. It was the romantic attitude toward love—the Rousseauian doctrine that the desires of the individual take precedence over the claims of society and the family—that stoked his ire. Goncharov was not alone among Russians in converting politics into an issue of morality. Economic and political theory inevitably seemed remote to people living in an underdeveloped country with a relatively simple economy and an authoritarian state system that decided political issues from above. Goncharov's choice of the family as the crux of the political question was also dictated by his personal psychology. Like many men, he idealized what he desired and could not find. Also, fearful of his feelings, and we can assume of his sexual feelings, with the passage of the years he found more occasion to give vent to a streak of moralistic prudishness that was part of his nature.

Outward compliance without strong inner conviction seems to have characterized Goncharov's religious faith as well. He never questioned the tenets of Orthodoxy, but he seldom affirmed them either. Some time in his youth he had ceased to observe the rites of his church. In later years he may have become more devout. He went to confession, may have resumed regular attendance of church services (the sources differ), and occasionally proclaimed his piety to his

[91] *Russkiy vestnik*, CCCV (October 1906), 579-583.

51

correspondents.[92] Goncharov certainly considered himself a believer, but his faith gave him little sustenance in his sufferings. Through a voluminous correspondence, which is at times an unceasing cry of despair, he almost never turned to God for support or justification of his sufferings.

On a few occasions Goncharov did attempt to explain the nature of his belief. In the "Introduction to the Novel *The Ravine*" (1869) he argued that though "moral imperfection" may to an extent depend on ignorance it is for the most part rooted in "an evil will." To correct the latter the Commandments and the Gospels provide "the sole guides." Happily, though, the roads of science and religion run parallel—one leads forward to the conquest of nature; the other to moral "perfection," which is presumably to be realized on earth.[93] Though Goncharov's view places large importance upon Christian teaching as the caretaker of man's moral nature, it also relegates the religious experience, which is central for a believer, to a secondary position. What we miss in Goncharov's professions of faith is a sense of the presence of God in the affairs of men, of a living and personal relation to Him, and of a hope for His grace. Instead, progress—the Enlightenment and widespread nineteenth-century faith of European man in the inevitable journey of the race to perfection—for which science and religion (and art) only furnish differing but parallel roads, became the central article of his belief.

Faith in progress is a comfortable theodicy. It reassures us that no matter how terrible the present, the world is still rational and the future happy. Did Goncharov really have his heart even in this highly rationalized and secular faith? Trust in the forward march of history intrudes into his literary work—he often judges his characters according to whether they avoid or further the process. But he also felt doubt as to the possibility or even the desirability of human perfection.

[92] See letter to N. A. Maykov, July 13, 1849, *Sobr. soch.*, VIII, 245; N. I. Barsov, "Vospominanie ob I. A. Goncharove," *Goncharov v vospominaniyakh*, p. 146; and Superansky, "Materialy," *Vestnik Evropy*, No. 11 (November 1908), p. 41.

[93] *Sobr. soch.*, VIII, 156-157. See also a letter to Vladimir Solov'ev, 1882?, *Zeitschrift für slavische Philologie*, XXXII (1965), 99-100.

He conveyed those doubts to Sofya Nikitenko, and he also described to her the plausibility of a world view diametrically opposed to the rational and ordered universe he postulated elsewhere. Sofya had urged him to resign himself to the logic of inevitability—his ideas always rebounded from her in the form of moralistic admonitions—and he offered her an alternative hypothesis. Suppose, he asked, that ants possessed consciousness and a human being capriciously stepped on one. The victim's fellow-ants might very well speak of "the intelligently arranged paths" of life and blame their brother ant because he had "left his path" where "everything that is created is created and arranged beautifully and for them. . . ." "Imagine," Goncharov continues, "if this were so, and perhaps it is so—how funny it is! Imagine that someone is looking down at us from above—and laughing. Imagine that all our joys, sorrows, and pains do not exist but have been dreamed, and, when we awaken and come to ourselves, we shall be told that there was nothing, that it was all a mirage, etc. etc. And we discourse about duty, lofty purpose, free will, and misuse of our possibilities."[94] The image is of an irrational and meaningless universe where the gods play with man. These two conflicting attitudes toward life—the scheme describing an intelligently ordered and purposeful world and the frightening sense of a hostile fate toying capriciously with human life—may very well have been the respective legacies of the novelist's two backgrounds, of the enlightened Nikolay Tregubov and the suspicious, superstition-ridden Goncharovs. The course of Ivan Goncharov's life suggests that the latter attitude, the sense of being helpless and forlorn before the contingencies of circumstance, dominated his mind, and his happy optimism was either a concession to his age or a means of self-justification.

Two events packed with emotional significance lay behind Goncharov when he began his descent into mental illness—the love affair with Elizaveta Tolstaya and the completion of *Oblomov*. One ended in failure, the other in success. Both may have had something to do with his difficulties. Elizaveta had represented the "thread of life,"

---

[94] June 29, 1860, *Literaturnyy arkhiv*, IV (1953), 137-138. See also letter of June 24 (pp. 127-130).

the "living nerve" that connected the artist to people and society. When the thread snapped he put all his hopes on art: "I frankly love literature," he wrote Turgenev in March of 1859, "and if I was happy in anything in life, it was in my calling . . . only this alone has remained; if only it has remained. . . ."[95] Love was a thread that led to life, but art served as a substitute for life: "[When writing] I sit down, like a musician at a piano, and I begin to imagine, to think, to feel, in a word, to live lightly, quickly, and originally and [I feel] almost as alive and real as in real life! . . . The evening, the morning passes imperceptibly; the force of electrical power expends itself— and I, like a discharged battery, become cold, without feeling, until the next day or the day after something again hits me—and I again can play—that is, write and live!"[96] Love had failed him, and after the great expenditure of creative energy upon *Oblomov* of the summer of 1857 a terror that he would prove unable to repeat the experience, that *The Ravine*—"this child of my heart"—was doomed to failure, overwhelmed him.[97] A loss of the ability to express himself in art was no small matter to a man who claimed to feel alive only in the act of creation. Turgenev was astute in perceiving that "Goncharov's strangenesses"—and Turgenev had ample opportunity to discover them—"can be explained . . . by too exclusive a literary life."[98] Love—the "thread of life"—had been severed, and now Goncharov stood in danger of losing his art, without which he felt like a desiccated battery cell—"cold, without feeling."

Goncharov's fear of failure was great. His fear of success may have been just as intense. It is perhaps no coincidence that the first tangible signs of Goncharov's paranoia—his suspicions that his friend Turgenev was stealing his ideas and plans—became manifest at the time *Oblomov* was appearing in print (in 1859). His censorship activity had thrust him into the public arena, and his novel quickly made his name a household word among literate Russians. Fame, however

---

[95] *Sobr. soch.*, VIII, 309-311.   [96] *Sbornik*, p. 133.

[97] The phrase appears in a letter to Fet, August 6, 1869, *Sobr. soch.*, VIII, 421.

[98] Letter to Ya. P. Polonsky, December 16, 1868, *Polnoe sobranie* (Moscow-Leningrad, 1960-1968), VII: *Pis'ma*, 260.

flattering, must have been also frightening to a man who had made it a major effort of his life to remain inconspicuous. In love Goncharov had dissociated himself from his feelings and tried to avoid responsibility by projecting them outward upon another—a fictional "he"—and in every area of his existence he made himself visible only with extreme reluctance and caution. He feared crowds and large social gatherings, avoided being photographed or posing for portraits, discouraged public celebrations of his literary fame, hesitated in publishing his works, and delayed their reprinting for many years. He continually belittled his own significance and expressed the wish to be forgotten.[99] His withdrawal into seclusion and private fantasies in his lonely flat on Mokhovaya Street in Petersburg was but a consequence of the logic of his life. Except in the realm of art Goncharov had denied himself usual human assertions of the self and, when art failed, nothing remained. The hostile critical reception of *The Ravine* in 1869 was merely the *coup de grâce* that put a seal of finality upon a slow drift away from human intercourse and action.

Early in 1859—while *Oblomov* was appearing in installments in the *Notes of the Fatherland* (*Otechestvennye zapiski*)—Goncharov accused Turgenev of plagiarism. He said that in 1855 he had shown his fellow-novelist his plans for *The Ravine*—he often sought Turgenev's advice and valued his literary judgments highly—and Turgenev had betrayed him by stealing some of his material for *A Nest of the Gentry* (January 1859). When *On the Eve* came out in January of the following year Goncharov made similar accusations. Turgenev demanded an impartial judgment of the dispute by members of the literary community, and on March 29, 1860 Pavel Annenkov, Alexander Druzhinin, Stepan Dudyshkin, and Alexander Nikitenko decided, sensibly enough, that whatever similarities existed between Goncharov's plans and Turgenev's novels could be explained by the

---

[99] Examples of Goncharov's self-effacement are so numerous as to create a depressing clutter for the author and his readers if cited fully. The opening statement of "Luchshe pozdno, chem nikogda" (". . . my time has passed and with it my compositions . . .") and the ensuing request that the public forget him and his works (while simultaneously reminding it in a lengthy defense of his art) is characteristic. *Sobr. soch.*, VIII, 64-65.

circumstance that they had arisen "on the same Russian soil." Nikitenko, who was drawn into the proceedings because he was close to Goncharov—Annenkov was presumed to be partial to Turgenev—gave an account of the incident indicative of the extent to which Goncharov had hurt himself in the eyes of his contemporaries: ". . . my friend Ivan Alexandrovich played a very unenviable role in this event; he showed himself to be some sort of petulant, extremely superficial and coarse human being, while Turgenev . . . conducted himself with great dignity, tact, refinement and that particular grace which is the property of decent people of highly educated society."[100] Upon hearing the verdict Turgenev broke off relations. A public reconciliation took place in January of 1864 at the funeral of Druzhinin. Goncharov, however, never felt reconciled and continued to nurture his suspicions and hatred in secret.

Why Turgenev? After all, Goncharov, though he later felt compelled to deny it, had admired his fellow-writer and had sought his approval and perhaps even his love. In the happiest moment of his adult life, perhaps its only happy moment—the Marienbad summer of 1857—it was Turgenev who was in his thoughts both as a literary authority he had to escape—"the thought that I am too simple in speech, that I cannot speak *in the Turgenevian manner* has ceased to frighten me . . ."—and as someone who inspired and would appreciate his achievement—"tell Turgenev . . . that when I wrote I heard his exhortations, his words, and that I dream of his broad embraces." ". . . I trusted Turgenev's taste and critical tact more than anyone else's," he added as a footnote to that strange and yet compelling account of his delusions, "An Uncommon Story" ("Neobyknovennaya istoriya"), and Turgenev's imagined perfidy appeared above all as a trust betrayed. Even after friendship turned into enmity, Gon-

---

[100] The correspondence is in *I. A. Goncharov i I. S. Turgenev po neizdannym materialam Pushkinskogo doma*, ed. B. M. Engel'gardt (Petersburg, 1923). See especially pp. 29-39. Goncharov's version may also be found in "Neobyknovennaya istoriya," *Sbornik*, pp. 7-189. The accounts of Annenkov and Nikitenko have been reprinted in *Goncharov v vospominaniyakh*, pp. 78-80, 116-118.

charov continued to assure the villain of his fantasies that they were still friends and performed sundry favors for the man he considered the cause of all his sufferings, as if he could not surrender completely the hope of returning to their formerly affectionate relationship.[101]

Envy had a great deal to do with the choice. Behind his cloak of diffidence Goncharov kept hidden a good share of vanity and ambition. He was not unaware of it: ". . . I am vain but my vanity appears in strange ways."[102] We have already observed his resentment of writers of the gentry who possessed an independent income giving them the unimpeded freedom to write and, in Goncharov's eyes, a more carefree existence than that enjoyed by a bureaucrat tied to the tedium of official routines. Also, those aristocratic qualities of grace, refinement, and sense of personal dignity Nikitenko found commendable in Turgenev only infuriated Goncharov. Turgenev's social ease, he recalled, made him a "common favorite" of the literary salons. Goncharov in comparison appeared stolid and secretive and felt friendless. "He has a throng of so-called friends," he complained; ". . . I lived alone—and probably shall die so!"[103] For a number of Russians, including Dostoevsky and Tolstoy, Turgenev's cultivated tact and moderation indicated only an absence of conviction; his urbanity, an alien effeteness. Whatever his talents—and these were also in dispute—Turgenev seemed to lack the passion, expansiveness, and seriousness of purpose that were supposedly the hallmark of the Russian writer. The great blocks of time he spent abroad and his close connection to Western literary circles fed the suspicions of his contemporaries. Though fluent in French, Goncharov rarely employed it in his correspondence and once chided a Russian gentlewoman for writing in its "pleasant and polite forms" instead of the more "sincere" Russian. French was reserved mostly for Turgenev and it gave a

[101] Letters to I. I. L'khovsky, August 2 and 22, 1857, *Sobr. soch.*, VIII, 291, 295. *Sbornik*, p. 168. Letter to Turgenev, January 22, 1868, *Goncharov i Turgenev*, pp. 57-60. Mazon, "Materialy dlya biografii i kharakteristiki I. A. Goncharova," *Russkaya starina*, No. 3 (March 1912), p. 106.

[102] *Sbornik*, p. 106.

[103] *Ibid.*, pp. 10, 171.

special bite to his scorn: "Oh, qu'il était magnifique, celui-là; oh, qu'il est beau—comme il porte majestueusement sa belle tête! oh, est-il grand, est-il superbe, ce premier poète de la Russie!"[104]

Professional rivalry also played a role in their falling-out. In the late fifties, when the dispute arose, there were virtually but two prominent novelists on the Russian scene—Goncharov and Turgenev. Gogol and Lermontov were dead; Dostoevsky was in exile; Tolstoy's early writings consisted of sketches and short stories or, like the work of Sergey Aksakov, stood on a borderline between autobiography and fiction. In "An Uncommon Story" Goncharov several times said with some accuracy that he was Turgenev's only rival. One of the major purposes of his accusation of plagiarism seems to have been, as Engelgardt has suggested, to discourage his rival from continuing in the genre of the novel, though his contempt for Turgenev's novelistic talents may also have reflected a sincere critical appraisal. From the beginnings of the sorry history Goncharov insisted energetically that Turgenev's true talent lay in lyricism or genre sketches (like those of *Notes of a Hunter*). Turgenev does not possess the patience, psychological depth, or persistence to pursue ideas and experience to their ultimate conclusions required of the novelist. Although Goncharov readily admitted lacking his colleague's facility, the implication is clear that the solider virtues of the psychological novelist are his: ". . . you slide through life superficially. . . . I . . . plough a deep furrow. . . ."[105]

As Turgenev continued to churn out novels and stories while Goncharov was bogged down on his final novel, delusions of plagiarism provided an excellent rationalization. After all, if Turgenev were stealing his best ideas and plans and rushing them into print before Goncharov, who felt it necessary to work slowly and stubbornly like "a harnessed ox,"[106] could get to them, it was perfectly understand-

[104] Letters to A. Ya. Koldkina, August 1866, *Sobr. soch.* (Pravda), VIII, 358, and S. A. Nikitenko, July 28, 1860, *Literaturnyy arkhiv*, IV (1953), 145.

[105] *Shornik*, pp. 32, 77. Letter of March 28, 1859 and Engel'gardt's introduction, in *Goncharov i Turgenev*, pp. 29-35, 17-18. As late as 1861 Chernyshevsky could write, "there are only two authorities in our literature: Mr. Turgenev and Mr. Goncharov." Quoted in *Chemena*, p. 65.

[106] *Goncharov i Turgenev*, p. 30.

able that the novel should be delayed and not meet with the applause
it deserved once it appeared. ". . . What an effect this novel could
and should have made," he lamented, "if only they [Turgenev and
his friends] had not run ahead with their copies!" Moreover, as his
delusions grew and multiplied, it became unnecessary to write or indeed do anything at all, for the very fact that talented people chose
Goncharov to steal from conferred greatness upon him. By the time
he came to write "An Uncommon Story" (1875-1878) almost all
contemporary French literature owed its success to the modest and
self-effacing bureaucrat from Simbirsk. The perfidious Turgenev had
passed his ideas on to his French friends—to Flaubert (*l'Éducation
sentimentale* is "simply an *abbreviated Ravine*"!), to the Goncourt
brothers, to Georges Sand, Alphonse Daudet, and others. Turgenev
in his monumental conceit had decided to play the role of the founder
and leader of an entire school of French literature. But since Turgenev stole from Goncharov, we can only conclude that the latter
deserves the credit. "Turgenev must . . . consider me a colossal talent
. . . if he spent half a lifetime in transmitting all this [his material]
to others. . . ."[107] Goncharov had few illusions about the actual
influence of *The Ravine*. His greatness was now a purely passive
phenomenon; it resided in his unrealized potential, in the quality and
magnitude of an imagination that Turgenev, through diabolical cunning and a network of agents, was able to divine. His comparisons of
himself to Turgenev always carried the implication that, though his
rival was facile, clever, and artful, he himself possessed depth, feeling,
expansiveness, and the richer imagination. Toward the end that rich
imagination ceased to be an active creative force. It became instead
a precious object others stole, a fruit they squeezed dry, a property
that enriched Turgenev, his friends, and even world literature, and
whose theft left the source dry and empty.

Such are the rationalizations neurosis contrives in order to ward
off the threat of failure or to turn its bitter pill into a fanciful triumph. However, they do not tell the whole story. Goncharov's crisis
went much deeper than injured vanity or even disappointment in art,
painful as the failure of *The Ravine* was. Indeed, it was an internal

---

[107] *Sbornik*, pp. 46, 84, 117 (italics removed).

catastrophe that doomed his talent and not the artistic failure that led to his malaise. Goncharov's illness had been long in preparation; it began well before his delusions appeared, though how early we cannot tell. It began the moment he decided that the best way to deal with his emotions was to project them away from the self and hide behind a protective mask of irony and diffidence. From his earliest surviving letters his despair centered upon a growing sense of being emptied. Along with "melancholy," words indicative of a loss of feeling and an emotional dullness—"apathy," "indifference," "ennui," "boredom," "coldness"—sound a continuing refrain in his correspondence. ". . . everywhere I bear with me an enervating boredom . . . , I feel a coldness close to repugnance . . ." (1847). "Some sort of heaviness, ennui, indolence, prosaicness, coldness . . . is becoming my lot . . ." (1849). "Melancholy has pursued me here also [on the journey to Japan]. . . . The sea has little effect upon me . . . ; perhaps the sea is not to blame, but old age [he is all of 40], coldness, and the prose of life" (1852). ". . . I have a plan . . . to try and see whether I can still complete my previous literary undertaking [*Oblomov*], if the coldness of life . . . has not taken everything away . . ." (1855). ". . . God forbid that apathy is my normal, inescapable condition . . ." (1858).[108] It was not. He could be warm and tender to the few he allowed himself to love; the fate of his nation and its literature concerned him deeply. The dull gaze emanating from those half-closed eyes, the roundish face with its heavy jowls, the phlegmatic movements of his corpulent body, which many took to be a perfect expression of Oblomovian laziness, were, like his cool mocking irony, a mask that hid a turbulent inner life and protected him from hurt. But as the years passed, his defenses in some terrible manner gradually became his inner reality. When the irony disappeared—and not a shred remains in "An Uncommon Story"—he was left with the coldness:

[108] To Yu. D. Efremova, *Sobr. soch.*, VIII, 238, *Nevskiy al'manakh*: "Iz proshlogo," II (Petrograd, 1917), 9; M. A. Yazykov, E. P. and N. A. Maykov, *Literaturnoe nasledstvo*, Nos. 22-24 (1935), pp. 346, 349; E. V. Tolstaya, *Golos minuvshego*, No. 12 (December 1913), p. 242; I. I. L'khovsky, *Literaturnyy arkhiv*, III (1951), 145.

... from the passage of the years, from experience, from—from—
the reasons are innumerable—a general cooling took place. Such
is my character and my entire nature: I am lively, receptive,
feverish both in my sympathies and antipathies, with a lively imagination; then I became tired, played out, grew dull, fat, and I feel
boredom and coldness from everything. This is not coldness to you,
or to another, or to a third party, but a general enveloping
coldness.[109]

These anguished words were written to Yuniya Efremova in July of
1859 at about the time Goncharov's delusions of persecution were
becoming manifest.

Freud in his classic paper on paranoia tells us that the

[paranoiac] patient has withdrawn from the people in his environment and from the external world generally the libidinal cathexis
which he has hitherto directed on to them. Thus everything has
become indifferent and irrelevant to him, and has to be explained
by means of a secondary rationalization. . . . The end of the world
is the projection of this internal catastrophe; his subjective world
has come to an end since his withdrawal of love from it. And the
paranoiac builds it up again, not more splendid, it is true, but at
least so that he can once more live in it. . . . *The delusion-forma-
tion, which we take to be a pathological product, is in reality an
attempt at recovery, a process of reconstruction.* . . . The human
subject has recaptured a relation, and often a very intense one, to
the people and things in the world, even though the relation is a
hostile one now where formerly it was hopefully affectionate. . . .[110]

To put it another way, the paranoiac, like the artist, creates an imaginary world—a fiction. His true illness does not lie in his delusions—
these are secondary phenomena—but in his emptiness, his absence of
feeling, which compels him to create a fiction in order to recapture

[109] Letter to Yu. D. Efremova, *Sobr. soch.* (Pravda), VIII, 320-321.
[110] "Psycho-Analytic Notes on an Autobiographical Account of a Case of
Paranoia (Dementia Paranoides) (1911)," *The Standard Edition of The
Complete Psychological Works of Sigmund Freud,* trans. and ed. James Strachey (London, 1958—), XII, 70-71.

"a relation . . . to the people and things in the world." Also, the relation that has been lost was once "hopefully affectionate"; "the person who is now hated and feared for being a persecutor was at one time loved and honoured." The paranoiac creates a relation based on enmity to replace one of warmth and affection that, for some reason, has become untenable.[111] But if the paranoiac behaves analogously to the artist in creating imaginary worlds, unlike the artist he no longer knows for certain that what he has conjured up is only a fiction; he cannot say with assurance, as Goncharov once did, ". . . if I know what Raysky is, if I am able to create him, it means that I am his critic, it means that I cannot be Raysky. . . ." Instead, the paranoiac tries to live his fiction and in the process loses himself in "a forest of conjecture" (the image is from "An Uncommon Story") where actuality and the hypothetical constructs of the imagination have become hopelessly confused. Goncharov had moved from the condition of the artist to that of the protagonists of his novels; he had created another fiction but he now perceived himself as merely a character manipulated by the whims of others. ". . . I cannot very well explain . . . where the author ends and the man begins," he lamented in the middle of "An Uncommon Story."[112]

The fiction his life had become even had its governing images— images of cold and warmth, light and dark, the sun and clouds. Like the deranged petty officials and declassé intellectuals who fill the pages of Russian literature from Pushkin's *Bronze Horseman* through Gogol and Dostoevsky to Bely's *St. Petersburg*, he suffered keenly

---

[111] *Ibid.*, p. 41. Freud (p. 59) felt that "homosexual wishful fantasies" played "an intimate (perhaps an invariable) relation" to paranoia. Goncharov's nephew Alexander reports an incident suggesting that the novelist may have projected such fantasies as a defense against homosexual wishes. See *Vestnik Evropy*, No. 11 (November 1908), p. 43. Freud's views have been amended to include the projection in paranoia of a wider range of emotions—see, e.g., Paula Heimann, "A Combination of Defense Mechanisms in Paranoid States," in *New Directions in Psycho-Analysis*, ed. Melanie Klein, *et al.* (London, 1955), pp. 240-265—and the evidence would indicate that Goncharov suffered from guilt over much of his emotional life, of which suppressed feelings of love for Turgenev surely played a part.

[112] *Sbornik*, pp. 108, 134.

from the "Petersburg illness." The gloom, the fogs, and darkness of that "unreal city" built on marshes and exposed to the cold winds of the Baltic oppressed him, provoked his hypochondria—Goncharov was a bundle of real and imaginary ailments—and intensified his melancholia. Foul weather, leaden oppressive skies, cold gray landscapes provided personal metaphors for the coldness and darkness within: ". . . some sort of foul cloud has stuck to the hills and transformed the forest and field into a swamp; it weighs upon a man's brain, holds back the blood in its flow and hardens all of him, makes him cold and indifferent to everything on earth. What is this? Do we live, or do we sleep through some sort of strange sleep and delirium?" "Yesterday the cold blew, clouds came—and all this lay upon my soul, and again turbid dregs floated to the surface; again I threw away my pen, hung my head and began to see, while awake, foul phantoms pursuing me! again friendly faces began to be transformed into enemies, to nod at me from the corners, to hurl filth, to put me into a pillory. . . ." His life, like that of Oblomov, turned into a search for warmth, light, and the sun. When the "caressing sun," as he called it, came into view and the sky cleared, he felt calmed, at times even cheerful, and was able to write. He fled the leaden skies and fogs of St. Petersburg, whenever his official duties permitted, to roam the watering-places and resorts of Europe—Marienbad, Baden-Baden, Kissingen, Boulogne-sur-Mer—in search of quiet and sunny spots where creative urges deadened by gray Russian winters could again come alive. ". . . I hunt the sun . . . ," he wrote Stasyulevich, and the hunt became a motif of his life and his masterpiece.[113]

Freud thought that the sun as a symbol represented the father.[114] Was Goncharov seeking the paternal love he lost in childhood with the death of his father? Did Turgenev, through what psychoanalysis calls "transference," become identified with his father or, more likely, with his aristocratic godfather, the indulgent and soft Tregubov? Was his suppressed affection for Turgenev the source of the guilt that made

[113] Letters to S. A. Nikitenko, June 24, 1860, *Literaturnyy arkhiv*, IV (1953), 129-130, and M. M. Stasyulevich, June 19, 1868, February 16, 1869, *Stasyulevich*, IV, 24-26, 68.
[114] *Stand. Edn.*, XII, 54.

him stifle the emotional side of his nature? Or was the "caressing sun," despite Freud, maternal?[115] Was Goncharov seeking the warmth and tenderness his mother seems to have been unable to communicate? Did an association with a maternal image compel him to turn the women in his life into ideals promising salvation and taboo for any relation aside from reverence or polite friendship? Every life probably raises more questions than can be answered. Goncharov's in particular must remain incompletely understood, for he has left us an account of his symptoms and the outlines of his dilemma as transformed into art, which is not the same as self-revelation, and very few keys to a full understanding of his plight. Of course he did not himself possess the answers, but he knew that men grow up crooked because of what they were deprived of as children. It was the first appearance of the "caressing sun"—of warmth, care, and tenderness—that was all-important.

And the light of a clear warm love should fall from somewhere on children's heads and, like the sun's rays, warm and comfort them so as not to intimidate them at the dawn of life, and, without disturbing their nerves with early storms, allow the germs of physical, intellectual and moral powers to develop.

What kind and tender hands are needed at a very early age to make out of children not oppressed and downtrodden cowards or humiliated, insulted, fainthearted, false people, but genuine, honest, courageous men and women, steadfast in life and, in addition, kind and trained for the fulfillment of every duty.[116]

Though the "bright and beautiful human image" of which Goncharov dreamed eluded him, he did find compromises that softened

---

[115] Freud (*ibid.*, p. 41) argues that ". . . the person to whom the delusion ascribes so much power and influence, in whose hands all the threads of the conspiracy converge, is . . . either identical with some one who played an equally important part in the patient's emotional life before his illness, or is easily recognizable as a substitute for him." In primitive myths the sun is chiefly parental but may be either maternal or paternal. See William Tyler Olcott, *Sun Lore of All Ages* (New York and London, 1914), pp. 35-36.

[116] Letter to S. A. Nikitenko, June 4, 1879, *Sobr. soch.* (Pravda), VIII, 467-468.

his dread of life. In a sense his delusions provided such a compromise, for, though they brought their own terrors, they also filled the emptiness with "a relation to the people and things in the world." Also several areas of normality remained. He still had a few close friends— Stasyulevich and his wife (except for those moments when his delusions expanded to embrace even him), Sofya Nikitenko, the Alexey Tolstoys, Anatoly Koni—who were able to temper his extravagant fancies with more realistic perceptions of his circumstances. After abandoning his large-scale literary ambitions and withdrawing from the competitive arenas of life, Goncharov, except for momentary returns of his imagined horrors, gradually began to calm down and settle into a humdrum existence. The letters of his last years are filled with commonplace banter—what he ate, where to find good cigars, the price of asparagus, whether the markets have carp. Most of his troubles were now *"petites miseries."* He continued to complain of old ailments—headaches, assorted tics, insomnia—but in addition his eyesight began to fail—he eventually lost the use of one eye—and he could read or work little. Europe was too distant for the aging writer, and from 1879 he spent his summers on the Baltic coast; almost to the very end he remained strong enough, when in Petersburg, to take his customary long strolls about the city. Despite his intentions to retire from literature, he could not tear himself away completely. The several efforts of his last years are for the most part an old man's exercises in nostalgia—reminiscences of his childhood, an idealized sketch of Moscow University, remembrances of Belinsky, and a fond account of the several servants who had cared for the bachelor's needs through the years. As an old man Goncharov also became a bit of a crank; he wrote short articles, printed anonymously, for a local Petersburg newspaper, the *Voice* (*Golos*), in which he complained of the noise in the city, recommended various measures for the restriction of stray dogs, hoped that sand would be sprinkled on the sidewalks in winter, and, in one article, offered a recipe for an ideal city where streets are clean and well-paved, doormen are civil, dogs leashed, and drunks have been removed from public places.[117] Such a blend of senile petulance and nostalgia may seem a

---

[117] A number of the *Golos* pieces have been reproduced by Mazon, in *Russ-*

tragic comedown for a writer who had once achieved greatness, but for Goncharov it represented an accommodation. He had transformed his longings and sufferings into art and now, when he gave up his longing, the suffering subsided: ". . . perhaps," he wrote Stasyulevich, "this peace comes from the fact that I have no desires except the desire—for peace."[118]

As Goncharov calmed down in surrendering his literary ambitions, he also felt more at ease because the dream of romantic love was no longer possible: "I hope that in the twilight of my days a good friend who abandoned me long ago, peace with quiet and reconciliation . . . will visit me, and not love . . . (to hell with it)."[119] Goncharov had failed to win his Olga, but, in another of those strange twists of fate whereby life seemed to follow on the heels of art, he in the end found his Agafya Matveevna. Alexandra Ivanovna Treygut was a woman of "the people"—the wife of Goncharov's manservant—who, when her husband died in 1878, took charge of the novelist's domestic affairs and cared for him in his declining years. He, in turn, after some initial trepidation, assumed responsibility for her welfare and the education and future security of her three children. It is difficult to tell exactly how Goncharov felt about Alexandra Treygut. He appreciated her efforts on his behalf, referred to her affectionately as "my nursemaid" and even in jest as "mom" (*mamochka*), but for the most part mentioned her only in passing. On one occasion he described her in terms that he could just as well have employed for his own mother. Alexandra Ivanovna was "an intelligent, solicitous mother, filled with love for her children, but such a love as they will appreciate in maturity. She cooks soup for them, sews, washes, working from morning to evening; she has neither time nor means to

kaya starina, No. 3 (March 1912), pp. 549-568, and No. 6 (June 1912), pp. 492-515.

[118] September 18, 1869, *Stasyulevich*, IV, 84. "Such are the events about which my stay in Paris turns," he wrote to Stasyulevich on July 18 of the same year after itemizing his assorted "*petites miseries*," "but I do not desire stronger ones; I fear them" (p. 81).

[119] Letter to I. I. Monakhov, June 7, 1876, *Sobr. soch.* (Pravda), VIII, 452.

indulge them, not even for caresses."[120] Indulgence was provided by Goncharov, as many years ago his godfather Nikolay Tregubov had indulged him in ways for which Avdotya Matveevna had neither the time nor, it seemed, the inclination. Perhaps the aging writer wanted to bestow upon these fatherless children the warmth of the "caressing sun" he had not had enough of in his childhood. "Goncharov," Koni recalled, "went to extreme limits in his completely selfless attachment. Concern about the children, their thoughts, feelings, habits, developing traits of character, the playful and tender nicknames he gave to them, the caresses of Sanya (so the oldest was called) aroused his warm gratitude. Gradually their lives set strong indissoluble roots in his existence."[121]

The bachelor had at last found a family. Alexandra and her children remained with him through the failing health of his last years. He suffered a mild stroke in 1890 and died a year later at the age of 79 after a brief illness. In his will the writer ignored his surviving relatives and left the great bulk of his wealth and earthly possessions to Alexandra Treygut and her children.[122]

[120] Letters to A. A. Muzalevskaya, April 18, 1878?, and S. A. Nikitenko, June 4, 1879, *ibid.*, pp. 463-464, 467. Alexandra Treygut's reminiscences are in an interview by Shpitser, *Istoricheskiy vestnik*, CXXVI (November 1911), 679-691.

[121] *Goncharov v vospominaniyakh*, p. 259.

[122] Alekseev, *Letopis'*, pp. 259-260.

CHAPTER II

Esthetic Views

GONCHAROV came to maturity in the romantic atmosphere of the thirties, and throughout his career he stressed the superiority of unconscious creation to conscious craftsmanship.[1] The role of the unconscious is central to his esthetics, though he may have overemphasized its importance in the face of the positivistic arguments of the sixties and seventies. In his famous *apologia*, "Better Late Than Never" ("Luchshe pozdno, chem nikogda") (1879), he quoted approvingly Belinsky's popular dictum, *"the artist thinks in images,"* but immediately added that the really important issue is whether he thinks consciously or unconsciously.[2] Apparently only the artist whose thought processes are unconscious "thinks in images," for "image"—an extremely loose term in the nineteenth-century vocabulary, which can signify anything from a metaphor to an artistic representation—is opposed to "idea," "conscious thought," and "intellect." Artists who depend upon their conscious minds usually turn out inferior work: ". . . the intellect furnishes what the image has left incomplete, and their creations are frequently dry, pale, and imperfect. They speak to the mind of the reader saying little to his imagination and feelings. They persuade, teach, convince, . . . touching us little."[3]

Goncharov did not usually perceive a middle position to the unconscious-conscious argument. Opposed to conscious artists are those who

---

[1] Goncharov's esthetic views have been garnered from his essays, memoirs, and letters. The essays and memoirs are listed and described below, in chap. ten.

[2] Belinsky's famous phrase reads, "The poet thinks in images. . . ." V. G. Belinsky, *Sobranie sochineniy*, ed. F. M. Golovenchenko (Moscow, 1948), I, 464. It was not original to Belinsky and came to Russia from the German romantics.

[3] *Sobr. soch.*, VIII, 69, 79.

have an "excess of imagination." In the work of such artists ". . . the image absorbs the meaning and the idea; the portrait speaks for itself. . . ." He unhesitatingly includes himself in this second group: ". . . I belong to the latter category, that is, I am primarily carried away (as Belinsky noted about me) 'by my ability to portray.' "[4] Occasional efforts at "conscious thought," he feels, constituted a fault in his fiction. The artist must not allow his intellectual judgments to intrude into the work of art, but "must speak through images." Intelligence in art is "the ability to create an image," "and in art only the image expresses an idea. . . ." "The author . . . is an external figure. He only looks at the faces of his heroes (in his imagination), listens to how they speak and what they say—and faithfully transmits it. Such are the conditions of the artist. . . ."[5]

The novelist found the ways of the unconscious to be unpredictable and elusive. Fond of opposing the terms "to compose" (*sochinyat'*) and "to create" (*tvorit'*), the artist as conscious craftsman (*poeta*) and as inspired genius (*vates*), Goncharov invariably used the former verb pejoratively and in a moment of difficulty with his own work defined "creation" as that which comes unbidden and unexpectedly: ". . . I am not creating, but composing, and that is why it is coming out badly, pale, weak. It is impossible to fabricate or compose the beautiful; it comes somehow unexpectedly, on its own, and this [quality] of the unexpected, that is, poetry, is missing (*etogo nechayannogo, to est' poezii, net kak net*)."[6]

Imagination, then, is associated with unconscious inspiration. It appears adventitiously, takes hold of the artist, and turns him into a passive vehicle who "faithfully transmits" its impressions. Imagination is also the *sine qua non* of the artistic process: "The truth in nature is given to the artist only by means of the imagination!" Art, like

[4] *Ibid.*, p. 70. Goncharov is referring to Belinsky's characterization of him in the essay, "Vzglyad na russkuyu literaturu 1847 goda." "Mr. Goncharov draws his figures, characters, scenes before all in order to satisfy his need and enjoy his ability to portray." Belinsky, III, 830.

[5] *Sobr. soch.*, VIII, 79, 107. *Sbornik*, p. 85. I. A. Goncharov, *Literaturno-kriticheskie stat'i i pis'ma*, ed. A. N. Rybasov (Leningrad, 1938), p. 315.

[6] In a letter to S. A. Nikitenko, June 28, 1860, *Sobr. soch.*, VIII, 343.

science, "shows the truth, but it has other means and devices; these means are feeling and the imagination."[7]

Goncharov's identification of the imagination with unconscious inspiration and even unconscious direction may seem surprising. Criticism has often characterized him as a realistic portraitist of social mores who rigorously avoided the subjective and personal. Though he certainly considered himself a realist, he avoided a narrow and dogmatic understanding of the term. If realism conflicts with the imagination, then the imagination takes precedence.

> . . . I am not such an adherent of realism as not to permit deviations from it. To please realism it would be necessary excessively to limit and even completely eliminate the imagination, which means falling into dryness, sometimes into colorlessness, drawing silhouettes instead of living images, sometimes entirely renouncing poetry and all in the name of a seeming truth. But imagination and with it poetry are granted to man by nature and enter into his being, consequently, into his life. Will it be right or real to omit them?[8]

He permits "deviations" from realism, and he also rejects definitions that would limit it to copying from nature.

> The artist does not portray only his subject but also that tone by which this subject is illuminated in his imagination. Realism, to speak the truth, endeavors to free itself of this, but it has no success. It wishes to achieve some kind of absolute, almost mathematical truth, but in art such a truth does not exist. In art the object itself does not appear save in the reflection of the imagination. . . . The artist does not even paint from the object itself, which no longer exists, but from this reflection.[9]

The relations between art and reality are indirect. The artist does not merely portray the objects of perception but an object that has become "illuminated in his imagination" and has acquired a certain "tone." It is impossible to duplicate nature and the attempt can only result in a

---

[7] *Ibid.*, pp. 106, 211.   [8] *Sobr. soch.*, VIII, 99-100.
[9] *Ibid.*, p. 195.

feeble product. "Nature is too strong and original to take it, so to speak, as a whole, to match one's strength with it and stand directly before it. It will not give. It has too powerful resources. A pitiful, impotent copy will result from a direct photograph. It permits an approach only by means of the creative imagination."[10] Though on occasion Goncharov will employ metaphors that describe art as a reflector or "mirror held up to nature," metaphors at least as old as Plato, he invariably adds that the mirror's reflection is "afterwards reworked in [the artist's] imagination." The writer "should write not from the event but from its reflection in his creative imagination, that is, he should create a verisimilitude which would justify the event in his artistic composition. Reality is of little concern for him."[11]

It is a startling sentence, but one that requires qualification. Certainly reality was of concern to Goncharov. He elsewhere stated that nothing had been contrived in his fiction, and that he had described "life itself."[12] Implicit in his seeming denial of reality is a belief that the order of a work of art is not equivalent to the order of nature. The artist chooses his materials from the actual world (the "object," the "event") but transforms them according to the dictates of his imagination into an autonomous structure with its own laws of necessity and probability ("a verisimilitude" that "justifies" the events of reality in terms of the artistic composition). Art represents nature not as a reflected but as a *refracted* image that has been filtered through the creative mind. What the artist conveys, then, is not "nature" or "reality," for these are too varied and "original" to be taken "as a whole," but an image of life in which the objects of sense perception are not only transformed but that is highly selective as well. "You," Goncharov wrote to Dostoevsky in 1874, "know how little artistic truth there is for the most part in *reality* and how . . . the meaning of creation is expressed namely through choosing several traits and indications from nature in order to create a verisimilitude, that is, to achieve artistic truth."[13]

The artist's method of refraction and selection, though primarily

---

[10] *Ibid.*, p. 107.

[11] *Literaturno-kriticheskie stat'i*, pp. 322, 310. Plato *Republic* x. 596.

[12] *Sobr. soch.*, VIII, 97.   [13] *Ibid.*, p. 459.

unconscious, is yet purposeful. It achieves "truth," though not the "mathematical truth" that those who misunderstand the nature of art seek. Instead, the authentic artist seeks "artistic truth"—a truth inseparable from the "tones" and "illuminations" provided by the eccentric imagination. As a result, ". . . artistic truth and the truth of reality are not one and the same."[14]

In rejecting the notion that art is a mirror of reality and in insisting upon the primacy of the unconscious in the act of creation, Goncharov was defending the uniqueness and integrity of the creative experience from the onslaughts of the materialistic and positivistic critics of the day. His fellow-novelists—Dostoevsky, Tolstoy, Turgenev, and others—differed greatly, but were united in perceiving a distinct region of "artistic truth." In formulating his defense, Goncharov was also repeating ideas that, though stated before, came into currency with the triumph of romanticism. The romantics, in their orientation toward self-expression (Wordsworth's "spontaneous overflow of powerful feelings") and interest in the workings of the individual creative genius, frequently either reversed traditional mirror-and-reflector metaphors for the creative process to turn the mirror inward from the physical world to the mind and emotions of the artist, or replaced the mirror entirely and conceived of the creative mind as a lamp, which does not passively reflect reality but emits its own radiance to the objects of sense (cf. Goncharov's use of "illuminated," above). Although belief in an external force taking possession of the poet and turning him into its instrument is, again, as old as Plato and was even implicit in neoclassical invocations to the muse, it is the romantic age that witnessed "the momentous historical shift from the view that the making of art is a supremely purposeful activity to the view that its coming-into-being is, basically, a spontaneous process independent of intention, precept, or even consciousness. . . ." It is also with the romantics that divine inspiration or the muse are internalized into a function of mind—i.e., the "unconscious."[15]

[14] *Ibid.*, p. 106.

[15] See M. H. Abrams, *The Mirror and the Lamp: Romantic Theory and the Critical Tradition* (New York, 1953), pp. 47-69, 187. Abrams, p. 210, credits Schelling "for making . . . [the unconscious] an ineluctable part of the

Goncharov also shared the romantics' use of organic analogies to describe the creative process—analogies and metaphors that were a natural corollary of a theory of unconscious inspiration.[16] The artist, he thought, cannot create what *"has not grown and ripened . . ."* in his mind. The emergence of a work of art, like the blossoming of a flower, depends upon accidental and unforeseeable factors: ". . . [a novel] demands propitious, almost happy circumstances, because the imagination whose participation is as unavoidable in a novel as in a poetic composition is like a flower; it unfolds and is fragrant beneath the sun's rays, and it develops from the rays—of fortune." Artistic creation is viewed as a natural process in which the artist's volition plays a secondary role: ". . . [characters] are given to the artist freely, almost independently of himself; they grow in the soil of his imagination. His labor is only one of cultivation, trimming, grouping. . . ." Even in the act of ordering into a final form ". . . a force independent of the author comes to his aid—his artistic instinct. The intelligence lays out the main lines, the situations, like a park or a garden. It invents the contingencies, but the above-mentioned instinct helps, and brings this to fulfillment."[17] Though Goncharov did not discard the role of the conscious intelligence that "lays out the main lines," or structure, of a novel and aids in the "cultivation" of an otherwise "natural" growth, he regarded problems of organization as difficult and at times overwhelming—an attitude that may have encouraged him to highlight the spontaneous aspect of artistic creation. The construction of a novel was for him "a gigantic labor"; it was, he lamented in the same words employed by his hero-artist Boris Raysky, "une mer à boire!"[18]

Another aspect of Goncharov's view of art had far-reaching conse-

---

psychology of art." For Plato (or Socrates) on the poet as "inspired and possessed," see *Ion* 533-534.

[16] Abrams, pp. 156-225, presents an extensive survey of organic theories.

[17] *Sobr. soch.*, VIII, 113. *Golos minuvshego*, No. 12 (December 1913), p. 245. *Sobr. soch.*, VIII, 112. Also, the above cited distinction between "composition" and "creation" recalls August W. Schlegel's famous antithesis of mechanical and organic art. See *Vorlesungen über dramatische Kunst und Litteratur, Sämtliche Werke* (Leipzig, 1846-1847), VI, 157.

[18] *Sobr. soch.*, VIII, 112; V, 43.

quences for his fiction. It may be related both to the uniqueness of his creation and to its limitations. He felt that it was impossible for literature to treat the contemporaneous. The life and the reality the artist portrays must be settled, stable, and formed over a long period.

> A serious and strict art cannot portray chaos, disintegration, all the microscopic appearances of life. . . . A true work of art can only portray a life that has settled into some sort of image, into a physiognomy. The very persons [represented in this image] should have been repeated in numerous types under the influence of various principles, customs, and kinds of upbringing. Some definite and permanent image of a form of life should have appeared and its persons should have manifested themselves with well-known principles and habits in a multiplicity of aspects and examples. And for this, of course, time is necessary.

> . . . it is difficult, . . . and in my opinion simply impossible, to portray a life that has not yet taken form, where its forms have not settled and characters have not been stratified into types.[19]

It is a position from which he attacks the "estheticians of the new generation" of the sixties and seventies "who limit the goal of art to extreme . . . utilitarian ends. . . ." Though Goncharov usually refrained from mentioning names, he had in mind Chernyshevsky, Pisarev, their radical followers, and the populist writers of those decades (he would have excepted Dobrolyubov, whom he credited with genuine sensitivity to literary facts). In an effort to distinguish them from his own generation of realists, he alternately refers to them as "neo-realists" or "ultra-realists," and dismisses their work as tenden-

---

[19] *Ibid.*, VIII, 212-213, 101. René Wellek in *Concepts of Criticism*, ed. S. G. Nichols Jr. (New Haven and London, 1963), pp. 240-241, gives a brief history of the concept of "type," from its romantic "sense of a great universal figure of mythical proportion"—what we might call today, "archetypal pattern," to its usage by the realists to denote a socially representative (or ideal) character—"social type." Goncharov, besides using type in its social meaning as here, also employed the term to describe a great literary character (Don Quixote, Lear, Hamlet, Don Juan, Tartuffe), who is able to give birth to "entire generations of related semblances in the creations of later talents. . . ."— a view closer to the romantic usage. *Sobr. soch.*, VIII, 104-105.

tious and sterile, if for no other reason than that they treat subjects of topical interest: ". . . they are not artists and their novels, lacking poetry, are not works of art but pamphlets, *feuilletons*, or journalistic articles representing the 'topical' " (*zloba dnya*). Goncharov, it should be added, also deplored governmental efforts to enlist writers in its support and the use by conservatives of literature as polemic.[20]

However, it is not merely the tendentious that Goncharov opposed, but the very effort to deal with the topical. He took to task even writers whom he generally admired for their attempts to depict the contemporaneous and the momentary. In 1873 he informed Pisemsky that his recent play, *Baal*, was not altogether successful, not through any fault of the author, but *"because of the novelty of the subject among us*; . . . the artist should wait a long time until everything takes form in typical traits of characters and life. . . . It is impossible to put contemporary, current life in such a solid and serious form as the drama. . . ."[21] The following year, while editing a literary anthology, Goncharov received a short story from Dostoevsky, lampooning the nihilists. He could not refrain from chastising his great colleague, and in the process explained his own conception of a literary type and literary creation.

> . . . if it is in the process of birth, then it is not yet a *type*. . . . A type is composed of many and lengthy repetitions or stratifications of occurrences and characters, where the likenesses of one and the other become frequent in the course of time and finally settle, congeal, and become familiar to the observer. Creation . . . can appear only . . . when life has settled; it does not manage with a new life which is coming into being. . . .
>
> . . . .
>
> As types I understand something very rooted, having settled over an extremely long period of time and sometimes encompassing a series of generations.[22]

[20] *Ibid.*, pp. 211-212. *Sbornik*, pp. 149-151.

[21] *Sobr. soch.*, VIII, 451-452.

[22] *Ibid.*, pp. 457, 460. The anthology was entitled simply, *A Collection* (*Skladchina*) and was published in Petersburg in 1874. The Dostoevsky contribution was "Small Sketches" ("Malen'kie kartinki").

In view of the frequency and conviction with which Goncharov reiterated his belief concerning the writer's proper subject, it would be shortsighted to dismiss it as merely a polemical attitude assumed in opposition to the radical critics and their demand for an immediate, socially and politically relevant literature. Far from being a contrivance for polemics, Goncharov's theory lies at the heart of his psychology of art. His insistence that literature treat only what has become familiar may have originated from the practice of the "natural school" of the forties and its fondness for drawing static ("congealed") portraits of characters readily recognizable as representative of their social milieu. It also reflected his personal psychology—his urgent need for order and stability, for what is known, "settled," and "very rooted." It is almost as if he wanted life itself to stop, hold still, and petrify into the "stratum" of a geological formation before he would dare to approach it.

Goncharov's view of character or type carries several extremely important implications for his art. If the life the artist describes has already settled and congealed through time into "a permanent image," then the experiences he treats must of necessity either belong to the past or be projected into it. The literary act becomes an act of recall, or reminiscence, a *recherche du temps perdu*. A large measure of artistic distance and detachment can be expected from an esthetic position that refuses to admit the uncertainties and "chaos" of life and demands remoteness between the artist and the objects of his perception. It is more than coincidental that in the midst of expounding his views to Dostoevsky, Goncharov chides his fellow-novelist for not portraying his character *sine ira*, a phrase that he elsewhere takes up as the motto of the artist and raises to a "law of objective creation."[23]

Most crucial, however, is the view of character as fixed and stable— what has "settled" and "congealed." Goncharov rejects characters subject to violent upheavals—to "chaos" and "disintegration," and perhaps even those capable of growth and becoming—"if it is in the process of birth, then it is not yet a type." He would include only "very rooted" types in his fiction, characters who are the final *results* of processes that took place "over an extremely long period of time,

[23] *Sobr. soch.*, VIII, 457, 94; *Sbornik*, p. 144.

sometimes encompassing . . . generations." Such a view apparently precludes dynamic and strongly dramatic literary modes, for dramatic conflict and tension usually depend (as in Dostoevsky) upon an instability and incompleteness of character—a split within the self that leaves open the possibility for alternatives of action or being. Instead we may anticipate that an interest in "rooted" characters and a life that has formed into "a definite and permanent image" will turn the novelist's attention to relatively static fictional structures.

While rejecting the tendentious and didactic, Goncharov also repudiated the slogan "art for art's sake," which he found "a meaningless phrase" and "a phrase not expressing anything." Art is far from a frivolous and idle exercise. It is a serious affair. One of its basic goals, if not its only one, is "to make men better." The devotees of art for art's sake are not true artists, because "they create that in which there is neither 'truth' nor 'life.' . . ." *Dichtung* and *Wahrheit* are viewed as inseparable. Several times Goncharov expressed reservations about Belinsky's critical contribution but readily commended his responsiveness to "the sound of truth and life in art." "*Notre cause commune,*" he proclaimed to Annenkov in 1870, is "art and truth." Rejecting the use of literature to further narrow sectarian interests or literature as idle play, Goncharov preferred instead to understand it in very ambitious (and very Russian) terms: ". . . [literature is] *enlightenment* in general, that is, *a written or printed expression of the spirit, mind, imagination, knowledge* of an entire nation. . . . *literature is only the organ, that is the language,* which expresses everything that the nation thinks, that it desires, that it knows, and that it wishes to know and should know. . . ."[24]

The conviction that literature should express an intangible (and undefined) "truth" or "life" made Goncharov extremely hostile to naturalism, which he understood to offer only a meaningless replica of reality. He attacked Zola, Flaubert (whom Goncharov, with *Bouvard et Pécuchet* in mind, took to be a naturalist), and others in very much the same terms he had used to reject the Russian radical writers. They make up the "extreme-realist" school; they "compose" and do

[24] *Sobr. soch.,* VIII, 162, 110. *Literaturno-kriticheskie stat'i,* p. 329. *Sobr. soch.,* VIII, 162, 164, 426, 436.

not "create," because they write with the intellect alone and not with the "heart"—an odd estimation of Zola, who was in practice, if not theory, the most committed of artists. The naturalists' impressive technical accomplishments, their ability to render a scene vividly and convincingly, are acknowledged: "You see before you a room, a garden, a road, a hut, the figure of a man or animal. You hear, it seems, even the intonation of a voice in conversation. . . ." But literature, Goncharov adds, should offer something more than convincing portraits. The naturalists' descriptions are "without rays of poetry . . . ; there is no idea, . . . no light or warmth!" Technique, though it is acquired only through long practice, "will never hide or fill the absence of ideas, of a serious and profound view of life. . . ."[25]

The objection to naturalism, though partly formal—fiction should include a lyrical dimension or "rays of poetry"—is essentially moral: fiction must offer "a serious and profound view of life." In the course of the same correspondence with Pyotr Valuev from which part of the above attack upon naturalism is drawn, Goncharov attempted to explain his own understanding of realism. Again, formal considerations are touched upon but the emphasis remains moral. In asking for the novelist's literary opinions, the aristocratic Valuev had complained about Pushkin's excessive use of concrete details and declared only his classicism praiseworthy. Goncharov replied that Pushkin's greatness lay precisely in his capacity to adjust to the "realism" of his century and appropriate its recently discovered techniques—i.e., the extensive use of concrete and specific detail—while at the same time keeping in touch with his classical heritage, with an older "realism" that avoids "extremes, every kind of coarseness, vulgarity, cynicism, or that dryness which the new belletrists pass off as real truth and which limits itself to a bare replica of reality. . . ." Realism, as we have already seen, should permit lyricism and subjective "tones" that make the work of art something more than "a bare replica of reality," but it should also endeavor to render the world in all its concreteness and specificity—as "modern" writers and the naturalists are able to so

---

[25] *Shornik*, p. 157. *Literaturno-kriticheskie stat'i*, p. 327. In his discussion with the writer Penkin, Oblomov levels similar complaints against the "natural school" of the forties. See *Sobr. soch.*, IV, 28-30.

convincingly. In addition, it must be, like the classical Pushkin, "sober and rational."[26]

These are obviously contradictory positions, but they are the stuff out of which Goncharov's fiction is made. We shall discover in it an uninhibited play of the imagination, and also formal structures that are carefully ordered, at times even excessively "rational." Though the close rendering of concrete reality became a trademark of Goncharov's art, lyricism is also part of his manner—indeed, he often perceived the concrete tangible world of everyday experience in lyrical or "poetic" terms. And as for Tolstoy, Dostoevsky, and almost every Russian writer of the century, a moral urge demanding that art act as "enlightenment," that it express "a serious and profound view of life" which will "make men better" left traces in his work. It led him to undertake ambitious projects that would confront serious moral issues, but it also made his art vulnerable to the very didacticism and tendentiousness he had deplored.

Essentially Goncharov viewed realism as a synthetic mode capable of absorbing diverse elements. His insistence upon inclusiveness and breadth is strongest when he speaks of the novel, which is of course realism's preeminent genre. "Life is a deep and boundless sea; it and art, its true reflection, cannot be exhausted or directed into some narrow channel!" The only literary genre capable of encompassing its breadth is the novel: "Everything that is included in life pertains to the novel. . . ." "The novel seizes everything. . . ." It embraces all the previous literary genres, assumes the moral function they once had, and tends to make them obsolete. With its inclusiveness it achieves a range that allows it to take in the broad expanse of life: "European literatures have come out of their childhood, and now not only do some kind of idyll, sonnet, hymn, sketch, or lyrical outpouring of feelings in verse have no effect on anyone, but even fables have little effect. . . . All this goes into the novel, whose boundaries include large episodes of life, sometimes the whole of life. . . ."[27]

---

[26] *Literaturno-kriticheskie stat'i*, p. 313. The correspondence (pp. 294-330) dates from 1877 through 1881.

[27] *Sobr. soch.*, VIII, 110. *Literaturno-kriticheskie stat'i*, p. 308. *Sobr. soch.*, VIII, 107, 211.

Several Soviet scholars have noted the presence of ideas of romantic origin in Goncharov's esthetic thought and, in an effort to maintain the general view of the novelist as the most "objective" of realists, have tried to explain them away. His writings have been scoured for possible influences, and Nadezhdin, the Maykovs, and even Winckelmann, who was hardly a romantic, have been made responsible for his "romantic" and "idealistic" tendencies.[28] On the other hand, Pushkin and Belinsky, particularly Belinsky, are credited with inspiring his "sober . . . critical thought," weaning him from the romantic excesses of his youth, and leading him to a proper and correct social realism. "Influence" is sometimes tantamount to direction, as Goncharov's novels are read as responses to *"an invitation which Belinsky made to leading Russian writers"* to take up a cudgel against romanticism. (Italics in original.)[29]

Not only are such descriptions bad history (Goncharov's recorded opinions remain unchanged through his career); they also give a misleading picture of the influential critic. Belinsky, as René Wellek cogently argues, "was a critic soaked in the views of the German [romantic] theorists."[30] He moved to a more "realistic" position toward the end of his career, but at one time or another he had shared every typically romantic belief held by Goncharov. Thus, for the young Belinsky, as well as for Goncharov, the true work of art "was not made, not composed, but created in the soul of the artist as if under the inspiration of a higher, mysterious power. . . ." Though the poet starts out with an idea or purpose, ". . . his activity is *purposeless* and *unconscious*." "The poet is the slave of his subject. . . ." Creation

---

[28] A. G. Tseytlin, "Goncharov-kritik," in *Istoriya russkoy kritiki,* ed. B. P. Gorodetsky (Moscow-Leningrad, 1958), II, 290, cites Winckelmann and the Maykovs; A. Rybasov, *I. A. Goncharov* (Moscow, 1962), p. 21, offers Nadezhdin.

[29] The quotations are from A. Lavretsky, "Literaturno-esteticheskie idei Goncharova," *Literaturnyy kritik,* Nos. 5-6 (May-June 1940), p. 34, and Tseytlin, *I. A. Goncharov,* p. 63. The thesis is almost universal in Soviet scholarship. For a more modest assessment of Belinsky's influence, we must go back to Soviet scholarship of the twenties. See V. E. Evgen'ev-Maksimov, *I. A. Goncharov* (Moscow, 1925), pp. 51-55.

[30] *A History of Modern Criticism* (New Haven and London, 1955-1965), III, 263.

proceeds "freely and independently of the creator. . . ," somewhat like "a dream" (1835). Much later, in 1843, the critic still held that, though the artist treats the "facts of reality," it is "not the fact copied from nature, but [the fact] led through the imagination of the poet. . . ." Belinsky also employed organic metaphors to express the unconscious and purposeless nature of art. A work of art is "an organic being *enclosed within itself*" (the example is a plant), which has an internal rather than an external cause (the seed), and which constitutes a natural unity (1840). That central thesis of romantic nationalism that gained such wide currency in Russia, the view that literature is the expression and symbol of the inner life of a nation, was enunciated by the critic at the very beginning of his career (1834). Belinsky, like Goncharov after him, proclaimed the novel "the widest and most universal genre of poetry . . . ," for "it unites all the other genres . . .—the lyrical and the dramatic . . ." (1848). In another passage strikingly similar to Goncharov's later critique of naturalism, he attacked literature that merely represents concrete reality in "portraits" that lack "rational thought" and a "rational goal" (1841)— once again, an apparent contradiction of the previously stated "unconscious" and "purposeless" nature of creativity, though Belinsky was aware of the Kantian paradox whereby art could be "purposive without purpose" (*Zweckmässigkeit ohne Zweck*).[31]

Despite striking similarities of ideas and even of phraseology, it is still impossible to ascertain to what extent the novelist took his opinions from the critic. Both Belinsky, who was a forceful critic but not an original thinker, and Goncharov were the products of the same age and atmosphere—an atmosphere that, to cite Wellek again, "was fairly charged with these ideas."[32] The age ended and its offspring surrendered some of their positions. But they retained others, usually minus their former metaphysical underpinnings. Many of the ideas and attitudes we continue to label as "romantic" survive through the first generation of realists—not only in Goncharov but also in his contemporaries, most notably Dostoevsky.[33] Indeed, concepts of the

---

[31] Belinsky, I, 127-129; II, 460; I, 560-561, 16; III, 802; I, 643.

[32] *A History of Modern Criticism*, III, 245.

[33] See Robert Louis Jackson, *Dostoevsky's Quest for Form: A Study of His*

unconscious sources of art, its organic autonomy, and capacity to il-luminate experience are very much alive today, though in the guise of a changed vocabulary. They have survived because they are valid (though not exclusive) ways of describing the creative process and its results. Goncharov did not cease to be a realist because he espoused certain romantic arguments; also he simultaneously held to other, more "rational" and classical notions. Literary traditions are always a mix of varying elements, some of which are survivals, and others new. Nevertheless, Goncharov's insistence upon the mixed and inclusive character of realism was particularly strong, and when we come to *Oblomov* we shall discover a book colored by dream and fancy, often veering to comic caricature, at times lyrical, and marked by those subjective tones or "deviations" he felt realism should embrace. His view of art undoubtedly began to take shape in the intellectual climate of his youth. In the following chapter we shall find that it also owed much to his experience in writing novels.

Philosophy of Art (New Haven and London, 1966), and Donald Fanger, *Dostoevsky and Romantic Realism: A Study of Dostoevsky in Relation to Balzac, Dickens, and Gogol* (Cambridge, Mass., 1963).

CHAPTER III

The Creative Method and the Writing of the Novels

The Creative Method

In "Better Late Than Never" Goncharov spoke at length about his method of work.

> While portraying, I seldom know what my image, portrait, or character means. I only see him as if alive before me and check whether I am portraying faithfully. I see him in action with others, sometimes far in advance as regards the plan of the novel, not yet foreseeing completely how all these parts of the whole, still scattered about in my head, will tie together. I hasten to sketch scenes and characters on sheets and scraps of paper so as not to forget, and I advance as if feeling my way. Initially I write sluggishly, awkwardly, monotonously . . . and I feel bored writing, until suddenly the light pours in and illuminates the ways where I am to go. I always have one image and with it a major motif. It leads me forward, and along the way I randomly seize at what falls under my hand, that is, what clearly pertains to it. Then I work with animation, briskly. My hand barely manages to write, until I again come up against a wall. Meanwhile, the work goes on in my head. The characters press themselves upon me; they pose in scenes. I hear bits of their conversations, and often it seems to me, may God forgive me, that I do not invent, but that all this is drifting in the air about me, and I only have to look and reflect deeply upon it.[1]

André Mazon, commenting upon the same passage, was struck by the repetition of such words as "image," "look," "portray," and, espe-

---

[1] *Sobr. soch.*, VIII, 70-71.

cially "see"—an observation that led him to deduce Goncharov's awareness of the essential nature of his talent: "the gift of seeing" (*le don de voir*).[2] Goncharov was indeed a fine observer, but, if we restrict ourselves for the moment to his self-description, we may wonder about the objects toward which his vision is directed. The artist "sees" an image, portrait, or character "alive" before him, but the image that guides him forward, the characters who hover in the air about him, whose conversation appears both real and menacing ("may God forgive me," he cries out) seem to derive at least as much from his inner world as from observation. What is only suggested in the above passage is made explicit in other contexts. Goncharov's essays and letters abound with remarks that indicate an artistic vision turned largely inward. In order to work, he tells us, he needs "gravelike silence . . . so that I can gaze intently and listen carefully to what is going on within me and write it down." ". . . silence is necessary to me in order to listen keenly to the music that is playing within me. . . ." "I have no curiosity. I have never wanted to know. I only wanted to see and to verify the pictures of my imagination, cancelling something here, adding something there. . . ."[3]

The description is of an imagination that, so to speak, feeds upon itself. It also holds a powerful sway over the artist. One commentator has detected a quality of hallucination in our citation from "Better Late Than Never,"[4] and Goncharov elsewhere attested to that complete submission to the workings of the imagination that characterizes a hallucinatory state. He claimed to have written *Oblomov* "as if by dictation" and described his work on *The Ravine* in a similar manner: "Yes, I am not writing the novel—. . . it is being written and is being dictated by someone to me." "Why should I necessarily write (*pisat'*) this or that," he asks a correspondent, "and not what writes itself (*pishetsya*)?"[5] The impression is of a force taking possession of

[2] *Ivan Gontcharov*, p. 293.

[3] From letters to M. M. Stasyulevich of June 9 and 7, 1868, in *Stasyulevich*, IV, 18, and *Sobr. soch.*, VIII, 385, and to Yu. D. Efremova, July 7, 1853, in *Literaturnoe nasledstvo*, Nos. 22-24 (1935), p. 390.

[4] Lavretsky, *Literaturnyy kritik*, Nos. 5-6 (May-June 1940), p. 36.

[5] From letters to Efremova of July 29, 1857, Stasyulevich of June 6, 1868, and Ekaterina Maykova of April 1869, in *Sobr. soch.*, VIII, 291, 382, 401.

the artist and turning him into its passive instrument: "Images . . . were present within me and instinctively [*sic*] guided my pen."[6] The creative imagination that held him in its grip offered as many terrors as his private fantasies: "What are these dreams that rise up, yes, rise up; the imagination is such a unique sort of boiler; may God only grant that the boiler does not burst!"[7]

Goncharov listened to his muse attentively and paid her due tribute. However, he does not describe his "possession" as the kind of poetic frenzy frequently described by the romantic poets. Nor was it Wordsworth's "spontaneous overflow of powerful feelings" that he experienced. Instead, there is a decidedly *passionless* quality about his description of the creative process—something detached, passive, "hallucinatory." The attitude is one of self-absorption rather than spontaneous overflow; reflective instead of passionate. As characters drift in the air about the artist, he has only "to look and reflect deeply" upon them and write down what they say "as if by dictation." Though his imagination is powerful enough to evoke characters who seem "alive" and independent of his will, the artist "gazes intently" and "listens keenly" in absorbed concentration.

It should be sufficiently clear that Goncharov's insistence upon the central role of the unconscious in the creative process reflected his experience. If we return to our key opening citation, we may detect how his use of organic images for the creative process also depended upon his method of work. The description was of a gradual accretion and extension of form. He begins with no definite idea of what his image or character means nor with a clear concept of the end product of his labor. Various fragments are scattered about in his mind. Suddenly, a light appears. A single image and major motif seizes control, points out the directions to be followed, and the heretofore random fragments are pulled into relation with the central image. It is a description that can easily accommodate itself to images of spontaneous germination, natural involuntary growth, and gradual ripening.

However, to call Goncharov's artistic method "purely instinctive," as Mazon does, is to exaggerate. Something akin to a hallucinatory

[6] *Ibid.*, p. 104.
[7] To Stasyulevich, May 30, 1868, in *ibid.*, p. 378.

state frequently accompanied his creative moments, but he has also told us of "the intelligence [that] lays out the main lines" of a novel, "the architectonics . . . [that] are enough to swallow up the entire intellectual activity of an author," and the "constant control" an artist must exercise.[8] "Instinct," or the unconscious, seems to have played a dominant role in the initial stages of creation, while the critical intelligence was reserved for problems of structure and undoubtedly for the smaller strategies of fiction as well.

The method had an element of risk to it. Everything depended upon the happy moment of grace—the ray of light that would illuminate the way. Meanwhile, the novelist would busily sketch scenes and characters on sheets of paper without foreseeing the ultimate purpose and unity of his work. He proceeded at the risk that the moment of insight would not come and he might be left with an accumulation of material, waiting futilely for inspiration to guide him. Or to pursue the organic analogy, germination might not take place, and the seeds of thought and imagination might be left strewn upon the ground.

THE WRITING OF THE NOVELS

Inspiration descended upon the artist at rare intervals. Approximately fifty years of literary activity witnessed the publication of only three novels, a book of travel sketches, a handful of short stories, and some miscellaneous writings. Of the novels, *A Common Story* seems to have presented the least difficulty. According to Goncharov's later account, the novel was conceived in 1844, written in 1845, and in 1846 there remained only a few chapters to complete.[9] It was published in the *Contemporary* in March and April of 1847 and in a separate edition in 1848. *A Common Story* remained the only one of Goncharov's novels to have an uncomplicated history in which writing and publication followed rapidly after conception.

Goncharov, on various occasions, dated the beginning of work on *Oblomov* to each of the years from 1846 to 1848. Most likely serious work on the novel did not commence until after the publication of

---

[8] Mazon, *Ivan Gontcharov*, p. 296. *Sobr. soch.*, VIII, 112.

[9] *Sbornik*, p. 7.

A Common Story in 1847.[10] A chapter of Part One entitled "Oblomov's Dream" ("Son Oblomova") was published as "an episode of
an uncompleted novel" in a collection put out by the *Contemporary*
in March of 1849.[11] The completed novel came out in *Notes of the
Fatherland* from January through April of 1859. A separate edition
was published in September of the same year. Thus there had been an
eleven- to thirteen-year interval between conception and final publication, and a ten-year hiatus between the publication of "Oblomov's
Dream" and the publication of the completed novel.

This long duration may leave the impression of slow meticulous
labor on what was to prove a masterpiece. There was nothing of the
sort. After commencing work in the late forties Goncharov put the
novel away for a considerable amount of time—probably until 1855.
Also, memory failed him when he later claimed to have completed
Part One in the late forties. In December of 1855 he was still occu-
pied with the initial section of the novel and felt that if he were "to
correct a bit and add about two chapters, then the first part will be
ready."[12] In spite of his optimism another year and a half passed, and
in April of 1857 he informed Mikhail Katkov, the editor of the *Russian Messenger* (*Russkiy vestnik*), that Part One was still not
completed.[13] Approximately a decade had passed, and Goncharov was
still involved in the first part of his novel—a little over a quarter of
the completed text. The impression is hardly one of deliberate and
steady progress toward a clearly defined goal. Goncharov was bogged
down. He was waiting, as he had expressed it to Elizaveta Tolstaya,
for "the flower" to unfold and "the rays of fortune" to strike.[14]

Elizaveta may unwittingly have helped hasten their arrival. Goncharov had not been able to get past the plotless "Dream" and the

[10] In "Better Late Than Never" and his "Autobiography" Goncharov associated the inception of work on the novel with the publication of *A Common
Story*. *Sobr. soch.*, VIII, 76, 223.

[11] The collection was entitled *Literaturnyy sbornik s illyustratsiyami*.

[12] *Sobr. soch.*, VIII, 223. The quotation is from a letter to Elizaveta Tolstaya,
Golos minuvshego, No. 12 (December 1913), p. 241.

[13] Quoted in Alekseev, *Letopis'*, p. 72.

[14] *Golos minuvshego*, No. 12 (December 1913), p. 245. The letter was
dated December 31, 1855.

comic play between Oblomov and Zakhar of Part One—among the most static or "congealed" sections of the novel. What he needed was an action that would permit character to develop, and his own disappointment in love may have heightened his sensitivity to the complications of human experience. Also, before the appearance of Turgenev's *Rudin* in 1856, Goncharov had few Russian models of a novel whose plot centered about a sustained central action. The plot of Gogol's masterpiece, *Dead Souls* (first part, 1842), furnished no more than a string upon which Gogol tied his brilliantly comic episodes and lyrical interludes; Lermontov's *A Hero of Our Times* (1840) was composed of five individual tales held together by the personality of Pechorin; Pushkin's great novel in verse, *Eugene Onegin* (1823-1831), may have been more helpful in that it follows a central relation between an irresponsible man and the strong woman who finally rejects him, but it is ultimately a poem—one whose appeal is in the brilliance of its verse, its ironic wit, and lyricism. Dostoevsky's novels had not yet been written; Tolstoy's work through the fifties consisted of short stories or reminiscences in the form of fiction. Though in his esthetics Goncharov assigned secondary importance to craftsmanship, purely technical problems may very well have contributed to his difficulties.

The good fortune he hoped for finally came in the summer of 1857. On June 21 of that year Goncharov, on a brief vacation from his censorship duties, arrived at his favorite spa, Marienbad. He left six weeks later—August 4. In the interval the novel that had lain dormant for so many years was virtually completed. It was a glorious summer of creative activity—one he was to recall and try to recapture in later years. "Part II and what follows, with the exception of the last two or three chapters which were finished in the winter in Petersburg, were written, so to speak, in a burst, almost in one sitting, in the summer of 1857 at the waters in Marienbad," he wrote toward the end of his life, and his letters at the time communicate the excitement of that unparalleled burst of creative energy.[15]

[15] A note on the manuscript made in 1888 and quoted in Mazon, *Ivan Gontcharov*, p. 438. Mazon, p. 30, found that later revisions did not affect the general design but were limited to the reworking of individual words and

Mazon found evidence in an early manuscript to suggest that those last few chapters (actually the last four) may have been written before the summer of '57. If so, the novel was written in a circle—beginning, end, and then middle. When we come to *Oblomov* we shall discover that experience in the novel also moves in a circle, so that Oblomov in the end returns to his beginnings.[16]

The Marienbad summer of 1857 was the great moment of Goncharov's life. A surge of creative energy had taken hold of the melancholic bureaucrat and had brought him the quickness of life.

How did it happen that I, a dead man, weary, indifferent to everything, even to my own success, suddenly undertook a task in which I had begun to despair? And how I undertook it, if only you could see! I barely contained my excitement; my head pounded; Luisa [a servant] found me in tears; I paced my room like a madman, ran along hills and through forests, not feeling the earth beneath me. There was nothing like it even in my youth.

He explained his accomplishment by referring to two of the cardinal principles of his esthetics—his belief in the organic, natural growth of a work of art and the power of the unconscious.

It will seem strange that almost the entire novel could be written in a month—not only strange, even impossible. But it is necessary to remember that it ripened in my head in the course of many years and almost all that remained was for me to write it down.

. . . .

It will seem unnatural that a man completed in a month what he could not complete in years. To this I answer that if there had not been years, nothing would have been written in a month. The fact

---

phrases. For a sampling of Goncharov's letters from Marienbad in 1857, see *Sobr. soch.*, VIII, 280-295.

[16] *Ivan Gontcharov*, p. 439. In a letter to Sofya Nikitenko of August 15, 1857 Goncharov spoke of having rough drafts for two scenes—"the final farewell of Oblomov and his friend [Stolz], and a conclusion. . . ." *Sobr. soch.* (Pravda), VIII, 301. Stolz's leave-taking of Oblomov is in Part Four, chap. nine, the same chapter in which Oblomov dreams that he has returned to Oblomovka.

is that the whole novel had matured up to the smallest scenes and details and all that remained was to write it down. I wrote as if by dictation. And truly, much appeared unconsciously; someone invisible sat next to me and told me what to write.[17]

The Ravine, Goncharov's last novel, was published in the first five issues of the *European Messenger* from January through May 1869. It came out in a separate edition in the following year. Before it was finally published, the novel had gone through a tortuous twenty-year history of conception and composition. As in the case of *Oblomov* Goncharov may not have proceeded consecutively, but the main lines of his progress can be reconstructed.

Though published ten years after *Oblomov*, *The Ravine* was conceived at about the same time. The idea for the novel came to Goncharov in 1849 while on vacation in his native Simbirsk. He also worked at it sporadically while involved with *Oblomov* and as early as 1858 had completed a considerable section of Part One.[18] However, it was not until the appearance of *Oblomov* that Goncharov began to work intensely upon his final project. In March of 1859 he informed Turgenev of his plans to return to Marienbad in the hope of recapturing the experience of '57: ". . . I will take up the task, if inspiration has not abandoned me, if it will be as easy abroad as it was in 1857, if—how many ifs!"[19] He tried to relive the Marienbad summer in 1860 as well, and in June the excitement returned for a brief moment: "I felt cheerfulness, youth, freshness, was in such an unusual mood, felt such a flood of productive power, such a passion to express myself, as I had not felt since '57." The significance of the second hero, Vera's lover (Mark Volokhov), had just become clear to him, and all the other characters had passed before him in a "two-hour poetic dream." Mark first appears in Part Two, chapter four-

[17] The quotations are from two letters, to Yu. D. Efremova on July 29, 1857, and I. I. L'khovsky on August 2, 1857, *Sobr. soch.*, VIII, 285, 291-292.

[18] *Sobr. soch.*, VIII, 71-72, 86. A surviving manuscript of the first sixteen chapters of Part One was copied by a nephew of the novelist in 1858. See O. Chemena, "Etapy tvorcheskoy istorii romana I. A. Goncharova *Obryv*," *Russkaya literatura*, No. 4 (1961), p. 198.

[19] *Sobr. soch.*, VIII, 310.

teen. An investigator has found a break in the manuscript after chapter seventeen, and it may mark the extent of Goncharov's progress through the summer of 1860.[20]

However, except for his "two-hour poetic dream," the Marienbad summers of 1859 and 1860 did not witness a creative outburst similar to that of the summer of 1857. On the contrary, Goncharov's letters of the period are filled with expressions of boredom, depression, and an abiding dissatisfaction with the progress of his work. In the 1859 summer he is merely "scribbling out of boredom. . . ." The experience of '57 refuses to return: "As for the desire for inspiration, this desire is in vain; it will not be granted . . . . it is impossible to think out and write a novel in six weeks: this is impudence and nonsense. Perhaps, two or three years ago it would have been possible. . . ."[21] The following summer found him still "scribbling." He is not "creating" but "composing," and it is coming out badly. There is "no hope of advancing the novel."[22]

The difficulty was not due to a collapse of the imagination or an inability to work. He was writing much, he informed Sofya Nikitenko, who was helping him rewrite his rough drafts. He was blocked instead by a failure to find a direction and a structure to organize the products of his thought: "Characters, figures, pictures are appearing on the scene, but I cannot, I am unable to group them, to find the idea, the connection, the goal of this drawing; *there is no necessity* according to which the whole novel should be created and which should penetrate it and tie it together. . . . how difficult it is—not to portray, no, that's easy, but to bring the portrayal to a center, to a goal. . . ."[23]

Overwhelmed by problems of organization, Goncharov decided to slow his pace of work and change his approach. Before leaving

[20] To Sofya Nikitenko and her sister Ekaterina, *ibid.*, p. 329. Chemena, *Russkaya literatura*, No. 4 (1961), p. 202.

[21] From letters to E. P. and N. A. Maykov, quoted in Alekseev, *Letopis'*, p. 97, and Yu. D. Efremova, *Sobr. soch.* (Pravda), VIII, 321.

[22] From letters to A. V. Nikitenko, *Russkaya starina*, CLVII (1914), 415, and to S. A. Nikitenko, *Sobr. soch.*, VIII, 343, 332, 335.

[23] *Sobr. soch.*, VIII, 336, 343. *Russkaya starina*, CLVII (1914), 413-414.

Marienbad to try his luck in other European summer resorts, he indicated to Sofya the state of progress and the tactics he had adopted. He has written much, and, though she will only see "evidence of a loss of power, a fading of the intelligence, and a slackening of talent," he is determined to complete the task and will proceed as follows: "But I wish to and I believe that I shall write to the end. Moreover, I am undertaking a huge labor—to begin to write anew from what has been written, planning each chapter, not rushing, and I shall devote a year, even two to this. But now, I hasten to write in order to later make use of what has been written as a plan, as material."[24]

Soviet scholars claim to find a change in Goncharov's intentions in the sixties—a change whose first indication is the discovery of Mark Volokhov's "significance" in June of 1860 and whose result was a decision to turn the novel into a polemic against the revolutionary left or, as they were called, the "nihilists" (Volokhov is the novel's radical). What is pertinent here, however, is an apparent change in procedure. Goncharov's method of writing "instinctively" until a flash of inspiration revealed the significance of his initial "image" and the direction to follow had brought unexpected success in the instance of *Oblomov*. He had tried to repeat it with *The Ravine* but failed. The singular experience of Marienbad had stubbornly evaded him. Now his decision was to start over from the beginning and work in a more systematic manner, rewriting each chapter slowly and methodically. Meanwhile he would continue to write in order to store up "material." He had apparently moved from principles of organic growth and submission to unconscious inspiration to a principle of collection and accumulation. Having failed to experience the illuminating moment, Goncharov would proceed by collecting and systematizing.

After the frustrating Marienbad summers of 1859 and 1860 he seems to have ceased intensive work on his novel for the next five years—a hiatus of approximately the same duration as that which *Oblomov* had undergone.[25] The summer of 1865 found him again

[24] *Literaturnyy arkhiv*, IV (1953), 139.

[25] Several fragments were published in 1860-1861: "Sof'ya Nikolaevna Belovodova," in *Sovremennik*, No. 2 (February 1860); "Babushka" and "Portret," in *Otechestvennye zapiski*, No. 1 (January 1861), No. 2 (February 1861).

in that now familiar haven of his creative memories and hopes—Marienbad. The tone of futility has become as familiar as the place: "I have begun to sort out my notebooks, write, or better say, scribble, and have scribbled out two-three chapters, but . . . but nothing is coming of it. . . ." He is still collecting: ". . . it turned out that I have only material which has been collected. . . ." The summer saw him get past the middle of Part Three.[26]

The problem continued to be a lack of a principle of organization, a means to bring unity to his store of accumulated material. Where the artist saw the development of *Oblomov* on the analogy of a growing organism, he began to conceive of bringing order to *The Ravine* as a process of "pasting": ". . . the whole trouble is that I cannot paste it together. If it was possible to throw it into print in fragments, about 150 pages would come of it. But all the rest is such dead stuff pasted together with chewed pulp. . . ." In the summer of 1866 he was again back in Marienbad, among other resorts, and still hoping. The "major goal" continued to elude him, and he feared that he might go on scribbling individual chapters and scenes *"ad infinitum."*[27]

Goncharov did not continue *ad infinitum*, though he often despaired of finishing. Early in 1868 he became acquainted with Mikhail Stasyulevich, the ambitious and energetic editor of the *European Messenger*. A series of readings of the work-in-progress took place in late March and early April at the home of Count Alexey Tolstoy. Stasyulevich was impressed and resolved that Goncharov should complete the novel and publish it in the pages of his journal. On April 22 the novelist agreed to give his completed manuscript to the *European Messenger*, and intensified labor upon *The Ravine* began.

The terms of the agreement with Stasyulevich stipulated that the novel was to be ready by September.[28] Goncharov kept his word. As was the case with *Oblomov*, a large share of a novel he had lived with

---

[26] To S. A. Nikitenko, *Sobr. soch.* (Pravda), VIII, 341. *Chemena* found the dates July 30, 1865 at the beginning of Part Three, chap. ten, and August 4, 1865 alongside Part Three, chap. fourteen of the manuscript. *Russkaya literatura*, No. 4 (1961), p. 199.

[27] From letters to Turgenev, in *Goncharov i Turgenev*, pp. 45, 51.

[28] *Sobr. soch.*, VIII, 378-379.

and worked on intermittently for many years—almost two decades—was completed in a brief span of time. The last report of progress from the summer of 1865 showed him in the middle of Part Three, and when he arrived in Kissingen three years later for another summer of literary work—for some reason he avoided Marienbad this time—he had not gone much further.[29] By the end of the summer the remainder of the work, a body of writing equivalent in length to an average novel, was complete save for last-minute corrections.

The letters of the Marienbad summer of 1857 had conveyed exuberance and joy over the unexpected emergence of creative power. Goncharov experienced nothing like it in '68. Instead, the correspondence with Stasyulevich provides a long and melancholy account of personal difficulties and creative anguish. Almost every letter is filled with complaints of an inability to write. The weather was bad, the hotels were too noisy, the novel would not progress. Several times he threatened to give it up completely, and at one point, in the middle of July, his despair was so great that he contemplated suicide.[30] There were no great "bursts" of writing as in the summer of '57. Goncharov later stated that *The Ravine* was written "in snatches, by chapters . . . ,"[31] and the reports of his progress through the summer of '68, like those of preceding years, describe the writing of a single scene, the completion of a single chapter. While the impetus to complete *Oblomov* stemmed from a deeply felt personal inspiration that Goncharov saw as the natural outcome of a long period of gestation, the drive to finish *The Ravine* seems to have been in great measure external. In regularly reporting the state of the novel to Stasyulevich, he more than once expressed his gratitude to the publisher: "My correspondence with you only arouses me to work: you urge me on with your energy as one spinning a top with a whip. . . ."[32] That he was able to finish at all, despite his difficulties and the large share of the

---

[29] In a letter to Stasyulevich from Kissingen, June 6, 1868, he informed the publisher that he had picked up the novel at the "shot and Mark"—i.e., the final two chapters of Part Three. *Ibid.*, p. 382.

[30] See the letters of July 16 and 19 in *Stasyulevich*, IV, 36-41. The complete correspondence is in this volume.

[31] *Sobr. soch.*, VIII, 230.   [32] *Ibid.*, p. 382.

novel that remained to be completed, may very well have been due to that store of "material" he had collected and was "pasting" together.

It took Goncharov twenty-five years to complete his three novels not because he indulged himself in Oblomovian indolence—he was a fairly industrious man pursuing two simultaneous careers over the course of his life—nor because of a painstaking quest for *le mot juste*, though he polished his style carefully and even compulsively after finishing his first drafts. Goncharov hesitated because he believed that a work of art required time to take shape in the imagination of the artist, and also because of his extreme sensitivity and morbid self-doubt. Writing, except for the great breakthrough of 1857, was a torturous activity.

> . . . I had an extreme lack of self-confidence. I incessantly tortured myself with the question: "Am I not writing nonsense? Is this suitable? Isn't it rubbish?" . . . And to this moment I am the same way. As soon as I sit down to write, I already begin to torment myself with doubts. . . . The torturous, slow process of labor in the creation of a plan, the thinking out of all the relations of the characters, the development of the action, became repugnant to me.[33]

The difficulties he describes, as we saw in the case of *The Ravine*, were not due to a poverty of imagination. He did not complain of a lack of what to say or the desire to say it. Instead, problems of organization and structure—"the creation of a plan," "the relations of the characters"—made writing "torturous" and "repugnant." Paradoxically, Goncharov seems to have suffered from what he had called an "excess of imagination."[34] While discussing his esthetic views, we noted a predilection for seeing literature in broad and capacious terms—a preference that caused him to esteem the novel above all other literary genres. His stress upon the unconscious and organic nature of creativity derived at least in part from his method of work, and his insistence upon largeness and inclusiveness was also not an abstract theoretical commitment but the consequence of the particular quality of his imagination. He had a mind that tended to see experi-

[33] *Sbornik*, p. 11. [34] See above, chap. two.

ence in epic proportions. It proved a mixed blessing. The particular cast of his imagination inspired him to ambitious undertakings and an ambitious conception of the role of literature, but it also presented problems of organization that appeared to him as gigantic and overwhelming. He had an especially fecund inner life. How to bring it into order and define its limits was an abiding problem.

> I wrote slowly because a solitary character, a solitary action never appeared in my imagination. Instead, an entire landscape with mountains, villages, forests, and a crowd of characters, in a word, a large province of some sort of full, complete life opened suddenly before my eyes as if seen from a mountain peak. It was difficult and slow to descend from this mountain, to enter into particulars, to look at all the phenomena separately and tie them together.[35]

"Organic" unity, epic largeness, and inclusiveness are terms that regrettably can be applied to only one of Goncharov's creations— *Oblomov*. *A Common Story* was written all of a piece, probably in 1845, and it is the tidiest and most orderly of his novels. Though not an unsuccessful work, its order is often mechanical; its scope small. *The Ravine* was conceived twenty years before its completion and was put together ("or pasted") slowly and laboriously, "in snatches," largely during the ten years prior to its publication (1858-1868). The result was a novel that never found its order, that remained fragmented and pasted. *Oblomov*, begun in the forties as were the other two novels, was, except for Part One and the concluding three or four chapters, written in the great burst of creative energy of the summer of 1857. In the intervening years it had "ripened" and "matured" in the mind of the artist. Obviously only that experience could have confirmed, if it did not provoke, Goncharov's belief in the organic growth of a work of art and the moment of epiphany, the sudden and unexpected ray of light that germinates the seeds of thought and illuminates the path for the artist. Of Goncharov's three novels only *Oblomov* consistently conveys a sense of having been written under the pressure of an inner urge for expression and a deeply felt vision of experience,

---

[35] *Shornik*, pp. 11-12. See also *Sobr. soch.*, VIII, 341. ". . . I suffer from a wealth of material and an inability to deal with it."

of having been "created" and not only "composed." Before attempting to justify these assertions, we must take a look at the writer's first literary efforts—several short stories written before *A Common Story*—to examine the development of his craft, for Goncharov, though he disparaged composition and complained about the difficulty of shaping form, was, like any artist worth his salt, also a craftsman.

CHAPTER IV

Early Efforts

OF the four stories Goncharov wrote before his first novel, only one—
"Ivan Savich Podzhabrin"—was published in the author's lifetime,
and he omitted it from his collected works of 1884; the others appeared originally in the Maykovs' handwritten manuscripts, and one
of these—"Nimfodora Ivanovna"—has not yet been published and
will not be discussed.[1] Though often amusing and entertaining, they
are slight pieces. Their importance lies in how they indicate future
developments.

"A Happy Error" ("Schastlivaya oshibka") (1839) is the most
fully developed of the group and also the most revealing of the problems Goncharov faced as a young writer and the paths he was to
take. The story is an extended anecdote whose outcome is determined
by a fortuitous circumstance—the "happy error." Egor Aduev has become disillusioned with his dissolute life and fears that his "heart" will
lose all capacity for feeling unless he finds true love. He sets out for
the home of an aristocratic young lady with the intention of proposing.
Elena is his "last chance" for happiness.[2] Unfortunately she does not
reciprocate his ardor, behaves coldly and coquettishly, and drives him
to distraction. Egor returns home in anger, inadvertently comes across

---

[1] "Ivan Savich Podzhabrin," written in 1842, appeared in *Sovremennik*,
No. 1 (1848); "Nimfodora Ivanovna" appeared in an 1836 issue of the
Maykovs' *Podsnezhnik* and is described by O. Demikhovskaya, in *Russkaya
literatura*, No. 1 (1960), pp. 139-144; "Likhaya bolest' " ("A Cruel Illness")
appeared in an 1838 issue of *Podsnezhnik* and was first published in *Zvezda*,
No. 1 (1936), pp. 202-234; "Schastlivaya oshibka" ("A Happy Error") was
in the Maykov almanac of 1839, *Lunnye nochi*, and was first published by
E. Lyatsky, in *Goncharov: zhizn', lichnost', tvorchestvo, kritiko-biograficheskie
ocherki* (3d edn.; Stockholm, 1920), pp. 321-355.

[2] *Sobr. soch.*, VII, 433-434.

a ticket for a ball at the Commercial Club, and decides to go in order to forget his troubles. The cabman, however, mistakenly takes him to a lavish affair at the residence of the Neapolitan envoy, where Elena has also been invited. They meet, imagining that each has come expressly for the other, and, after a brief interval, kiss and decide to marry, blissfully unaware of their common misconception. Egor's eventual discovery of the nature of his "happy error" does not prevent the couple from living happily ever after. The entire action is compressed into less than twenty-four hours.

"A Happy Error" belongs to the romantic style of the thirties, and, because of its playful manner, anecdotal plot, and its setting (the world of the aristocracy), to a sub-genre Russians call the "society tale" (*svetskaya povest'*).[3] The hero moves from a state of initial "disenchantment" to a final "enchantment," a movement antithetical to the central tendency of nineteenth-century realism, where the typical plot (and that of Goncharov's first novel) followed the reverse direction—from "great expectations" to "lost illusions."[4] The diction is often extremely elevated: a horse pulling Egor's sled becomes "an intrepid grey trotter" and "a noble beast"; Elena's dressing room is "a goddess's temple"; she has "black, always lively, radiant, lightning-flashing eyes." The vocabulary is conventionally romantic: "passion" (*strast'*) is a key word; it resides in the "heart" (*serdtse*), another repeated term; it is usually "ardent" (*plamennaya*) or "a flame" (*plamya*), though it can also be "stormy" (*burnaya*) or "seething" (*kipuchaya*). When such emotive epithets appear in clusters, they lend an exaggerated, overemphatic quality to the prose: ". . . she listened to the stormy outpourings of seething passion with a melancholy smile. . . ." The protagonist is constantly at a high pitch of emotion: love

---

[3] For a description of the genre, see M. A. Belkina, "Svetskaya povest' 30-kh godov i 'Knyaginya Ligovskaya' Lermontova," *Zhizn' i tvorchestvo M. Yu. Lermontova*, ed. N. L. Brodsky (Moscow, 1941), pp. 518-524.

[4] A. G. Tseytlin, " 'Schastlivaya oshibka' Goncharova kak ranniy etyud *Obyknovennoy istorii*," *Tvorcheskaya istoriya*, ed. N. K. Piksanov (Moscow, 1927), p. 143. Fanger, in *Dostoevsky and Romantic Realism*, p. 8, remarks that "the process, which forms the plots of most of the great novels of the nineteenth century, might be summed up in the juxtaposition of two of their titles—*Great Expectations* and *Lost Illusions*."

promises Egor "a whole world of bliss"; when it is unrequited, "melancholy (*toska*) pierced deeper into his heart; the worm of despair stirred stronger in his breast. . . ."[5] The first-person narrator occasionally interrupts the course of the narration with rhetorical exclamations and lyrical asides made in the same emotionally heightened and hackneyed manner: "What demon answered in her stead with sarcasms to Aduev's proposal? what angel forced her to weep now?" "Oh, how I love the twilight (*sumerki*), especially when I am borne away in thought to the past! Where are you, golden time?"[6]

But Goncharov hardly takes his characters' intense emotions seriously and much of the prose may be intentionally inflated. The narrator now and then intrudes into the action to dissociate himself from his protagonist and to remind the reader that the story is mere artifice: "Come to think of it, what name does one give to Elena's conduct? Aduev, in a paroxysm of frenzy, called it—take note, please, *mesdames*, Aduev, and not I—called it. . . ."[7] Moreover, the narrator in his intrusions often evinces a distinctly prosaic cast of mind that further sets him apart from his ecstatic hero and makes his own hyperboles of lyricism or rhetoric suspect. The story opens with a lengthy evocation of Petersburg at twilight, which, in apparent imitation of Gogol, blended lyricism—"Oh, how I love the twilight . . ."; hyperbole—"Conversation, heretofore rolling slowly like a brook over pebbles, took hold once again; like a powerful river it beat against its banks, became louder, more tumultuous"; a mock-sentimental tone— "Isn't this, I blush to say, the time of the sweet whisper, the timid avowal, the clasping of hands, and—all sorts of things?"; slice-of-life observations of characteristic "physiognomies" from the passing scene—"Here a subordinate boldly takes the measure of his superior from head to foot; a lover boldly devours with glances the beauty of his beloved . . ."; and an attempt to capture the mysterious atmosphere

---

[5] *Sobr. soch.*, VII, 429, 445-446, 432, 438, 456. Dmitrij Čiževskij, in *Romanticism in Slavic Literatures*, trans. D. S. Worth ('s-Gravenhage, 1957), pp. 25-51, includes "plammenyy" and "burnyy" in a vocabulary list of words given particular emphasis by the Russian romantics and notes the special importance of "serdtse" and "strast'." Scholarship identifies the style with that of Marlinsky. See Tseytlin, *I. A. Goncharov*, pp. 42-43.

[6] *Sobr. soch.*, VII, 439, 428.   [7] *Ibid.*, p. 433.

of the darkening city—". . . light struggles with darkness . . . ; the street is empty; houses lurk like giants in the darkness; nowhere is there any light; all objects merge into an indefinite color; nothing disturbs the silence; . . . only sleds, as if by stealth, continue to weave their eternal pattern along the Nevsky Prospect." The passage, however, concludes with what reads like a disavowal of this highly elaborate and colored style. As Petersburg assumes its more conventional aspect after the mysterious moment of twilight, an anonymous voice implores the narrator to "remain only an observer of twilight"—a favorite hour of the romantic mood—and other voices respond with the common sense qualification that "it is inconvenient . . . to observe in the twilight. It is dark." The narrator readily subscribes to this prosaic view and begins the narrative proper with a terse matter-of-fact summary, lowering the heightened description to the ordinary and usual: "Once in winter, at twilight, accompanied by all the above-stated conditions, that is, falling of snow and silence on the streets. . . ."[8]

The young Goncharov soon became aware that he could not continue to imitate Gogol's highly intricate and expressive prose, if he had not already recognized the fact while trying to duplicate it in "A Happy Error." Though many tried, Gogol's uncanny brilliance of stylistic improvisation proved inimitable and, besides, Russian prose was shortly to turn into an altogether different channel. After "A Happy Error" Goncharov abandoned "subjective" forms of narration characterized by a first-person narrator who intrudes into the tale with rhetorical and lyrical asides or digressive comments intended to establish his superiority to the fictional world before him (i.e., "romantic irony"). An omniscient third-person narrator who rarely comments upon the action narrates all his future fiction in a prose that is usually neutral and restrained. But if Gogol's verbal pyrotechnics turned out to be a dead end for those who followed him, the art of that singular genius included other ingredients more compatible with the realism waiting to be born—coarse and even vulgar details of common life, comic caricature, and delicious parody. The ironic pattern that occasionally comes to the surface in "A Happy Error"—the juxta-

---

[8] *Ibid.*, pp. 427-429.

position of lyricism, hyperbole, or an emotionally heightened perception with the ordinary and commonplace—became an essential feature of Goncharov's fiction. It had also been characteristic of Gogol's.[9]

There are moments in "A Happy Error" when the contrast appears in the context of the narrative and does not depend upon the narrator's gratuitous interventions. Thus Egor dreams of a "lost bliss" and "poetic haven"—"a home that is a miracle of comfort, taste, and luxury; a charming garden where art contends with nature; of how he and Elena would separate themselves . . . from the whole world; [and] he would lie there with a magic mirror at the feet of his Armida" while scratching his ear and playing with the button of his jacket. The passage concludes with an abrupt paralleling of the poetic dream and the prosaic gesture: " 'And everything has perished! the magnificent edifice of dream has crumbled!' He ripped off the button completely and scratched his ear. . . ."[10]

Other characters also serve to delimit Egor's flights of rhetoric by opposing a more ordinary view of things. Elena responds to his eloquent advances by mimicking him, commenting upon his manner of speech—"How emphatically spoken!" or by turning her attention to such mundane matters as the time of day during the course of his fervent speeches. Again Goncharov highlights the parallel: " '. . . I know that there is no hope for happiness; it has passed as everything passes in its turn!' Aduev fell into thought. Elena looked at the clock."[11] Finally, the anecdote itself depends upon an implicit parallel between two levels of reality—the grand ball of the Neapolitan envoy and the decidedly more ordinary affair at the Commercial Club.

The organization of the story's action, if we disregard the narra-

---

[9] For traces of Gogol's influence in the early stories, see O. A. Demikhovskaya, "Rannee tvorchestvo I. A. Goncharova," *Materialy yubileynoy Goncharovskoy konferentsii*, ed. P. S. Beysov (Ul'yanovsk, 1963), pp. 72-86. For some general remarks on Gogol's influence see V. Desnitsky, "Trilogiya Goncharova," *Izbrannye stat'i po russkoy literature XVIII-XIX vekov* (Moscow-Leningrad, 1958), pp. 296ff. The subject has hardly been exhausted and would make an interesting study.

[10] *Sobr. soch.*, VII, 450. Armida is an enchantress in Torquato Tasso's *Gerusalemme Liberata (Jerusalem Delivered)*.

[11] *Ibid.*, pp. 434-438.

tor's intervention, displays a meticulous orderliness that not only is unromantic, but which characterizes a good deal of Goncharov's fiction. When Egor first enters Elena's elegant residence he is struck by the circumstance that its inhabitants are all sitting "in pairs" and resolves to seek out Elena "for symmetry—we too shall be a pair."[12] Like Egor, "A Happy Error" strives for perfect symmetry. Characters appear in pairs and so do the incidents. Egor's headlong ride through the streets of Petersburg to Elena's house opens the action; a second ride on the same grey trotter, now with hopes realized, provides a frame at the conclusion. The avowal of love takes place in twilight, the time of day when lovers feel unrestrained; the temporary break between the lovers at twilight's end, furnishing a second frame to enclose half the action of the story—from the avowal to the separation. The lovers' first and second interviews, the quarrel and the reconciliation, take place in the same room, a coincidence the narrator feels compelled to comment upon (the reconciliation scene, though begun at the ball, is completed in Elena's home).[13]

The story's "returns," because they occur under changed circumstances in the lovers' affairs, give an ironic twist to the denouement. "Congratulations!" his friends shout to Aduev at the conclusion, ". . . you have gone from one extreme to another," referring to the happy error that brought him to the Neapolitan envoy's ball instead of the Commercial Club, but reminding us that Egor's situation also turns from extreme to extreme—from unrequited to realized love.[14] But in changing his circumstances Egor remains the same person. He begins his story as a romantically infatuated youth and has not changed at the conclusion. Aduev's return to his original psychological state is emphasized by another repetition that frames the second half of the action—from separation to union. After the unsuccessful interview Egor resolves to turn his energies from love to business and, as part of his new resolve, communicates a number of extremely harsh decrees for the administration of his estate to his elderly steward, causing

[12] *Ibid.*, pp. 430-431.

[13] *Ibid.*, p. 459. Tseytlin's interesting article in *Tvorcheskaya istoriya*, ed. Piksanov, was helpful in pointing out the story's symmetry. See p. 145.

[14] *Sobr. soch.*, VII, 464.

the old man to remark that the young master takes after his father. He also treats his personal servant with similar harshness (the steward and the servant constitute another pair). At the conclusion Egor reverses himself, asks the servant to forgive him, rescinds the decrees, bestows extremely generous gifts upon his peasants, provoking the steward to exclaim that, no, he does not resemble his father at all.[15] As Egor's external circumstances change, his mind merely returns to the ideal "world of bliss" that had captivated it at the opening of the story.

This enclosing symmetry, created by a series of parallel actions and circular returns, diminishes, if it does not altogether preclude, the possibility of a psychological development of character. Incident—the twists of circumstance, the happy errors—prevails, and characters are manipulated to provide its ironies. That the protagonists' states of mind also form symmetries in turn reduces the possibilities for conflict. Except for Elena's momentary display of "coquettishness," which prevents her from reciprocating Egor's intense emotions (and without which there would be no story), the lovers undergo the same experiences simultaneously. They suffer together; they commit the identical "happy error"; they finally submit to the same raptures of love ("What is this? The same things are happening with her now, as happened previously to Egor Petrovich"). "Elena Karlovna was kind and amiable; Egor Petrovich was amiable and kind," the narrator had declared at the opening of the story, and what separates them, Elena's momentary display of aristocratic frivolity, takes on the quality of an illusion, a legerdemain as trivial as the inversion of adjectives in their descriptions. Elena's vanity, we are told, is merely another "error," one that is quickly rectified at the conclusion, as the two lovers become one: "Both hearts beat powerfully; both barely drew a breath. . . . Both their eyes reflected happiness."[16]

In the last sentence of the story the narrator informs us that the Neapolitan envoy, whom Egor had failed to recognize at the ball (another "error") and had insulted, has forgiven him and is coming to the wedding. The reader is also invited. As "A Happy Error" tends

[15] *Ibid.*, pp. 449-450, 460-463.   [16] *Ibid.*, pp. 457, 434, 444, 460.

toward perfect esthetic symmetry, it also moves to a perfect unity of the social world.

I have dwelt at length upon this early story not for its intrinsic merit, but because it is especially significant for Goncharov's later work. *A Common Story* and *Oblomov*, as we shall see, also display a symmetry of parallel presentations and circular returns, though in *Oblomov* Goncharov discovered new ways to complicate habitual patterns. Moreover, we shall discover the same stability of character, its resistance to change, and an urge to mitigate, if not completely dissipate, conflict throughout Goncharov's fictional corpus. Characters will appear, as Elena and Egor do, in pairs—Pyotr and Alexander Aduev (the repetition of the surname points to the many continuities between "A Happy Error" and Goncharov's first novel),[17] Stolz and Oblomov—each member of which initially seems irreconcilably opposed to the other; as their stories evolve the novelist will either reveal the differences to be illusory or (in *Oblomov*) attempt to bring his characters together in spite of them. Because he generally refused to acknowledge important conflicts of character, Goncharov was compelled to seek other kinds of tension and distance for his fiction. In "A Happy Error" he established a distance between the ironic first-person narrator and the unitary fictional world—a narrative form he was to abandon. However, "A Happy Error" contains another sort of tension, one that remains undeveloped in this early story but that was to be elaborated and refined in the novels. The important conflicts of Goncharov's fictional art usually result not from opposed motives of individuals but from the confrontation of differing modes of the literary imagination and disparate categories of existence—the poetic and the prosaic, the ideal and the commonplace, the exceptional and the usual—sometimes as represented by several characters, at other times as embodied in a single individual.

Such patterns of opposition may be parodic in nature, though parody in Goncharov is not usually directed against an identifiable literary source and may not be intended merely to deride a specific literary

---

[17] See Tseytlin, in *Tvorcheskaya istoriya*, ed. Piksanov, pp. 124-153.

movement (romanticism), as criticism often maintains.[18] Instead, the parodic, as in "A Happy Error," becomes a formal principle of the literary composition itself, as one level of the work (the prosaic) comically deflates the other (the poetic).[19]

"A Cruel Illness" ("Likhaya bolest' ") (1838) is clearly a piece intended for the initiates of the Maykov circle. It good-humoredly spoofs the Maykovs' (they are called the Zurovs) enthusiasm for outings to the environs of Petersburg through a string of anecdotes describing their ill-starred picnics. Their enthusiasm constitutes the "cruel illness," and it has the force of an epidemic, as friends, relatives, and acquaintances are drawn into the family's frenzied search for the joys and peace of nature. The narrator does not share the Zurovs' passion, and apparently neither does the author. The bucolic retreats of the tale, instead of offering peace and solitude, become the scene of a series of minor catastrophes: children fall into ditches, tobacco into the tea; dogs attack the picnic baskets; carriages overturn; it rains. The story of the family's misadventures is told in a mock-hyperbolic manner, not dissimilar to that of sections of "A Happy Error." The central hyperbole is, of course, the "cruel illness" that holds the family in its grip and from which they finally perish.

Goncharov again deflates the enthusiasms of his characters by juxtaposing them with prosaic perceptions, though in "A Cruel Illness" the target of his parody is the idyll of pastoral instead of romantic love. Zinaida, a young lady who has joined the Zurovs, grows rapturous over the rural scene—all those "havens of simple bliss, labor, contentment, love, and family virtue"—only to discover that the rustic bridge she has been admiring is lined with manure, the lake that appeared from a distance as "smooth and glistening like a mirror" is only a puddle, and the foam on its surface is an accumulation of soap bubbles

[18] See, e.g., N. I. Prutskov, *Masterstvo Goncharova-romanista* (Moscow, 1962), p. 6, and B. Engel'gardt, introduction to "Putevye pis'ma I. A. Goncharova iz krugosvetnogo plavaniya," *Literaturnoe nasledstvo*, Nos. 22-24 (1935), p. 342.

[19] Yu. Tynyanov, in an introduction to *Mnimaya poeziya* (Moscow-Leningrad, 1931), p. 8, argues that parody may be used as "form" without a parodied object. See also Tynyanov's brilliant "Dostoevsky i Gogol' (k teorii parodii)," in *Arkhaisty i novatory* (Leningrad, 1929), pp. 412-455.

caused by soldiers washing their dirty linen. Later, when the fence of a brick factory looms before her to disrupt another picturesque scene, she can only exclaim in exasperation: "People everywhere, everywhere!"[20]

Zinaida's exclamation might serve as a motto for the novelist's art. Nature in Goncharov is "impure"—it seeks a human presence. Nature descriptions appear in his fiction, but he usually seems little interested in them. They may not all be as perfunctory (or ironic) as the description by enumeration the narrator provides at one point in "A Cruel Illness," but they are seldom very much more. "... I shall only say that we descended into five valleys, skirted seven lakes, clambered up three ridges, sat beneath seventy-one trees of an extensive and dense forest, and stopped at all the remarkable spots."[21]

Thus far we have encountered characters caught up in enthusiasms of emotion or hyperboles of language. "A Cruel Illness" introduces a character who, instead of merely adopting an exaggerated pose, is himself an exaggeration—so to speak, a hyperbolic character. His name is Tyazhelenko ("Heavy").

> ... he was famous from his youthful years for his unparalleled methodical laziness and heroic indifference to the world's bustle. He spent the greater part of his life lying in bed; if he sometimes sat, it was only at the dinner table. . . . He . . . seldom left his home, and, because of a life spent in a lying position, he had acquired all the attributes of an idler: a large belly curved out majestically like a hill and flourished bountifully; his entire body fell into folds like those of a rhinoceros, forming some sort of natural dress.[22]

Tyazhelenko is a pure caricature—a distillation of a single trait, "laziness." Though the narrator calls his idleness "an illness,"[23] he does not take the diagnosis seriously or grant his character a psychology. Tyazhelenko's function in the story is only to highlight that other "cruel illness," the Zurovs' passion for strenuous activity, by opposing his own monumental passivity. The narrator, despairing at his failure

[20] *Sobr. soch.* (Pravda), VII, 389-390, 393.
[21] *Ibid.*, p. 393.   [22] *Ibid.*, p. 375.   [23] *Ibid.*, p. 378.

to dissuade the Zurovs from pursuing their ventures into the country-side, has invited his friend to assist him. Tyazhelenko, though he meets with as little success, nevertheless proves a powerful ally. A good deal of the potency of his argument lies not so much in what he says but in what he is—a perfect exemplar of "methodical laziness and heroic indifference to the world's bustle." He opposes the busy world largely by ignoring it but also, and more importantly, by mimicking its forms in an absurdly narrowed sphere. A caricature himself, Tyazhelenko in turn caricatures the Zurovs' enthusiasms. He, like them, exercises, but his exercises take the form of daily walks along the corridor that leads from the bedroom to the anteroom of his apartment; he seeks fresh air but obtains it without bothersome excursions to the country— merely by placing his face beside an open window and inhaling.

As Goncharov narrows the range of Tyazhelenko's physical ac-tivity, he allows him to expand in another direction—verbally. Tya-zhelenko, we are told, is "eloquent." He spends his eloquence, how-ever, in inflating the Zurovs' conventional pastimes into dangerous undertakings of heroic proportion (it is Tyazhelenko who coins the phrase, "cruel illness").

> "Imagine, what they have come to! If they remain at home on a summer's day . . . something lies heavily upon them, gives them no peace; some sort of invincible force draws them to the city's outskirts; an evil spirit settles into them, and now they"—here Tyazhelenko began to speak heatedly—"now they swim, leap, run and, swimming, leaping, running, they come close to death. . . ." Here he accompanied each of these notions with a colorful gesture. "They rush to ford streams; they sink into marshes; they make their way through thorny bushes, clamber up the highest trees; how many times they have come close to drowning, fallen head-long into abysses, sunk into slime, grown numb with cold, and even—O, horrors!—suffered hunger and thirst!"[24]

Tyazhelenko embodies two extremes, both of which are perceived comically—an extremely narrow range of physical activity and an equally extreme verbal expansiveness.

[24] *Ibid.*, p. 378.

He, of course, anticipates Goncharov's great creation—Ilya Ilich Oblomov. Oblomov also begins his novel as a grotesque caricature given to the same extremes of verbal exuberance and almost total physical passivity. In the novel, however, Goncharov will not remain content with presenting isolated comic gestures but will explore the discrepancy between the words (or thoughts) and actions of his hero, and the implications of a life lived almost entirely in verbal constructs.

As "A Cruel Illness" includes presentiments of the character who was to dominate Goncharov's sole masterpiece, "Ivan Savich Podzhabrin" (written in 1842) suggests the situation its hero will confront at its opening. Podzhabrin, though a more active character than Tyazhelenko, also experiences moments of total lethargy that he seeks to escape through a series of short-lived love affairs.[25] He has a constant companion in his romantic adventures, a prosaically obtuse servant, who is completely uncomprehending of the master's enthusiasms and concerned only with the practical exigencies of existence. Like Oblomov and Zakhar after them, Podzhabrin and Avdey are compelled to vacate their apartment (in this instance the master's interest in the neighbors' wives has brought about their difficulties) and set out to find a new home. Characteristically, in examining vacant apartments, the servant checks the heating, plastering, and furnishings, while the master concerns himself only with the female neighbors. Podzhabrin, in spite of his easy susceptibility to feminine allures, very much fears marriage, and the story ends with master and servant in flight from a second apartment because one of the neighbors took his advances seriously. As at the opening, they are again homeless.

"Ivan Savich Podzhabrin" is written in the more "objective" manner of the forties. Goncharov subtitled the tale "sketches," and it belongs to the genre of "physiological sketches," an early example of literary realism that was made popular in Russia in the forties by Nekrasov, Grigorovich, Vladimir Dahl, and Ivan Panaev, and whose influence can be felt in the early work of Turgenev, Dostoevsky, and

[25] Cf. Egor Aduev, who is oppressed by "a death-like peace," which he calls "sleep" (*Sobr. soch.*, VII, 442), and which he seeks to escape through Elena. All three protagonists of Goncharov's novels experience the same condition and seek to escape it through love for a woman.

others.[26] In the manner of the physiological sketch, "Podzhabrin" presents a series of "slice-of-life" (*byt*) portraits of ordinary life in Petersburg—i.e., the "physiology" of the city. The structure is very loose, falling into a series of discrete scenes that describe Podzhabrin's successive affairs and the social milieux of his partners. The story is told by an omniscient third-personal narrator—Goncharov's usual narrative manner—who avoids the lyrical or rhetorical interventions and, except for occasional lapses—". . . the spirit of knowledge flew over his head without its wing casting a shadow"—the contrived diction of the tales of the thirties. Instead, he narrates the story in a restrained and unobtrusive manner, allowing the characters to speak for themselves (much of the tale is in dialogue, which lends it a theatrical quality). The narrator limits himself largely to descriptions of character and, occasionally, of place. Where the previous stories admitted "low" detail only for comic contrast, the landscapes of "Podzhabrin" belong entirely to a prosaic realm: "Master and servant set out for another courtyard; a peasant dragged after them as an observer. Two geese and five chickens strayed about the yard. An old woman was washing a tub in one corner; in another a coachman was chopping wood."[27]

The characters take on the aspect of social types or, more accurately, caricatures of social types. Where the tales of the thirties centered upon the aristocracy (the Maykov milieu), Podzhabrin's adventures take him through the various levels of the Russian social hierarchy, from a "lady" (*baryshnya*) of the lower gentry, to a baroness and "distinguished lady" (*znatnaya baryshnya*), to a servant girl, and finally to the ward of a low-ranking government official (*chinovnik*). Podzhabrin, also an inconsequential bureaucrat, displays an exaggerated pride of caste—"Who am I? . . . I am an . . . of-

[26] For a survey and description of the Russian physiological sketch and its French antecedents, see A. G. Tseytlin, *Stanovlenie realizma v russkoy literature: russkiy fiziologicheskiy ocherk* (Moscow, 1965). In the forties Goncharov also wrote an anonymous article in the style of the physiological sketch, "Pis'ma stolichnogo druga k provintsial'nomu zhenikhu," in *Sovremennik*, No. 11 (1848). See *Sobr. soch.* (Pravda), VII, 67-87.

[27] *Sobr. soch.*, VII, 9-10.

ficial!"—identifies the objects of his seductive wiles by their social position and regulates his enthusiasms accordingly. Goncharov presents an extended description of his "daily manner of life," which consists in avoiding work and going on "sprees," and implies that such manners are typical of his class: "[These activities] signified for Ivan Savich and those like him *leading a gay life.*"[28]

Besides social class, characters are identified by a single distinctive characteristic of speech or appearance—a device that was to become an important component of Goncharov's fiction. Though he employed such identifications for several purposes in the novels, in "Podzhabrin" they serve to narrow the characters down to the single level of comic caricature and to provide the mechanical repetitions of comedy. Ivan Savich's pet phrase is one we have seen, "to lead a gay life" (*zhuirovat' zhizn'yu*), though he reiterates other choice expressions of his philosophy such as "life is short" and "the service is dry stuff" with almost the same frequency. His distinctive physical feature, which is continually stressed and which gives him great pride, is his long sideburns. The servant Avdey can muster little more than an uninspired "I don't know" as commentary upon each of his master's successive amorous projects. The lady of the lower gentry responds to Ivan Savich's eager advances with an ecstatic, "Oh, what bliss!"; the ward of the government official conveys the inherent modesty of her social milieu with a repeated, "Oh, my God."[29]

It would be mistaken, however, to understand the new elements that appear in "Ivan Savich Podzhabrin"—the "objective" omniscient narrator, genre portraiture, social typicality—as signifying one step in a steady line of progress to artistic maturity and literary realism— concepts that much Goncharov criticism confuses by treating them as synonyms. "Podzhabrin" is different, but it is not necessarily better. More to the point, Goncharov, as we shall see, returned in *Oblomov* to lyrical modes of expression (though a lyricism of a different sort from that of the first stories), revived a character whose habits of life and thought are so extreme and individual that it becomes difficult, if not impossible, to perceive him as only a social type, and even intro-

[28] *Ibid.*, pp. 16, 9.
[29] See *ibid.*, pp. 26-30, 64-68, for a representative sampling.

duced elements of fantasy usually eschewed by realistic writers. Also, though the novelist was again to employ "slice-of-life" presentations, the careful structural symmetry of "A Happy Error" is more indicative of the pattern of *A Common Story* and, in a loosened and freer form, of *Oblomov*, than is the casual accumulation of incident exhibited by "Podzhabrin." Goncharov's several early stories, instead of indicating a linear development toward a specifiable goal, reveal an artist testing various approaches and stratagems while keeping an eye on current literary trends. Goncharov, as Tseytlin wrote in regard to "A Happy Error," "had not yet found his style."[30] Such is the case with apprentice writers, but the mature Goncharov continued to test varied approaches, sometimes to accommodate a personal vision, at other times in response to the contemporary literary scene. What he eventually discovered was not so much a distinctive kind of novel, though there are some qualities that are properly "Goncharovian," as a single great novel that conflated with much sophistication the various elements—lyricism and prosaic detail, hyperbole and irony, structural order and the mimetic rendering of ordinary experience—first explored in these slight tales.

If anything remains fairly constant in Goncharov's work (and even here qualifications will have to be made when we come to *The Ravine*), it is an ironic conception of character and an inclination to parody. In "A Happy Error" and "A Cruel Illness" parody took the form of a lowering of the ideal and poetic to the ordinary and prosaic. In "Podzhabrin" Goncharov momentarily abandoned the immediate paralleling of two levels of experience, probably because the story does not require it. The world of "Ivan Savich Podzhabrin" is in itself a lower order of existence, so dominated by coarse appetites and vulgar ambitions that any attempt on the part of its characters to simulate cultural refinement results in parody-like comedy. Ivan Savich, who has been compared to Gogol's Khlestakov,[31] habitually masks his sensual preoccupations with an affected diction: "She was—how may one express it?—a dear apparition, so to speak, a dream—she diversified the melancholy of a dead life." He interlards his speech with a

---

[30] Tseytlin, *Tvorcheskaya istoriya*, ed. Piksanov, p. 135.

[31] See Tseytlin, *I. A. Goncharov*, p. 47.

few memorized French phrases (*mon cher* is a favorite), though, unlike Khlestakov's, his pretensions are "philosophical" rather than literary. At times, like Gogol's great verbal improviser, he seems merely
to be providing the ladies with what they want to hear.

"Oh yes," she said, "you presented a brooch to my niece. I am
wearing it—you see?"

"Very pleasant—only, I am embarrassed; it is unworthy of such
a breast—if only I knew—"

"What else do you occupy yourself with?"

"I frequent the theater."

"The theater! Oh, fortunate fellow! What can be more delightful than the theater? Oh, bliss! . . . You read, of course?"

"Er, yes, yes—of course."

"What, Pushkin? Oh, Pushkin! 'The Robber Brothers'! 'The
Prisoner of the Caucasus'! poor Zarema! how she suffered! and
Girey—what a monster!"

"Er, no, I read philosophical books."

"Ah! what sort? . . ."

"The compositions of Homer, Lomonosov, the *Encyclopedic
Lexicon*. . . ."

"It's one of them, I suppose, who said 'life is short'?"

"Er, yes."

"Beautifully said!"[32]

[32] *Sobr. soch.*, VII, 37, 28. The lady has confused her literary references—
Pushkin is correct, but Zarema and Girey belong to "Bakhchisarayskiy fontan."
The *Entsiklopedicheskiy leksikon* appeared in the late thirties; N. I. Grech
was an editor.

CHAPTER V

A Common Story

Early in the novel a youthful Alexander Aduev arrives in Petersburg from the provinces with high hopes for success and glory in the great city. He calls upon his uncle, Pyotr Aduev, a successful bureaucrat and industrial entrepreneur, for protection and advice. The uncle soon observes that there is a "great difference" between them. Alexander's enthusiasms are wholeheartedly "for friendship, for the delights of life, for happiness"; the uncle lives for work (*delo*).[1] *A Common Story* is the history of the abolition of this difference. It traces Alexander's progress, despite a number of temporary setbacks, to the condition of his uncle. Disappointed in his several attempts to find love and to prove himself a writer, Alexander regularly returns to Pyotr for instruction in the art of urban living. A Socratic dialogue between the sophisticated uncle and his naive nephew dominates much of the work.

For the literary imagination educational problems may be reduced to the task of mastering a proper language, a style. Though Pyotr in the course of the novel instructs his provincial nephew in all the civilities and stratagems of city life—proper dress and table manners, the respectful distances to observe with strangers, how to manage women, the quickest way to "career and fortune"—he devotes the greater part of his educative energies to Alexander's language. For Pyotr, "le style c'est l'homme." His instructional method approximates the traditional procedure employed by writers who are trying to wean themselves or their audiences from atrophied literary conventions—parody.

The parody proceeds in a number of ways. The novelist places the

[1] *Sobr. soch.*, I, 41.

uncle's colloquial speech alongside the nephew's affected and self-consciously literary prose. After their initial meeting they simultaneously report their impressions of each other to friends:

> [Alexander:] My uncle . . . is very prosaic. . . . It is as if his spirit is chained to the earth and never rises to a pure reflection, isolated from earthly squabbles, of the phenomena of the spiritual nature of man. For him heaven is inseparably bound to earth, and he and I, it seems, will never merge our souls completely.
>
> .   .   .   .
>
> [Pyotr:] . . . he's a quiet fellow. He has his odd points—he throws himself upon me to kiss me, speaks like a seminary student—well, but he'll get over that, and it's a good thing he isn't hanging on my neck.[2]

More frequently Goncharov allows the uncle to be the conscious agent of the parody. Pyotr parodies by completing the predicates of Alexander's sentences,

> Life is like a lake. . . . It is full of something mysterious, alluring, concealing in itself so much—
> Slime, my good fellow. . . ;[3]

by substituting his own subjects,

> I gaze at the crowd as only a hero, a poet, and a lover made happy by mutual love, could gaze.
> And as madmen look. . . ;

by repeating Alexander's stock phrases such as "friendship and love" in a coarse and colloquial context,

> . . . dreamers like you: they sniff around with their noses to see whether it doesn't smell anywhere of eternal friendship and love.[4]

---

[2] *Ibid.,* p. 44.

[3] Alexandra and Sverre Lyngstad, in their recent *Ivan Goncharov* (New York, 1971), pp. 48-51, trace a series of references to flight and fall into various forms of filth. The Lyngstads' book appeared too late for me to comment upon its many interesting observations or to indicate those places where our views coincide.

[4] *Sobr. soch.,* I, 53, 70.

He mocks his nephew's favorite expressions by frequently repeating them under the principle that the repetitive, when it is not simply tedious, is comic. "Sincere effusions," "colossal passion," and "sweet bliss" are Alexander's favorites and supply his uncle with vulnerable targets. In addition, Pyotr has at hand an arsenal of prosaic gestures—a puff on a cigar, a shrug of the shoulder, a raised eyebrow, a yawn—that he regularly employs to deflate his nephew's rhetorical flights.

At times Pyotr's commentaries are less oblique. He assumes the role of literary critic and comments directly on Alexander's language.

> [Alexander:] And I thought you were bidding farewell before your wedding to your true friends, whom you sincerely love, with whom you would recall for the last time your gay youth, and, perhaps, on parting, would press fast to your heart.
>
> [Pyotr:] Come now! In those several words of yours there is everything that does not and should not exist in life. . . . Really! You say *true friends* when there are simply friends and *goblet* when people drink out of wineglasses or ordinary glasses and embraces *on parting* when there is no question of parting. Oh, Alexander![5]

Pyotr would have Alexander call things by their proper names. He wishes his nephew to speak "more simply" and to give up his "wild language."[6] The pedagogical method by which he teaches Alexander to speak "like everyone else and not like a professor of esthetics"[7] relocates the nephew's speech into a radically different and "lower" linguistic level where it appears incongruous. "Eternal friendship and love," though not in itself a reprehensible phrase, becomes ludicrous when the uncle asks if it "smells" (*pakhnet*). Such verbal displacements are the method of parody. A linguist has read the novel as "a

---

[5] *Ibid.*, pp. 83-84.

[6] *Ibid.*, pp. 41, 51. "Wild" (*dikiy*) is Pyotr's usual epithet for his nephew's speech.

[7] *Ibid.*, p. 41. The reference may be to Nadezhdin.

collision between two speech styles. . . ."[8] It is also the subversion of one by the other.

Occasional parodic touches had appeared in the early "romantic" stories, but in the novel Goncharov limits romantic inflations of language to one character and never allows them to appear without an accompanying ironic deflation. Parody in the novel is not only more systematic and thoroughgoing; it is also more self-conscious. *A Common Story*, published in 1847, the approximate birth-date of Russian realism, has been called Russia's first true prose novel. As such it reflects the polemical stance realism adopted toward romanticism and provides another example of how often realism originates in parody.[9] It mocks the romantics' penchant for an emotionally heightened language and their thematic conventions as well. Alexander dreams of becoming a writer, and, disheartened by his uncle's cool reception of his efforts at poetry, he turns to prose. The story he produces is strewn with the standard equipment of romantic fiction—exotic landscapes and a lonely hero who experiences tragic passion outside the conventional limits of society: ". . . the furnishings were luxurious: American nature, mountains, and in the midst of all this an exile (*izgnannik*) who has abducted his beloved." Alexander invokes the shades of Byron, Goethe, and Schiller to support his view that literature should concern itself only with exalted heroes—"a corsair, a great poet, an artist." He reads French romances to his uncle as evidence that to love means to dwell in the infinite and the ideal. The

[8] V. B. Brodskaya, "Yazyk i stil' romana I. A. Goncharova *Obyknovennaya istoriya*," *Voprosy slavyanskogo yazykoznaniya*, III (L'vov, 1953), 145.

[9] Brodskaya identifies Alexander's speech with the style of Marlinsky. *Ibid.*, pp. 131ff. Marlinsky is mentioned in the novel. *Sobr. soch.*, I, 30. N. I. Prutskov, "Romany Goncharova," in *Istoriya russkogo romana* (Moscow-Leningrad, 1962-1964), I, 521, finds "*A Common Story* the first Russian prose novel in the direct and exact sense of the term." Previous novels were novels in verse (Pushkin's *Eugene Onegin*), novels as cycles of stories (Lermontov's *A Hero of Our Time*), the novel as a prose "poem" (Gogol's *Dead Souls*). Mirsky, *A History of Russian Literature*, p. 169, dates the birth of Russian realism to 1846-1847. Harry Levin, *The Gates of Horn: A Study of Five French Realists* (New York, 1963), p. 47, describes realism as originating in parody.

deliberate absurdity of the language immediately discredits the argument: "In the ideal world . . . surpassing in luster and splendor every luster and splendor."[10]

The word "common" forms part of the novel's title, and the argument directed against Alexander's views of art (and self, for they are intimately entwined) constitutes an effort to reduce the artificial to the natural, the exalted to the ordinary, the "uncommon" to the "common." Pyotr, after restlessly hearing out his nephew's exuberant readings, wonders about the authenticity of the experiences depicted: "Can there have been an age when people in all seriousness thought and did all that? . . . Can it be that everything they write of knights and shepherdesses is just an insulting concoction?" He concludes that the heroes of Alexander's favorite fiction are "exceptions, and exceptions are almost always bad." Similarly, in attempting to dissuade his nephew from taking vengeance upon a rival in love (Alexander's story centers on a love triangle; the tales he reads to his uncle are about bloody acts of vengeance), Pyotr converts the extraordinary and exotic to the usual and commonplace. Petersburg is not the Kirghiz steppes, he argues, and a duel in "our age" is not conducted with weapons but with wit and cunning whose purpose is "to present the rival in a common aspect, to show that the new hero is 'so-so'. . . ." When Alexander perceives the comments "excessive ardor, unnaturalness, . . . there are no such people . . ." on the rejected manuscript of his American story, he asks himself, "Can I be expected to portray these vulgar heroes one meets at every step, who think and feel like the crowd, who do what everyone does—these pitiful characters of everyday, petty tragedies and comedies, who are not marked by a special seal?"[11] The novel itself provides the answer, for *A Common Story* is Alexander's "common story," the story of how he abandons his dreams of an exceptional fate and an extraordinary personality and becomes ordinary, "common," "like everyone else."

A Common Story is, then, to a significant degree, a programmatic novel. Alexander's conversion to the values of his uncle assumes the aspect of a literary conversion. His abandonment of an abstract, in-

[10] *Sobr. soch.*, I, 103, 161.
[11] *Ibid.*, pp. 161-162, 137, 102-103.

flated, and conventionally romantic diction and final discovery of "the poetry *of a grey sky, a broken fence, wicket gate and a muddy pond . . .*"[12] mark a progression from a language divorced from things to that language of things that characterizes literary realism (*res*, it will be remembered, means "thing"). Similarly, the deflation of the extraordinary and the unusual to the ordinary and usual, though perhaps less immediately apparent as such, also reflects a particular view of the nature of art. Popular usage has so accustomed us to evaluate novels according to criteria of verisimilitude and actuality that we easily forget that an insistence upon presenting common incidents and characters from ordinary walks of life, though it had appeared before, was part of the program of a specific literary movement called realism.[13]

A Common Story also signifies a personal development of the artist. The poems Goncharov ascribes to his protagonist and ruthlessly parodies in the novel are examples of his own early attempts at poetry. Alexander's elevated diction exaggerates and caricatures the style of the thirties that Turgenev had dubbed the "pseudo-sublime"—a style Goncharov had indulged in, not without some irony, in several of his earlier stories.[14] *A Common Story* is in part a self-parody, as Alexander's weaning through parody from the affectations of a literary

[12] *Ibid.*, p. 290. The italics are Goncharov's. Alexander is paraphrasing several lines from the uncompleted chapter of Pushkin's *Eugene Onegin*, published under the title, "Excerpts from Onegin's Journey ("Otryvki iz puteshestviya Onegina"). Pushkin has just taken leave of the romantic imagery of his youthful years and is celebrating the discovery of more homely pictures from the Russian landscape, though in the following stanza he expresses shock at having fallen into, in Nabokov's version, "Prosy divagations,/ the Flemish School's variegated dress!"

[13] Cf. Walter Scott, who in 1818 distinguished the new style of novel that had recently made its appearance in England from former narrative fiction in "the art of copying from nature as she really exists in the common walks of life, and presenting to the reader . . . a correct and striking representation of that which is daily taking place around him." Sir Walter Scott, Review of Jane Austen's *Emma*, cited from *Novelists on the Novel*, ed. Mirriam Allott (New York, 1959), p. 65.

[14] I. S. Turgenev, "Vospominaniya o Belinskom," *Sobranie sochineniy* (Moscow, 1961-1962), X, 86.

school already deep in decline and his progression to a "poetry of things" duplicates the novelist's progress.

When Pyotr Ivanych advises his nephew to avoid extremes and "take instead the middle" in his writings,[15] he provides us with a description of the narrative style Goncharov adopted in *A Common Story* and held to through his literary career. It is a style that for the most part carefully avoided extremes of heightened rhetoric or the blatantly colloquial and dialectical. Instead the novelist chose "the middle"—a language emotionally neutral, syntactically and grammatically correct, carefully literary, smooth, measured, and unobtrusive.[16] The choice anticipates the major tendency of the realistic novel, which generally avoided all attempts at "fine writing" and strove for a transparent prose merely adequate to the thing described.[17] Critics often cite Goncharov's prose as an extreme instance for its severe limitation of the expressive possibilities of language, but we shall note in *Oblomov* not only an important exception but also a successful adaption of language to certain modes of feeling.

Although parody in the stories of the thirties remained an incidental mannerism, in the novel it became an important element of the structure. The major action of *A Common Story*—Alexander's becoming his uncle—evolves steadily toward a final "comic reversal" in which *both* uncle and nephew change roles. The course of the parody closely parallels the course of the action and serves as one of the many markers of the comic resolution as well as its agent. As Alexander

[15] *Sobr. soch.*, I, 49.

[16] For the best study of Goncharov's language see V. K. Favorin, "O vzaimodeystvii avtorskoy rechi i rechi personazhey v yazyke trilogii Goncharova," *Izvestiya Akademii nauk SSSR: otdelenie literatury i yazyka*, IX, No. 5 (1950), 351-361. Also see L. A. Bulakhovsky, *Russkiy literaturnyy yazyk pervoy poloviny XIX veka* (Kiev, 1957), p. 146. ". . . perhaps, not a single work of the period under study [the first half of the nineteenth century] presented in the sphere of language and style that middle of quality, that equilibrium of lexical and syntactic elements of artistic speech. . . ." Also, S. A. Vengerov, "Druzhinin, Goncharov, Pisemsky," *Sobranie sochineniy*, V (St. Petersburg, 1911), 72-73. "Goncharov's style is remarkably smooth and even . . . , [his] sentences are rounded periods, built upon all the rules of syntax. . . ." For a more detailed look at Goncharov's style, see below, chaps. seven and eight.

[17] See Mirsky, p. 171.

approaches the reversal, the positions of uncle and nephew in the parody begin to change. The cocksure uncle becomes weary of his compulsive commitment to practical and efficient work and begins to assume Alexander's rhetoric of sentiment (of "love and friendship"), while Alexander turns on him with the uncle's favorite critical epithet: "You are speaking wildly, uncle, wildly." One of the uncle's means of mockery, the ever-present cigar he employs to distract the nephew from his transports of poetic fancy, passes over to Alexander, as, with his offer of stylistic advice, he proffers Pyotr a cigar to mark their changing positions in the development of the plot. Finally ready for the reversal, Alexander reports that, among other things, he has given up his former prose style: "You are surprised, isn't that so? It seems strange to you to hear this from me? To read these lines written in a calm tone so uncustomary for me?" In the epilogue Alexander finally speaks his uncle's words: "Uncle, . . . You see, I am citing your very words."[18] The novel is, on one level, a language lesson. The nephew becomes like his uncle by giving up his own language and adopting the other's. He is brought to the reversal by the force of parody.

A Common Story is a novel written with a great deal of self-consciousness about literature, literary tradition, and the novelist's position in that tradition. Literary allusions and references to a score of literary personalities—from the rank of Goethe, Byron, and Balzac to lesser luminaries like Marlinsky, Mikhail Zagoskin, and Jules Janin—dot its pages.[19] The frequent literary references often bear no relation to the parody. Alexander constantly quotes poetry and cites the authority of novelists and poets—most often Pushkin, a figure Goncharov, for all the ironic bent of his imagination, revered too much even to contemplate parodying. The constant literary quotations and allusions in Alexander's speech indicate a character who sees himself and others in literary terms. At times a literary polemic and almost a literary manifesto, *A Common Story* is also a novel about Alexander Aduev.

[18] *Sobr. soch.*, I, 227, 292, 309.

[19] Mikhail Zagoskin (1789-1852) was a minor historical novelist; Jules Janin (1804-1874)—a contemporary French novelist.

It relates Alexander's story, however, through formal devices analogous to its parodic method. As the parody deflates Alexander's exalted rhetoric to common usage, the novel organizes experience so as to deflate his dream of an extraordinary fate to his eventual "common" lot. Not only does the overall scheme follow a deflationary course, but practically every individual chapter in some way lowers Alexander's hopes and enthusiasms—from the opening chapter in which Evsey, his manservant, somewhat like the servants of classical comedy, mimics the master's sentimental leavetaking of home, mother, and sweetheart on a socially lower and coarser level of sensibility, to the epilogue where he surrenders his dreams altogether.[20]

A love scene with Nadenka, one of his several infatuations, furnishes a typical example.[21] The chapter opens with Alexander at his desk in the government office where he has found temporary employment, evading his duties and dreaming of love and perfect happiness. After a brief walk through a stifling hot Petersburg, which seems dead in the summer's heat—a deadness that echoes his depressed mood—he sets out across the Neva to one of the islands where Nadenka and her mother have retreated for the summer. As Alexander's boat approaches "the promised land," his expectations rise. His face brightens, the soles of his feet burn with impatience, and, with a wish to be able to walk upon the water in order to hasten the journey, his eagerness reaches its apex. He tips the indifferent and obtuse boatmen generously to encourage them to speed their rowing. The tip is immediately effective as the tempo of both the rowing and the prose quickens until the first of a series of comic deflations: "How they set to work; how they leaped in their places! . . . The oars shimmered so across the water. . . . Alexander and Nadenka smiled at each other from a distance and did not take their eyes from one another. Aduev stepped out with one foot into the water instead of onto the shore. Nadenka laughed."[22]

Evening descends and the young lovers find themselves alone in a

---

[20] The germ of the Oblomov-Zakhar relation may be felt in the Aduev-Evsey association. Also cf. the relation of master and servant in "Ivan Savich Podzhabrin," above, chap. four.

[21] Part One, chap. four.   [22] *Sobr. soch.*, I, 86.

garden, having finally eluded Nadenka's intrusive and gossipy mother. The scene is a rare lyrical exception in this relentlessly ironic novel.

> Night fell—but what a night! . . . All about, it was still. The Neva seemed to be asleep. Now and then, as if in its sleep, it splashed a gentle wave against the shore and again fell into silence. And suddenly a late breeze would rush over the sleepy waters, but could not wake them, merely rippling the surface and fanning Nadenka and Alexander with its coolness or bringing them the sounds of a distant song. And again everything would fall silent, and again the Neva would be motionless like a man asleep, who opens his eyes for a moment at a slight noise and immediately closes them again, and sleep seals his heavy eyelids more firmly.

The brief description contains, besides the closing simile comparing the Neva to a man asleep, five different words related to the condition of sleep (*spala, vprosonkakh, sonnymi, spyashchiy, son*) and three indicating silence (*tikho, zamolchit, smolknet*). The next two sentences, which have been omitted here, include another two words denoting silence. The following paragraph reveals the scene for what it is—"a sleep of nature." Little interested in nature, Goncharov was moved to lyrical expansiveness only by landscapes suggestive of perfect repose and peace. It is noteworthy that the narrator, generally aloof in the debate between duty, work, achievement, and idle dreams that dominates the novel, though an active agent of the ironic treatment of Alexander's dreams, momentarily places himself on the side of the useless dreams that arise during "the sleep of nature": "Yes, useless, but it is only in those moments that the soul dimly perceives the possibility of happiness which men so assiduously seek at other times and do not find."[23]

The idyllic moment proves short-lived, as the pattern of deflation quickly reasserts itself. Alexander, at the apex of his infatuation, leans over "with a trembling heart" to steal a kiss. The narrator interrupts: " 'It's improper!' strict mamas will say. . . ." A second ecstatic kiss and the narrator's qualms are conveyed to Nadenka: "I shall tell mama!" she exclaims, as "Alexander fell from the clouds." To re-

[23] *Ibid.*, pp. 94-95.

123

assure Nadenka, who has premonitions that the moment of bliss is doomed never to be repeated, Alexander insists upon its permanence. He promises her a perpetual idyll: "We shall always be alone; we shall put ourselves far away from others; . . . even rumors of sorrow and misfortune will not disturb us, just as now, here in the garden, no sound disturbs this triumphant silence." Alexander's simile is premature: " 'Nadenka! Alexander Fyodorych!' resounded suddenly from the porch, 'Where are you?' " And a moment later: "Alexander Fyodorych! . . . your yogurt has been on the table for a long time." Alexander ruminates about the vagaries of his destiny: "A moment of inexpressible bliss—and suddenly yogurt! . . . Is it possible that all of life is like that?"[24] His question might well be asked by each of the heroes of Goncharov's three novels, whose moments of exaltation and dreams of a permanent idyllic state are constantly interrupted by or contrasted to the usual and commonplace.

The scene is enclosed by a return to the obtuse oarsmen who must be tipped once again, now to slow down their rowing, so that Alexander may prolong his moment of bliss—a return that provides the kind of tidy symmetrical frame and ironic reversal we observed in the early story, "A Happy Error."

The movement of the chapter, then, is from a state of withdrawal, evasion of responsibilities, and daydreaming, to an attempt to capture the dream in actual experience, to an ironic deflation. The deflation occurs through the intrusion of the prosaic and ordinary (the first part of the Russian compound for yogurt—*prostokvasha*—can mean "ordinary") into a poeticized experience. The scene with Nadenka is not an isolated instance, as practically every chapter in the novel follows the same pattern.[25] The regular and repeated patterning of experience, besides imparting a symmetrical shape to individual chapters, results in a rhythmic presentation of action. Experience falls into a curve, rising from withdrawal and daydreaming to excited anticipa-

[24] *Ibid.*, pp. 95-98.

[25] The exceptions are negligible. They include the frame chapters (see below), the epilogue, and the final chapter of Part One in which Alexander's misanthropic mood is sustained throughout. Part One concludes with Alexander at the nadir of his fortunes; the novel, with Alexander at the summit—another instance of symmetry.

tion, and descending to ironic deflation. The rhythm is yet a sub-sidiary element of the structure, which is dominated by the larger action—the linear plot of Alexander rising to the condition of his uncle. Each renewed elevation of hopes and expectations only retards the ultimate outcome. Alexander's enthusiams hinder him from be-coming like his practical and efficient uncle; when he is completely exhausted and disillusioned he will be ready for his conversion. In *Oblomov* we shall note a similar rhythmic pattern, but there the curve of Oblomov's smaller actions is recapitulated by the curve of the total action.

Threaded through the novel are a number of frequently repeated words and gestures that serve as leitmotifs of the action. The bulk of these may be divided into two categories—those that indicate Alexander's persistence in his romantic infatuations and those that denote Pyotr's refusal to grant his nephew recognition as long as he persists. Among the former are the phrases "sweet bliss," "sincere effusions," "colossal passion," and Alexander's dismissal of money offered him by his uncle as "filthy lucre." Among the latter are Pyotr's evasions of his impetuous nephew's attempts to embrace and kiss him, his repeated questioning of Alexander's motives in coming to Petersburg since his uncompetitive and sentimental values are more appropriate to a rural setting, and, what is most obviously a refusal to grant recognition, an inability or unwillingness to remember the names of his nephew's romantic attachments (Nadenka becomes successively Marya, Anyuta, Sofya, Katenka, Yuliya, Varenka, Verochka, etc., etc.). "Career and fortune," another repetition, is what the argument of the novel is ostensibly about. Alexander's in-fatuations block his path to career and fortune; his uncle will not recognize him until he has a career and a fortune.

The leitmotifs also denote the comic reversal. Shortly after Alex-ander decides that he is "not a madcap, nor a dreamer, nor disillu-sioned, but simply a man like those of which Petersburg is full . . . ,"[26] he reminds Pyotr of his promises and finally asks for money and a position in the service (i.e., "career and fortune"). When the nephew appears in the epilogue as a duplicate of his uncle ("You resemble

[26] *Ibid.*, p. 293.

me completely . . ."), Pyotr wonders what has become of his "colossal passion" and "sincere effusions." Convinced that Alexander has indeed achieved a career and fortune, he at last permits him an embrace. The uncle recognizes the nephew as his own. " 'And a career, and a fortune! . . . And what a fortune! And all of a sudden! Everything! Everything! Alexander!' he added proudly, solemnly, 'you are of my blood, you are an Aduev! All right—embrace me!' "[27] They embrace, the uncle offers Alexander "filthy lucre," and Alexander accepts. The resolution of the plot is accompanied by a tying together of the various strands embodied in the leitmotifs.

Northrop Frye, in *Anatomy of Criticism*, locates the theme of the comic in "the integration of society, which usually takes the form of incorporating a central character into it."[28] Thus far the structure of *A Common Story* has indicated a classic example. The uncle is the representative of "the age," "the crowd," and "the new order"[29]— Goncharov probably has in mind a Russia modernized on Western lines. The nephew is unwilling or unable to conform and become respectable (*poryadochnyy*) like the rest of his contemporaries. The comedy is resolved with his incorporation into the correct and decorous society. However, an important factor in the novel complicates the simple linear plot of the nephew becoming his uncle. The complication is also marked by a leitmotif—yellow flowers.

Yellow flowers grow along the banks of a lake lying at the center of Alexander's rural estate—Grachi. Pyotr recalls them in the course of the novel and employs them as an emblem of that absolute faith in the powers of poetry and "love and friendship" he finds so distasteful in his nephew. He associates the yellow flowers with the tokens of love and fidelity that Sofya, Alexander's country sweetheart, had bequeathed the nephew as, in our hero's inimitable diction, "tangible

---

[27] *Ibid.*, pp. 313-314.

[28] *Anatomy of Criticism* (Princeton, N.J., 1957), p. 43. The view of comedy as socially integrative does not, of course, originate with Frye. It is a venerable idea and was central to Bergson's famous essay on comedy. See Henri Bergson, "Le Rire," *Oeuvres* (Paris, 1959), pp. 383-485.

[29] *Sobr. soch.*, I, 41. References to "our age" and "the crowd" run through the novel.

signs of intangible relations."[30] Yellow flowers become a symbol for what is left behind—the easy ways of gentry life in the country and a value system built around an ethos of sentiment rather than labor and achievement.

But, though Pyotr tries to project the associations tied to the yellow flowers onto his nephew, they, as we know from the opening of the novel and as Alexander discovers at its conclusion, refer instead to what the uncle left behind. A letter from Alexander's aunt, Marya Gorbatova, has informed us that seventeen years before Alexander's departure for Petersburg Pyotr had also left his native Grachi to make his way in the great city. Before leaving, he walked with Marya about the lake and plucked a large yellow flower from its edge as a token of his love. He was twenty at the time—exactly Alexander's age at *his* departure. At the conclusion of the novel, when an Alexander grown wise in the ways of the world gleefully reveals his pragmatical uncle's secret history of sentiment—"yellow flowers," "sincere effusions," avowals of love, and even tears—he is thirty-four, approximately the uncle's age at the opening. *A Common Story* is only apparently the story of two characters diametrically opposed to each other. Actually, it is a novel where one character recapitulates the history of the other.[31] The uncle's "common story" took place before the novel began.

As one strand of the novel extends into the past, another leads beyond its formal conclusion and into the future. When we encounter Pyotr Ivanych in the epilogue, he has declined both physically and morally. The decline began late, immediately after Alexander underwent the last of his successive disillusionments. It was marked by a chronic backache—one of the finer comic touches in the novel, which gradually grew into an emblem for the failure of the uncle's ultrarationalistic, calculated, and emotionally sterile life. When in the epilogue a greying, slightly stooped, and unsteady Pyotr Ivanych con-

---

[30] *Ibid.*, p. 45.

[31] See V. F. Pereverzev, "K voprosu o monisticheskom ponimanii tvorchestva Goncharova," *Literaturovedenie*, ed. Pereverzev (Moscow, 1928), p. 211. "The story of the uncle is the story of Alexander Aduev; the character of the uncle is only the completion of that course along which the nephew moves."

fronts a fat, rosy, balding, and successful Alexander, the reversal is apparently complete. However, Alexander's own decline has already begun.

> You resemble me completely. Only the backache is lacking!
> I already have a stitch there sometimes. . . .

When nephew and uncle at last meet, it is but for a moment. The novel ends with the embrace and the exchange of "filthy lucre."

> "At last! For the first time!" Pyotr Ivanych declared.
> "And the last, uncle. This is an uncommon incident."
> said Alexander.[32]

Uncle and nephew have pursued the same course—from a sentimental view of the world to disillusionment and a subsequent practical success in business (*delo*) to a decline, or, in Alexander's case incipient decline, which is a price of that success. The novel, rather than presenting two views of existence irreconcilably at odds, tells the story of two identical careers spread out over different time intervals, each commenting ironically on the other. We view Alexander's romantic infatuations from the standpoint of his uncle's more worldly view of experience, Alexander's success with the knowledge of the price Pyotr has paid for a similar success. Similarly, Pyotr's self-assured and mocking denial of the claims of sentiment is undermined by our knowledge of his secret affinity with his nephew—his past of "yellow flowers."[33] Goncharov received a great deal of abuse from a number of Russian critics writing before the Soviet period, who read the "message" of the novel in Pyotr's calculating rationalism, practical efficiency, and denial of the efficacy of poetry and sentiment.[34] An examination of the structure of the novel, rather than a reliance upon isolated statements of individual characters, finds no basis for locating the author's point of view in either of his protagonists. *A Common*

---

[32] *Sobr. soch.*, I, 313-314.

[33] There is some similarity here to the Stolz-Oblomov relation, which is also not merely one of direct opposition.

[34] The view was widespread at the turn of the century. For its most explicit articulation, see Vengerov, V, 67-96, *passim*. Similarly, Stolz is read as the author's voice in *Oblomov*.

Story is instead the "ironic deadlock" that Frye describes as a version of the comedy of manners. It is a comedy about coming of age, the loss of illusions, and the compromises of maturity as they are repeated in the lives of the two major characters, not as an object lesson, but as a perception of "the way of the world" or, in the title of the English translation, "the same old story." The novel treats both the normative society, as represented by the uncle, and the excluded nephew ironically.[35]

Immediately before the final resolution of the epilogue—the coming together of uncle and nephew—Alexander contemplates another solution to his difficulties, which deserves mention. He returns to the idyllic estate of his childhood, a place characterized by peace and material abundance, where, Alexander's mother had asserted, he was "first in the world."[36] Upon his return Alexander compares the city and the country—all to the country's favor. The city is an arena of constant competition, where he was unable to find "a role" and was tormented by his "implacable uncle." Life there is so rationalized that it leaves no "expanse for feelings, passions and dreams and . . . poetical charms. . . ." The estate offers all these, and, in addition, time for contemplation and "reminiscence" under the protective "unsleeping eye of maternal love." The country/city opposition seems also to be an opposition of maternal and paternal attitudes—of Alexander's mother and his father-substitute uncle (Alexander's father, never mentioned, is apparently dead). Alexander exchanges his "tight foppish tail-coat" for "a broad home-made dressing gown" (a *khalat* like the one Oblomov wears) and for a while settles into the unchanging routines of life upon the estate. However, he soon tires of this idyllic but uneventful existence. The guilt he feels about abandoning his mother is dissolved by her sudden and convenient death. The brief sentence that reports her death, when we recall the narrator's earlier encomium to motherhood,[37] seems very curious: "He

---

[35] Frye, p. 48, ". . . an ironic deadlock in which the hero is regarded as a fool or worse by the fictional society, and yet impresses the real audience as having something more valuable than his society has." The translation is by Ivy Litvinova, *The Same Old Story* (Moscow, 1957).

[36] *Sobr. soch.*, I, 9.   [37] *Ibid.*, p. 10.

tossed about in anguish and did not know how to tell his mother about his intention to leave. But his mother soon saved him from this difficulty—she died."[38] In *Oblomov* these brief scenes of an idyllic condition (which one seeks to escape!) are expanded and treated with great imaginative power. From the glimpse of another possibility that Alexander catches in the process of his relentless disillusionment, Goncharov will move to the full presentation of an alternative way of life—one that will contend with the competitive and rationalized workaday world for the hero's (and our) allegiance.

Goncharov divided his novel into two parts of approximately equal length and an epilogue. He further divided each part into six chapters. This purely arithmetical symmetry is symptomatic of an almost total esthetic symmetry. We have already noticed a symmetry of the smaller parts—the regular and recurring pattern into which individual chapters fall and the framing of individual scenes within repeated actions (the boatmen in the above example). The entire novel (excluding the epilogue) is similarly framed by two chapters—Alexander on his country estate before and after his sentimental education in Petersburg. In addition to the recurring leitmotifs, a repeated action encloses the novel, as Alexander, in informing his uncle of his changed attitudes, promises to bring him a gift of honey and dried raspberries, and letters from his provincial neighbors—the same items he carried with him to the city eleven chapters and some fourteen years before.[39] Alexander's reminder, like most of the novel's "returns," occurs under changed circumstances, providing an ironic commentary upon his former state instead of a mere automatic repetition. The plot also evolves symmetrically, as both uncle and nephew follow the same route, only at different intervals. The final resolution ties together every thread of action and structure—the difference between uncle and nephew is overcome; the leitmotifs that embodied the difference are brought together and resolved of their tension; the parody that was the means of overcoming the difference is successfully concluded. *A Common Story* is a novel that leaves no loose ends.

The total effect of these procedures, aside from contributing to the "patently artificial structure" that critics from Apollon Grigorev

---

[38] *Ibid.*, pp. 288-292.   [39] *Ibid.*, pp. 26, 296.

on have noted, is to impart a static quality to the novel.[40] Though it is called a history (*istoriya* may mean both "story" and "history") and its action proceeds through fourteen years of Alexander Aduev's life, *A Common Story* fails to communicate either a sense of the passage of time or a suggestion of unfolding experience. Instead, Goncharov presents a single situation, the gulf between uncle and nephew that must be bridged, which he continually plays upon while retarding the inevitable denouement—inevitable because it repeats the pattern of deflation to the "common" the smaller sections of the novel have led us to expect. The leitmotifs, the comedy via mechanical repetition, and the returns enhance what becomes an abiding sense of *déjà vu*. The novel, though it covers a substantial part of Alexander Aduev's life, leaves the impression of a single event neatly enclosed within its symmetrical frames and ironic returns, its scenes in turn neatly enclosed in their frames.[41]

A Common Story has a theatrical quality, which the concentration upon a single action or event heightens. For much of the novel several characters—Pyotr and Alexander, who are occasionally joined by Pyotr's wife, Lizaveta Alexandrovna, in Part Two—stand on stage speaking their parts before an unspecified backdrop. Descriptions and histories of characters are usually terse, if given at all. The most detailed presentations of place occur in the frame chapters, which do not constitute part of the action proper (and which describe an estate of the gentry—almost the only social location Goncharov ever presents in concrete detail). These concretely rendered scenes depicting Alexander pampered by his mother and servants in the idyllic countryside might have provided an explanation for his later behavior and a sense of temporal continuity to his life, but the causal connection remains undeveloped. Instead the passage of time is conveyed largely by sign posts placed at various intervals—"Two weeks passed," "Several months flashed by," "More than two years passed," "Here is what happened to the main characters of the novel four

[40] Apollon Grigor'ev, "Russkaya literatura v 1851 godu," *Sochineniya* (St. Petersburg, 1876), I, 31.

[41] Tseytlin, *I. A. Goncharov*, p. 85, writes of "the single leveled plot of *A Common Story*: one image, one conflict, one intrigue dominates."

years after . . ."—very much like the announcements that appear
between scenes in vaudeville, or notes in a playbill.[42] Secondary characters walk out onto the stage where the comedy is played and
promptly vanish when no longer needed. The narrator notes important events in the lives of the protagonists in the same incidental manner. Thus a casual remark by Pyotr informs us that he is engaged
and a later, terse, "My wife is angry at you . . ."[43] is all we have by
way of a wedding report, although Lizaveta, who has not yet appeared, plays an important role: her expressions of dissatisfaction with
her husband and of sympathy for Alexander provide a third perspective that prevents us from identifying the novelist's point of view with
the uncle. As in comedy designed for the stage, the major focus is on
comic action and incident.[44]

The systematic subordination of the novel to a central comic situation, the restriction of the time plane to an immediate present, and
the tight ironic design of the plot vitiate any attempts to explore and
complicate character. Pyotr and Alexander, despite the fact that they
dominate almost every moment of the novel, remain flat and one
dimensional. They become mere vehicles and passive agents of the
plot. One is the object of the parody and the systematic comic deflations; the other, its source. The parody is the thing and not its victim
or perpetrator. Alexander, who persists in his romantic posturings in
face of the most awkward humiliations, turns into a rigid comic
type.[45] He is a position to be maintained, out of which comedy is
made, rather than a character perceived in his potential psychological

---

[42] *Sobr. soch.*, I, 43, 68, 63, 297.   [43] *Ibid.*, p. 102.

[44] As a young man Goncharov was a theater enthusiast. See Lyatsky, *Roman
i zhizn'*, pp. 74-75. In a letter to P. D. Boborykin, October 7, 1876, he recalled
his youth as a time when ". . . literature and the theater went hand in hand;
. . . and the old classical repertoire was still in vogue. . . ." *Sobr. soch.*, VIII,
483. Farce and vaudeville were also very popular on the Russian stage of the
thirties and forties, and the comedy of *A Common Story* often displays a light
farcical quality.

[45] The constancy of the comic type is a frequent theme in writings on comedy. See Susanne Langer, *Feeling and Form* (New York, 1953), pp. 335-336.
Also, Bergson, p. 396, ". . . rigidity is the comic. . . ." The "reduction to
absurdity" in Alexander's posturings is at times so extreme as to approach

complexity. The absence of a past causally linked to the present in which the comedy is enacted and of a sense of the passage of time turn what happens at the conclusion of the novel into an exchange of comic masks rather than the necessary result of a consistent psychological development. This reduction of personality to a single position in an argument or a single trait of character—Goncharov wrote that "an author's aim is the dominant element of a character . . ."— implies a corollary generalization and abstraction. Alexander is ever in danger of ceasing to be Alexander and becoming "romantic youth"; Pyotr, "the practical man of the world"; the novel that contains them, "the same old story."[46] It is the latter irony, the comic reversal that indicates "the way of the world," rather than exploration of character, that is the central concern of the novel. Grigorev put it well: "Everything here was sacrificed to . . . irony."[47]

A Common Story has been compared to Balzac's *Illusions perdues* and included in the tradition of the novel of systematic disillusionment, which is, perhaps, the characteristic form of the nineteenth-century realistic novel, especially in France.[48] A closer look at the two novels will reveal instead Goncharov's tenuous connection to the tradition. Some superficial similarity exists between the two works, and it is possible that Goncharov took his general format from Bal-

---

burlesque. ". . . he [the writer of burlesques] converts a manner into a mannerism." Kenneth Burke on burlesque, in *Attitudes Toward History* (New York, 1937), I, 70.

[46] See Grigor'ev, I, 31. "The author brought forth two figures—one, pale, thin, weak, with a label on its forehead: romanticism, . . . and the other, blooming with health, calm as a mathematician, with the label: a practical mind." Goncharov's statement that "an author's aim is the dominant element of a character; the rest is up to the reader," appears in a letter to I. I. L'khovsky, August 2, 1857, *Sobr. soch.*, VIII, 291. It is of great importance for understanding his fiction, and we shall return to it.

[47] Grigor'ev, I, 31. Ian Watt, in *The Rise of the Novel* (Berkeley and Los Angeles, 1957), p. 279, states "a principle of considerable significance for the novel form in general: namely, that the importance of the plot is in inverse proportion to that of character." As with many literary principles, exceptions immediately spring to mind—namely, Dostoevsky.

[48] See Mazon, *Ivan Gontcharov*, pp. 73-74. Levin, *The Gates of Horn*, p. 48, defines realism as a "technique of systematic disillusionment."

zac's novel. Lucien de Rubempré and Alexander Aduev are both young provincials on the make in the great city. They have similar artistic ambitions and temperaments without the requisite talent and will to realize their aspirations. Each novelist leads his hero through a series of disillusionments brought about by a faulty understanding of the "real" nature of the world, though, characteristically, Alexander's more intensely felt disappointments are in love and art, while Lucien's derive from a quest for position and power. Balzac, like Goncharov, treats his hero ironically and even comically. The novels evince a slight similarity of structure. Where Alexander's encounter with Petersburg is framed by two chapters depicting the provincial at home, *Un grand homme de province à Paris*, the central novel of Balzac's trilogy, is framed by two novels, *Les deux poètes* and *Ève et David*, describing Lucien in the provinces before and after his failures in Paris.[49]

The most evident difference between the two novels lies in their endings. Alexander joins the society whose values he had previously opposed; Lucien remains an outsider. The difference is not essentially a matter of the success or "conformity" of one and the failure of the other.[50] Alexander's "success" is dubious and ironic; Lucien's failure is never total. The end of the novel finds Lucien looking forward to yet another attempt to climb the ladder to success and power. The respective endings, though they do not in themselves establish the difference between the two novels, are symptomatic of it. Alexander's abrupt reversal into a solid bourgeois is consistent with the overall comic pattern of the novel. The total effect of his comic deflations strips him of his illusions and dreams, and when finally naked, he is ready to put on a new suit of clothes (or a new comic mask). Balzac avoids the finality inherent in such a climactic reversal of character. Lucien's successive catastrophes neither change him nor close the door upon new possibilities within the limits of *Illusions perdues* or in further novels of an ever-unfolding *Comédie humaine*.

---

[49] The Lyngstads, p. 71, have also noted the use of the image of yellow flowers in Balzac's novel.

[50] Renato Poggioli, "On Goncharov and His *Oblomov*," in *The Phoenix and the Spider* (Cambridge, Mass., 1957), p. 36.

Lucien exists as a kind of potentiality—a potentiality Balzac continually thwarts only to revive our belief in its reality. Though, like Alexander, he displays a certain psychological (and comical) obstinacy, predictably falling back into the trap of his illusions after each successive disappointment, he remains a different sort of character from Goncharov's hero. The distinction resides not so much in their essential personalities as in the fictional structures that express them. While *A Common Story* is enclosed into a single comic situation in terms of which character is defined, an accumulation of episodes constitutes *Illusions perdues*. Lucien, unlike Alexander, is defined in a multiplicity of situations, "those bustling combinations of material circumstances" that form the heart of a Balzac novel.[51] The novel is not reducible to a single complication of circumstance but equals the totality of events in Lucien's life. Every encounter carries its own complications and has its own particular drama. As a result Balzac's novel avoids the closed and static quality that characterizes *A Common Story*. *Illusions perdues* evolves into what Goncharov's novel only promises to be—a "history." In telling his story through a succession of encounters in the world, a world that is in turn manifested in a host of characters and social situations—from the scenes of Lucien's impoverished youth through the intricate network of Parisian life, and finally to Vautrin and a sinister realm outside conventional society—Balzac manages to capture the sense of a human life in process. Where experience in *A Common Story* becomes a digression from the central ironic situation of Alexander's becoming his uncle, Lucien is conceived entirely in experiential terms. If there is any inevitability in Balzac's novel, it grows out of a sense of Lucien's character as it manifests itself in the course of his progress through the world, and not from the dictates of a controlling plot. The shape of Goncharov's novel determines character and limits its possibilities; in Balzac's work experience determines the shape of the novel.

Paul Goodman, in *The Structure of Literature*, defines novelistic plots (as distinct from tragic, comic, and epic) as centering not upon an action but on "the fixing of character" from an original "sentimental disposition" or "potential character" through a sequence of

---

[51] Levin, p, 166.

occasions. The heroes of such novels may "come to abiding commitments or rejections and the ensuing dramatic actions," but in the novel he takes as his model, Flaubert's *L'Éducation sentimentale* (another work to which *A Common Story* has been compared), the resolution is entirely in the "fixing of character." The protagonists of these novels belong to Aristotle's third category of possibilities—they are neither above nor below "our own level of goodness," but "just such as we are."[52] I may add that such novels, with their accumulation of incidents (occasions), their evasions of a final conclusive action and resulting open-endedness, strive to imitate the tendency of usual life. Though Balzac's novel fits the general terms of his argument, *A Common Story* is a throwback to older comic forms. Its hero's character is "fixed" from the very beginning. He is a "given," an ossified humor, continually deflated through parody and irony until brought to his comic reversal.

Both novels deal primarily with manners, but in totally differing contexts. For Balzac, as for Lionel Trilling, manners are "a culture's hum and buzz of implication . . . , the whole evanescent context of its explicit statements."[53] His characters always imply a dense social fabric larger than their individual destinies. In Lukács' description, they "live and act within a concrete, complexly stratified social reality, and it is always the totality of the social process that is linked with the totality of the character."[54] In the manner of many a socially oriented novel, his characters are situated topographically and as such become representative (or "typical") of their locations in the novel.[55]

---

[52] *The Structure of Literature* (Chicago, 1954), pp. 127-135. "Sentiment is the response of a person on a temporary occasion. . . . Attitude is his more permanent feeling . . . with regard to the objects. But character is the emerging unity among his attitudes, so that we can speak of character apart from any particular objects." Aristotle's divisions are in *Poetics* 2.

[53] Lionel Trilling, "Manners, Morals, and the Novel," in *Forms of Modern Fiction*, ed. William Van O'Conner (Bloomington, 1959), p. 145.

[54] George Lukács, *Studies in European Realism*, trans. Edith Bone (London, 1950), p. 55.

[55] Fanger, *Dostoevsky and Romantic Realism*, p. 30. "Balzac, by situating his characters topographically, situates them socially as well." Fanger, p. 9, makes an interesting and pertinent observation about social typicality in the nineteenth century: "The seriousness of this belief meant taking the characters

Every character evokes the social grouping to which he belongs, and his novels turn into a system of social, rather than exclusively individual, oppositions. Ultimately it is the panoramic view of society that is Balzac's true interest.[56] This panoramic view is achieved in a number of ways, but chief among them is the intervention of an ever-present and incredibly busy narrator. Almost every major character and even many minor figures receive a detailed background that is a personal history and a piece of the history of France as well. Place is always specified with an abundance of detail demonstrating "that sensitiveness to actuality which is the secret of Balzac's power as a novelist of manners. . . ."[57]

Goncharov's novel, like most nineteenth-century novels, also takes as its starting point a specific historical moment—the reaction against romanticism and idealism in Russia of the forties. As an outcome of the reaction much of the Russian intelligentsia turned to political radicalism to seek ways to overcome Russian backwardness, and Goncharov, a son of merchants and a government official, erected the part bureaucrat and part industrial entrepreneur Pyotr Aduev as an image of a new practical Russian. The opposition of the uncle's impersonal rationalism and the nephew's defense of sentiment and familial affection also reflects an antagonism between the Europeanized bureaucratic society of the capital and the more traditional rural gentry.[58]

as well as the milieu seriously, and here the break with comic tradition is most evident."

[56] Levin, p. 199, ". . . society comes first and last for Balzac, with psychology crowded in between."

[57] Frederick C. Green, *French Novelists: From the Revolution to Proust* (London, 1931), p. 169.

[58] In "Luchshe pozdno, chem nikogda," *Sobr. soch.*, VIII, 73, Goncharov declared the theme of the novel to be "the necessity of *work* . . . and of *lively activity* in the struggle against Russian stagnation." V. Pereverzev, in "K voprosu o sotsial'nom genezise tvorchestva Goncharova," *Pechat' i revolyutsiya*, No. 1 (January 1923), pp. 32-35, and No. 2 (February-March 1923), pp. 34-47, interpreted the novel as a conflict between bourgeois and patriarchal values, with the former triumphing, but Pyotr Aduev strikes me as more a bureaucratic member of the gentry than a true capitalist—Western-style capitalists were very rare in Russia of the time. In *Literaturovedenie*, p. 201, Pereverzev extended his thesis to include all three of Goncharov's novels.

Nevertheless, Goncharov's characters tend to drift out of time and history, while Balzac's remain firmly rooted in them. Those various mechanisms that combine to place Balzac's people in an actualized social milieu—the extensive biographies of his characters, the busy narrator reporting events from a world outside their private concerns, the broad spectrum of social hierarchies—are absent from *A Common Story*. Instead Goncharov presents genre scenes of a rural estate whose denizens are seen as quaint and curious but hardly as part of a configuration of social interaction, and then transports his hero to a severely abstract city to argue with his uncle in a house that is not once described, though it is the scene of most of the action. Where a Balzac novel follows a wide range of characters moving through fluid and changing social relationships, *A Common Story* concentrates its social world into two characters who conduct a debate between opposed value systems on an empty stage in what seems like a continual present. As a result of their isolation they become identified with absolute moral positions rather than specific social reflexes. If not for the light, at times farcical, treatment of Alexander and the ironic deadlock of the resolution that precludes a didactic reading, the two antagonists might easily be taken for allegorical figures in a timeless debate of romantic dreamer and practical man.[59] Their story takes on the aspect of a universalized tale—"a common story," "the same old story," as it evolves from a portrait of Russia at a particular moment into a story of coming of age as it is repeated with every new generation; indeed, uncle and nephew both undergo the same old story. Though Balzac's novels are preeminently social—*Comédie sociale* would undoubtedly describe them better than *Comédie*

[59] Dmitry Pisarev's description, though overstated, deserves citation: "The characters of Goncharov's novels [*A Common Story* and *Oblomov*] continually revolve in an indeterminate atmosphere, and stand in such relations to one another as depend on the peculiarities of their personal characters and not on conditions of time and place." "Pisemsky, Turgenev i Goncharov," in *I. A. Goncharov v russkoy kritike*, ed. M. Ya. Polyakov (Moscow, 1958), p. 129. Grigor'ev, I, 31, read the novel as an allegory with "compromise" as its lesson. He was more acute when, in "I. S. Turgenev i ego deyatel'nost' (po povodu romana *Dvoryanskoe gnezdo*)," *ibid.*, p. 416, he compared Pyotr Aduev to the *raisonneurs* of classical comedy.

humaine—the abstract quality of Goncharov's first novel, its meticulous symmetry, rigid view of character, and concentration upon a single comic situation, which is pointed toward a final enclosing resolution, recall classical and neoclassical comedies of manners rather than the nineteenth-century novel of manners for which Balzac has served as our example.[60]

A Common Story is a closed and tight little world. This is in itself not a criticism; many comedies of manners are. Works of art should be judged according to what they set out to do and not by some elusive absolute standard. Not every novel is *The Brothers Karamazov* or, for that matter, *Oblomov*. A more serious complaint that can be levelled against Goncharov's comedy is that it shows not enough of the qualities of wit, charm, and elegance we associate with better examples of the genre. It is an entertaining book, especially at first reading, but its witticisms are too often heavy-handed and over-calculated (the reader may judge for himself from earlier examples). The limitation of much of the comedy to the dialogue between uncle and nephew and to a single set of comic devices—the systematic deflations of Alexander—eventually induces a wearisome repetitiveness. The novel is simply too long. The reader comes away with the feeling that Goncharov took some of the mannerisms of his earlier "society tales" and blew them up to novel length, while furthering their incipient, parodic tendencies.[61] Also, the relentless ridiculing of Alexander's illusions has an element of cruelty, almost of sadism, about it. In comparison to the values of the sterile social world about him, Alexander's faults at times acquire the qualities of virtues. However, Goncharov had not yet learned to handle the ambiguity of the situation. In his next novel he again held to an essentially comic view of experience, but the comedy of *Oblomov* is broader, less circumspect and contrived, than the drawing-room banter of *A Common Story*, and marked by warm, human sympathy for its subjects.

[60] See Mazon, *Ivan Gontcharov*, p. 77. ". . . un roman admirablement logique, pareil au drame le plus ingénieusement agencé . . . un système de composition tout classique. . . ."

[61] Goncharov's first novel, like most of his early work, was first read in the Maykov salon. See Starchevsky, in *Goncharov v vospominaniyakh*, pp. 52-55.

Late in *A Common Story* there begin to appear a number of literary strategies and thematic concerns, indicating that the novelist was already moving toward a different and larger kind of novel. Yuliya, the second of Alexander's Petersburg loves, receives a lengthy history that is both psychological and social in import; it explains her romantic nature (she is Alexander's double) in terms of a faulty education, which indiscriminately mixed imported Western elements, and implies its typicality for a generation of Russians.[62] In the later pages of the novel the relationship between Pyotr and Alexander begins to manifest itself in an increasing seriousness of tone. An Oedipal conflict submerged in the comic opposition of uncle and nephew surfaces briefly, as Alexander solemnly pledges to destroy his "giant" uncle, to demonstrate that "he is not a child but a man," and to reverse their roles so that he may be the "experienced master" while the uncle "will play the role of pitiful pupil."[63] As Alexander's determination to reverse roles in the comedy intensifies, so does the seriousness of his withdrawals and depressions. He falls into "an apathetic sleep," "a complete drowsiness," and "a slumber of the soul"[64] so intense that even his skeptical uncle begins to fear for his nephew's welfare and has second thoughts about his rigorous educational methodology. The loss of a comic posture now threatens to become a loss of identity.

Concurrent with the increasing psychological interest of Part Two, the novelist somewhat reduces his reliance on comic dialogue and begins to enter Alexander's inner world through interior monologue. The longest of the excursions into Alexander's mind concludes with a fleeting question that will prove a central and crucial problem for

[62] *Sobr. soch.*, I, 199-205.

[63] *Ibid.*, pp. 173-174. Frye finds "a comic Oedipus situation" underlying New Comedy. Northrop Frye, "The Argument of Comedy," in *Theories of Comedy*, ed. Paul Lauter (New York, 1964), pp. 450-451. Lizaveta, Pyotr's wife, who is approximately his nephew's age and exceptionally beautiful, on occasion thinks of deceiving her husband to reveal the inefficacy of his much-proclaimed system of rational control. The reviewer of the *Northern Bee* (*Severnaya pchela*) anticipated a cuckolding of Pyotr by Alexander as a logical outcome of the plot. Quoted in Tseytlin, *I. A. Goncharov*, p. 92.

[64] *Sobr. soch.*, I, 232.

his literary successor, Ilya Ilich Oblomov. Alexander momentarily frees himself from his mold of comic rigidity and allows himself the kind of self-doubt out of which novelistic complexity can grow: "There are so many of them, these paltry beings. . . . And I am alone. Can it be—that all of them—are empty—are wrong—and I?—"[65] Finally, and perhaps most important for his next novel, Goncharov on occasion discovers a continuous narrative mode to suggest the passage of time. Instead of the earlier sign posts, changes in nature now convey its passage.

> Dark evenings descended. She [Liza, the third of Alexander's Petersburg loves] still waited. . . .
> Autumn came. Yellow leaves fell from the trees and dotted the river banks. Foliage faded. The river took on a leaden color. A cold wind blew carrying along a fine drizzle. The banks and the river were deserted. . . . Boats and barks stopped scurrying to and fro. . . .
> And Liza still waited. . . .[66]

Oblomov follows many of the comic patterns of this first novel, except that it is a comedy taken out of the drawing room and into a larger world placed in time and history.

[65] *Ibid.*   [66] *Ibid.*, p. 250.

CHAPTER VI

A Prosaic Imagination:
The Journey of the Frigate Pallas

. . . what will you say, my friends, reading this—this "letter" from England? . . . You will say, of course, that I am repeating myself, that I —did not leave. I'm at fault—native and familiar roofs, windows, faces, and customs keep flashing before my eyes. I see something new and alien and in my mind I immediately measure it by my own yardstick. . . . We have grown our roots so deep at home that wherever and for whatever length of time I may travel, I shall everywhere carry on my shoes the soil of my native Oblomovka and no oceans will wash it away![1]

The Frigate Pallas: Notes of a Journey may be Goncharov's second-best work; indeed, the author regarded it as his favorite.[2] An official log Goncharov kept as secretary to the admiral on his journey to the Far East from 1852 to 1855 and, to a greater extent, a personal diary and letters to friends provided the material for this volume of travel sketches. The published version is still in the form of letters and diary entries, but Goncharov reworked his material extensively to give it the shape of a book.[3]

[1] *Sobr. soch.*, II, 73.

[2] See D. N. Tsertelev, "Iz literaturnykh vospominaniy ob I. A. Goncharove," in *Goncharov v vospominaniyakh*, p. 190.

[3] Goncharov's travel sketches initially appeared from 1855 through 1857 as individual sketches in *Otechestvennye zapiski, Sovremennik, Biblioteka dlya chteniya, Morskoy sbornik,* and *Russkiy vestnik.* For full citations, see *Sobr. soch.,* III, 449, and Alekseev, *Bibliografiya.* The sketches were published as a book in 1858. The letters have been published in *Literaturnoe nasledstvo,* Nos. 22-24 (1935), pp. 309-426, with an excellent introduction by B. Engel'gardt. Goncharov frequently indicated that he regarded the notes and letters written

142

The Frigate Pallas

The Frigate Pallas is something more than a travel book, but even
as an account of a cultivated Russian's impressions of England and
once exotic places like the west coast of Africa, Java, the Philippines,
China, Japan, Siberia, among others, it holds interest despite some
over-long sections. Goncharov could be an intelligent and sometimes
acute observer, and his smooth, lightly ironic prose was made for a
travel book. The sections on Japan, which were originally published
as a separate volume and may still be read as such, have a particular
charm.[4] The refinement and dignified bearing of the Japanese nobles
and officials he encountered strongly attracted Goncharov; their
elaborate ceremoniousness proved irresistible for a writer always on
the watch for the comic possibilities of the curious and eccentric. A
number of delightful pages are devoted to what he calls the Japanese
"ballet"—a series of involved maneuvers the Japanese adopted to
keep the Russian intruders at bay. To sit or to stand during official
encounters, how and where to sit or stand, how to come ashore—on
Japanese or Russian sloops—to eat together or separately or at all,
became the subject of protracted negotiations and the author's playful irony.

Also, Japan was sufficiently different—which was more than could
be said for most of the other places Goncharov visited. Every traveler
on his first journey from his native country sets out with certain
expectations, and the European image of the Orient in the nineteenth
century was often of something exotic, sensual, primeval, and pristine—in a word, "romantic." Goncharov, if he did not fully share
such views, was well aware of them: "No, I don't want to go to
Paris . . . or to London, or even to Italy, . . ." he begins his travel
sketches,

I want to go to Brazil, to India; I want to go where the sun
calls forth life from stone and nearby transforms all that it touches
with its fire back into stone; where, like our forefathers, man reaps
unsown fruit, where the lion roars, the serpent creeps, where eter-

on the trip as raw material that required reworking. See e.g. *ibid.*, pp. 407,
416, and *Sobr. soch.*, VIII, 266-267.

[4] *Russkie v Yaponii v kontse 1853 i v nachale 1854 godov* was published
in 1855. The sections devoted to Japan may be found in *Sobr. soch.*, III, 7-188.

143

nal summer rules—there, to the bright temples of God's world, where nature, like a bayadere, breathes sensuality, where it is sultry, terrifying and fascinating to live, where the enfeebled imagination grows numb before a finished creation, where one's eyes will not weary of gazing, and the heart throbs.[5]

Instead, except for Japan and a few other isolated spots, he found a world hopelessly similar to the Europe he had left behind, an Orient that under the rule of the several colonial powers had begun to achieve a pedestrian sameness, an East not of mystery and allure but of squalid ports, shabby European hotels, and sullen natives.

Out of this discrepancy between the expected and the actual Goncharov made his book. Everywhere the ordinary, the mundane, the "common" stalk this most unlikely of world travelers as they did his fictional hero Alexander Aduev before him. He came ashore on his first tropical island, one of the Cape Verde group off the west coast of equatorial Africa, only to discover the natives lying on the sand playing a local variant of a card game popular in Russia. Souvenirs of his stay on the Cape of Good Hope turned out to be imports from England. Manila promised "something flowering, . . . luxury, poetry," but offered initially only foul smells. The Chinese were disappointing—they all looked monotonously alike. Too much of what he saw was merely a second-hand Europe: "I expected something more. What? Perhaps brighter and warmer colors, more poetic fancies and more of a life unknown to us Europeans—a distinctive life; and I found that here [Manila] they dance, and dance much, they also sleep much, and they are embarrassed about everything that resembles their own ways." What was unmistakably indigenous was often dull: "You see one or two [Korean] villages, one or two groups [of natives], and you've seen them all." At the end of his trip, when he found himself on a surprisingly well-traveled and fairly safe Siberian trail that failed to substantiate "dark legends [of Siberia] as a land of brigandage, extortion, and unpunished crimes," he could only exclaim somewhat wistfully, "Alas! Where is romanticism?"[6]

[5] *Sobr. soch.*, II, 14. Oblomov also dreams of a land of "eternal summer." See below, chap. seven.

[6] *Ibid.*, II, 119, 139; III, 224; II, 270; III, 272-273, 315, 382.

"Romanticism" could not be found at sea either. Goncharov had heard from "the poets"—from Byron, Pushkin, Vladimir Benediktov, and others—that the sea is "boundless, somber, gloomy, infinite, immeasurable, and indomitable." Experience taught him that it was "salty, boring, ugly, and monotonous. . . ."[7] On a Russian sailing vessel ill-equipped for the long and difficult journey to Japan, it was mostly uncomfortable.

On one occasion Goncharov thought he had found what he was ostensibly seeking—that idyllic land of "eternal summer," those "bright temples" of nature in which creation had assumed a "finished" or completed form. The account of his journey to this land of "the golden age"—an island of the Ryukyu chain south of Japan—reflects in miniature the pattern of the book, with the sole difference that Goncharov for some time retains the enthusiasm of his expectations. The expectations are literary—what "the poets" had taught him to anticipate. The traveler initially views the island through a prism of art and literature: its ordered and decorative landscapes resemble a Watteau; playful silvery streams and clamorous cascades seem "theatrical"; forests and ravines, "picturesque"; friendly shepherds recall the Chloes and Daphnis of Theocritus and Gessner; life here is as the Bible and the Odyssey of Homer describe it.[8] The place appeals so strongly to Goncharov because nature, to which he was usually indifferent, has had the hand of art applied to it. It is not yet the overcivilized city—all those smelly ports—nor is it, like the monotonous sea, mere formless nature. Instead, this island Arcadia belongs to the "middle distance" of the pastoral tradition—a landscape where nature has been wedded to art to form a perfect harmony. Everything in this "fairytale landscape," Goncharov writes, was "measured, cleared, and beautifully arranged," so that each tree, even each leaf, appeared distinct and was not "lumped together in an accidental disorder as nature usually contrives."

Another view of this idyllic land follows, and it is sinister. Accord-

---

[7] *Ibid.*, II, 76-77, 89. V. G. Benediktov (1807-1873) was a minor Russian romantic poet popular in the 1830s.

[8] *Ibid.*, III, 190-199. Salomon Gessner (1730-1788), a Swiss poet and painter and author of pastoral idylls.

ing to a local missionary, the several apparently friendly natives who follow the Russian visitors about the island are actually spies; the local inhabitants are courteous only because they are afraid; the "innocent" shepherds are prone to drunkenness, gambling, and violence. Goncharov is at first skeptical, but he has also become skeptical of his literary source.[9] When he later encounters the local chief, a gray-haired old man with all the signs of "a great lack of continence"—misshapen features, blue and reddish veins about a red nose—he is forced to exclaim in familiar accents of disillusionment, "Alas, fare-well idyll!"[10]

The similarity of the pattern of *The Frigate Pallas* to Goncharov's earlier fiction is obvious. Like *A Common Story* and the early stories (and, as we shall see, *Oblomov*, and to some extent *The Ravine*), *The Frigate Pallas* dwells upon the discrepancy between expectations or imaginative projections, often of a literary origin, and actual experience. Though a volume of travel sketches, it is also a book built upon similar principles to Goncharov's other parodic structures. It debunks romantic myths of the sea, the exotic, and that recurring object of Goncharov's irony, the nostalgia for an idyllic condition of life, "the golden age."

Also, *The Frigate Pallas* reveals a conscious concern with literature and literary problems akin to what we have found in the fiction. Very early in his book Goncharov complains about the difficulties of writing travel sketches: the writer has more "room" than in any other literary form and yet as a result feels confined; the rhetoricians, from Aristotle through Lomonosov, have given us no rules or guidelines; the reading public is uninterested in mere factual accounts, which it can get from scholars, and has come to expect, under the influence of sentimental and romantic travel literature, "wonders, poetry, fire, life and color." But the world is really not as previous travelers perceived it, or it has changed, and as a result

---

[9] Goncharov's source on the Ryukyu islands was Basil Hall, *Account of a Voyage of Discovery to the West Coast of Corea, and the Great Loo-Choo Island* (London, 1818).

[10] *Sobr. soch.*, III, 204-211.

, . . . poetry has changed its sacred beauty. Your muses, dear poets, the lawful daughters of the Parnassian Camenae would not proffer to you the obliging lyre, would not point out to you that poetic image which throws itself in the eyes of the contemporary traveler. And what an image! Neither of brilliant beauty, nor with attributes of power, nor with a spark of demonic fire in his eyes, nor with sword or crown, but simply in a black frock coat, round hat, white vest, and with an umbrella in his hand.[11]

The man wearing the black frock coat and carrying an umbrella becomes in the course of the book a running sight-joke of the kind we saw in *A Common Story*. He appears everywhere and in the most incongruous places—on the sands of Africa, on tea plantations in China, upon the shores of remote tropical islands. He is a representative English merchant and colonizer and Goncharov's symbol for the increasing uniformity and prosaicness of the world, as "everywhere this image . . . stands above the elements, above man's labors, and triumphs over nature!" The frequent parody and irony of *The Frigate Pallas* is a response to the problem of writing a travel book in a world dominated by this unprepossessing image; it represents Goncharov's solution to the question posed at the beginning of the book: how to find a suitable form, or in his words, "a poetic image," when everyone anticipates "wonders" but there are no wonders and "everything is approaching a prosaic level."[12]

[11] *Ibid.*, II, 18-20. The "dear poets" addressed here are Benediktov and Apollon Maykov.

[12] *Ibid.*, II, 18-20, 107-108. Tseytlin argues that *The Frigate Pallas* parodies Karamzin's *Letters of a Russian Traveler. I. A. Goncharov*, pp. 136-138. In one of the letters that served as material for the book Goncharov remarked that the passage he had just written to his correspondents was "simply a parody of Karamzin. . . ." To E. P. and N. A. Maykov, November 20, 1852, *Literaturnoe nasledstvo*, Nos. 22-24, p. 354. Engel'gardt, who regards the work as "a pamphlet against romantic traditions in the description of nature and the notorious romantic *couleur locale*," notes that in the fifties the romantic tradition of travel literature was still alive and the public expected something on the order of Marlinsky. *Ibid.*, pp. 309, 330. Cf. Druzhinin's reaction in his excellent review in *Sovremennik*, No. 1 (1856), Part III, pp. 5-6.

Faced with the increasing predictability and sameness of the world about him, Goncharov put himself—or, better, a mask of himself—at the center of his book. The external world, all those supposedly romantic spots, gradually recede into the background and the author as world traveler steps to the fore. Sentimental travelers such as Karamzin and Sterne—if Sterne was really a sentimentalist—also placed themselves at the center of their travel books, but Goncharov, though the image of himself he presents may be just as self-consciously literary, is a different sort.[13] In letters home to friends he jokingly talked of calling his work "Oblomov's Journey" or signing it "I. Oblomov,"[14] and the "hero" of *The Frigate Pallas* confronted by the great and varied world often displays a stolidity and imperviousness to experience not unlike that of his fictional hero faced with the smaller social world of Petersburg. *Often* but not always, for the author of the travel sketches at times was genuinely interested in the lands he visited. Though Goncharov in *The Frigate Pallas* speaks in his own voice, it would be naive to conclude that here we at last have him in his entirety. Instead, he presented a partial image of himself—ironic, diffident, prosaic—that recalls the narrator of the early story "A Cruel Illness," who was more obviously a literary artifice, and that is not too dissimilar from his other fictional narrators. In that early story the narrator by his matter-of-fact and ironical manner threw the exaggerated enthusiasms of the other characters (also for "travel," though on a much smaller scale) into an ironic perspective—a function performed by all of Goncharov's fictional narrators. In *The Frigate Pallas* the narrator again opposes a prosaic self to the enthusiasms of others—to those of previous travel literature, of his correspondents and hypothetical readers, and himself. Setting out upon his journey, Goncharov wondered how he might reconcile the two self-images, or in his words "the two lives," that had suddenly been thrust upon him—that of "a modest bureaucrat in an official

---

[13] Karamzin's *Letters of a Russian Traveler* tries to be informative as well as an expression of the author's sensibility. See Henry M. Nebel, Jr., *N. M. Karamzin: A Russian Sentimentalist* (The Hague, Paris, 1967), pp. 154-176.

[14] To M. A. Yazykov, August 23 and November 3, 1852, and to E. P. and N. A. Maykov, November 20, 1852, *Literaturnoe nasledstvo*, Nos. 22-24, pp. 348, 356.

frock coat quailing before his superior's glance, fearing colds, locked up within four walls with several dozen faces and uniforms all similar to each other," and the image of "the new Argonaut in a straw hat . . . hurtling over the depths in search of the Golden Fleece in an inaccessible Colchis. . . ."[15] He solved his dilemma as he solved it in the autobiographical "Pour et contre" and in the novels, which also reflect the split of his personality into a "prosaic" and a "poetic" self, by playing one image against the other: here, the indifferent bureaucrat against the eager Argonaut. In the process he created a book that is not only a travel sketch but another comedy in his unfolding comic perceptions of himself in the world.

Both images, the expectant Argonaut and the dull bureaucrat— the Alexander and Pyotr Aduev of this book—are viewed ironically. As distant lands never coincided with the illusions of the adventurer, the bureaucrat never proved quite up to the adventures of the world he has reluctantly set out to explore. Goncharov continually highlights, even exaggerates, the incongruity of his own position—the timid Petersburg official cast upon the great seas, the landlubber who insists upon calling the deck "a street" among men for whom the sea is home, the world traveler plagued by rheumatism, weariness, boredom, and homesickness. The "Argonaut" had embarked upon a quest for those idyllic lands of "eternal summer"; the bureaucrat's voyage turned into a quest for a moment of comfort upon inhospitable oceans, a brief period of respite from incessant motion. At sea he paid little attention to its "gloomy" and "indomitable" character; instead he worried about how to keep his balance, how to eat while the ship was rocking frantically, how to arrange for an unauthorized extra ration of fresh water. If the scenery of a place attracted him he remained painfully conscious that reaching it over muddy potholed roads could be "true torture in spite of picturesque ravines and hills." At times a dull indifference, an obtuseness that was perhaps as much an ironic pose as it was a reflection of his weariness, overtook him. At such moments he stayed on board and let the sights go unseen: "So what," he exclaimed in a not uncharacteristic fashion when urged by his excited shipmates to come and inspect a crocodile, "I'll see it at

---

[15] *Sobr. soch.*, II, 15.

Zam's [zoo] when I return to Petersburg; . . . they have a small one there; it will have grown up by that time."

Traveling by its nature was problematical—what the traveler sought was a comfortable room with a peaceful armchair, adequate ventilation, and a pleasant view, but no sooner had he found it and begun "to sink his roots" than he again had to return to the endless and dull sea.[16] Through it all—stormy seas that dashed him against the cabin wall, torrid tropical heat and numbing Siberian cold, nasty mosquitoes and lizards fond of crawling into his bed, showers that refused to work, a cigar factory where he had difficulty getting a cigar, Siberian towns where he could not find a fur coat—through all his privations and discomfitures, there remained the abiding consolation of good company and good food. Alexander Herzen, who was born in the same year but had little else in common with Goncharov, complained that the author of *The Frigate Pallas* journeyed around the world in order to present a list of what he ate, and indeed a good part of the book has the character of a menu, as Goncharov describes with relish innumerable meals including everything from English roast beef to exotic Chinese dishes that sent him into raptures of praise.[17]

Another means of gaining consolation was to see the exotic world before him in familiar terms. While setting out Goncharov reassured himself that his route, however long or difficult, could not after all be compared to the intrepid voyages of a Magellan, a Vasco da Gama, or a Columbus across uncharted seas. The contemporary traveler would surely find French hotels and English porter on the Sandwich Islands, decent carriages in Australia, Chinese wearing Irish linen, Africans with white gloves, Indians who all spoke English—in a word, "everything except savages."[18] His hopes, as we have seen, were at least partly realized, so that much of what he encountered, if it was not always comfortable, was at least familiar. Moreover, Goncharov strove to present it as such. Wherever he went, he sought

[16] *Ibid.*, pp. 198, 262, 242.

[17] A. I. Gertsen, "Neobyknovennaya istoriya o tsenzore Gon-cha-ro iz Shi-pan-khu," *Sobr. soch.*, XIII, 104.

[18] *Sobr. soch.*, II, 16-17.

out aspects of life not too different from what he knew at home. His eye is not on the spectacular but on the ordinary—upon those homely habits of everyday life that men hold in common. No matter how exotic or wild the place, whether it be in Africa, the East Indies, China, or on the Russian frigate in the midst of the empty sea, he managed to find something comparable to a Russian estate, a street in Petersburg, or at least unexotic England.[19] Even when what he saw was authentically different, Goncharov often attempted to project upon it qualities of the familiar—if only in his imagination. In a revealing passage the traveler, gazing at the charming and picturesque scene of Nagasaki and its environs, tells us that "... in my thoughts I covered all these hillocks and groves with temples, cottages, pavilions and statues, and the waters of the harbor with steamships and thickets of masts; I populated the shores with Europeans; I already saw paths of a park, galloping horsewomen, and closer to the city I envisioned Russian, American and English factories."[20] Raw nature was for Goncharov a vacuum he abhorred and felt compelled to fill.

His abhorrence of the uncultivated and taste for the comfortable and familiar provided the basis of a philosophy he expounded in *The Frigate Pallas*—the fullest statement of his social views to be found in his writings. It can be summarized as "bourgeois," imperialistic, and, in its naive optimism and unquestioning faith in inevitable material and social progress, conventionally "nineteenth-century." Three trying years at sea had confirmed Goncharov's confidence in the virtues of soft easy chairs, clean linen, fine cuisine, and all the attributes of a well-furnished middle-class home, and he gladly would have the rest of the still-benighted world share the blessings he has known. In a central passage he compares the concepts of luxury and comfort— all to the favor of the latter. Luxury is aristocratic—its pleasures can be enjoyed only by a privileged few, as in the despotic Orient or Renaissance Venice and Spain (or, he might have added, in contemporary Russia); its demands are excessive and presuppose the poverty and misery of the majority. Comfort on the other hand is rational and democratic. It is but the fulfillment of "the reasonable needs of

---

[19] See e.g. *ibid.*, II, 119, 125-126, 148, 242; III, 238-239.
[20] *Ibid.*, III, 151.

the majority." Through world trade and development its pleasures become accessible everywhere. "Comfort and civilization are almost synonymous, . . ." Goncharov declares. Later he adds that he would have the non-European world become Christian as well as comfortable, which may account for the "almost." The manifest destiny of the European is to carry to less fortunate peoples "the banner of security, abundance, peace, and that well-being which [the traveler] enjoys at home. . . ." This heroic undertaking of the European world has already begun to bear fruit so that ". . . what was inaccessible luxury for the few is, thanks to civilization, becoming accessible to all: in the north a pineapple costs 5 or 10 rubles; here—a half-kopeck. The task of civilization is to transport it quickly to the north and drive the price down to 5 kopecks, so that you and I may enjoy it."[21]

The modern reader is more likely to be amused by the quaintness of Goncharov's description of civilization than shocked by its banality. Nevertheless, there is vision at work here. Having derided one version of the golden age—the idyll of the "natural"—Goncharov postulates another and quite different idyllic condition. His vision is of a world that has become perfectly tamed and domesticated, where all the wildernesses and deserts are covered with tidy farms, comfortable homes, clean hotels, and well-provisioned restaurants, presumably moderately priced; where roads are plentiful and paved and seas offer few hazards to swift steamships; where strange peoples with names difficult to pronounce have become courteous and respectable burghers barely distinguishable from their European models. It is perhaps a pedestrian and narrow vision, certainly egocentric, but in some ways it foresees the actual shape of our modern world with its widespread industrialization, increasing uniformity, and almost universal desire for the "comforts" that in the past were the luxuries of a few. It is hazardous to speak for others, but we may even venture that many of us, if not most, would prefer or would at least feel more "comfortable" in Goncharov's utopia—and despite its homely middle-class quality the vision is unquestionably utopian—than in some other versions of utopia propagated in the nineteenth century.

[21] *Ibid.*, II, 284-287. See also II, 164-165, 208, 251; III, 81, 130-131, 145-146, 207, 300-304, 379-400.

However that may be, it is more important for the purposes of our study to point out that his vision was a response to profound psychological needs. Goncharov's contemporaries, whose enthusiasms he often did not share, tended to see him as conventional and humdrum, but there was an intent to his prosaic imagination that they often missed. The writer who, when invited by his excited shipmates to admire and describe a lightning-spangled southern sky, could only exclaim "deformity, disorder!" was of course a literary parodist constantly countering conventional responses—here the lyrical reflex to nature—with a prosaic observation. He was also a man with a compulsive urge toward what is represented by the roots of those words minus their negativizing prefixes. Face to face with pristine nature, which lacked "form" and "order," Goncharov felt profoundly uneasy.[22] In *The Frigate Pallas* he expressed his hope to see a world where everything was orderly, familiar, and safe. Oblomov expresses the same hope though in different terms and with more complex implications.

Also, Goncharov was aware of some of the possible limitations of his hypothetical utopia. In a world become totally rationalized, human spontaneity may be lost. Leaving England, which for Goncharov was the model of the future, he summoned up a nostalgic image of a modest Russian estate and its master. The Russian master is the exact opposite of the frock-coated Englishman. Where the Englishman is energetic, punctilious, and mechanical in his approach to life, the Russian is indolent, disorderly, and yet blessed with the gift of spontaneity in his relations with his fellowmen. The opposition of course echoes that of Alexander and Pyotr Aduev, as it anticipates the confrontation of Oblomov and Stolz. While in his conscious mind Goncharov looked to the future and those rationalistic mechanical men who served as its emblems, nostalgia continually drew him back to an image he could not leave entirely behind—those native Oblomovkas that he carried with him everywhere.[23]

[22] *Ibid.*, II, 254-255. [23] *Ibid.*, II, 66-73.

CHAPTER VII

Oblomov

The Comedy of Alienation

Estragon: And all that was yesterday, you say?
Vladimir: Yes of course it was yesterday.
Estragon: And here where we are now?
Vladimir: Where else do you think? Do you not recognize the place?
Estragon: (*suddenly furious*) Recognize? What is there to recognize? All my lousy life I've crawled about in the mud! And you talk to me about scenery!

Waiting for Godot, Samuel Beckett

THOUGH AT first glance Oblomov and Zakhar may seem to be no more than eccentric curios, they belong to a respectable and durable literary tradition, stretching back to Don Quixote and Sancho Panza—their most similar antecedents—and forward to various alienated figures of modern literature.[1] Like their literary analogues, Goncharov's master and serf adopt modes of behavior and pursue private visions that set them apart from normal society. They are lost, "superfluous" in the common epithet of Russian criticism, and yet in the course of the novel they manage to touch us in important ways.

In Part One their isolation is almost total. The master and his serf have found a temporary refuge from the world on Gorokhovaya Street in Petersburg and no longer venture outside. Oblomov has

---

[1] Several critics have made comparisons to Beckett. See V. S. Pritchett, "An Irish Oblomov," *The Working Novelist* (London, 1965), pp. 25-29, and Frederick J. Hoffman, *Samuel Beckett: The Language of Self* (Carbondale, Ill., 1962), pp. 13-19. For some parallels to Don Quixote, see Henry Gifford, *The Novel in Russia: From Pushkin to Pasternak* (New York, 1965), p. 58, and Poggioli, *The Phoenix and the Spider*, pp. 42-43.

further restricted his existence to a single room of their four-room apartment. In the small confines of the Gorokhovaya flat almost all activities, save those absolutely essential to maintain life, have ceased. Dust becomes an emblem of the stagnation that has settled upon Oblomov's tiny realm. It is everywhere—on the heavy and graceless mahogany furniture, on the carpets, the walls, around the several pictures. Thick layers have coated the yellowed pages of books left open at that point in the past when reading stopped, and lie upon newspapers bearing the dates of other years. Time itself seems to have come to a standstill in the Gorokhovaya apartment. The dust has coated the apartment's windows, and Oblomov relies upon occasional visitors, not only for news of the outside world, but even to ascertain the time of the year: "Don't come near, don't come near; you are from the cold!" he cries out to each of his successive guests, only to be told that it is a beautiful May first and that the sun is warm.[2]

Both the outside world and the inner world—larger reality and the confines of his psychic retreat—terrify Oblomov. He fears crowds, movement and bustle, traveling. But the withdrawal to the single room, his blanket, and dressing gown bring him little solace. Attacks of "nervous terror" descend upon him; he fears the very silence he has sought; "supernatural apparitions" appear in the dark corners of his room.[3] Clearly a victim of a profound psychological malaise, Oblomov, however, never becomes the object of a clinical investigation. The moments of terror and hallucination return, but essentially Oblomov's alienation as well as his evolving relation to the larger world are perceived comically.[4]

The comedy of Part One, written in the forties, is composed of static set scenes played out between Oblomov, his servant, and his visitors, which convey a theatrical quality reminiscent of Goncharov's other writings of the forties, *A Common Story* and the earlier tale "Ivan Savich Podzhabrin." It is enacted within the narrow limits of

---

[2] *Sobr. soch.*, IV, 19-20, 23-24, 27, 34-35.

[3] *Ibid.*, p. 63.

[4] For the best psychological study of the three novels, see Leon Stilman, "Oblomovka Revisited," *American Slavic and East European Review*, VII (1948), 45-77.

the Gorokhavaya apartment. Amid the dust, cobwebs, and plates
with yesterday's gnawed chicken bones, the master and servant
vainly try to maintain the semblance of a home, but the skills of
housekeeping and the arts of living together totally escape them.
Though a central motive of the novel later becomes the search for
a more comfortable and truer domesticity, in Part One Oblomov's
and Zakhar's ineptness only provides an occasion for playful, at times
farcical, comedy. The humor is broad, frequently bordering on slap-
stick. Zakhar, dropping a trayload of dishes one by one in a vain
attempt to retrieve an initial sliding plate, or heroically trying to navi-
gate an apparently impenetrable doorway, is an artist of ineptitude, a
truly Chaplinesque figure. An incessant domestic squabble dominates
the lives of master and serf—Oblomov scolds, cajoles, becomes ex-
asperated at his bumbling servant; Zakhar is alternately repentant
and recalcitrant. The two have been inseparably joined in their curious *ménage*, and, though they cannot live without each other, they
do not manage very well together. The argument that runs through
Part One predictably concludes in a deadlock: "They both had ceased
to understand each other, and finally each himself."[5]

The comedy at a more important level depends on differing attitudes toward reality. In a number of ways Oblomov and Zakhar are
very much alike: both are inept; things in the literal and metaphorical
sense escape them—much of Part One is taken up by a hunt for
missing handkerchiefs, letters, food, money, etc.; both live in memories of a former glory and abundance on their manorial birthplace,
Oblomovka. But despite their similarities, the master and servant perceive the world from different points of view—a circumstance that is
the source of their mutual incomprehension and of the comedy they
enact. As helpless as his master, plagued by things gone out of control, Zakhar is nevertheless totally circumscribed by the concrete objects and material needs that constitute his immediate environment.
The servant's complaint against the master, to whom he is otherwise

[5] *Sobr. soch.*, IV, 97. Richard Freeborn, in his recent intelligent *The Rise
of the Russian Novel: Studies in the Russian Novel from Eugene Onegin to
War and Peace* (Cambridge, 1973), pp. 144-146, points out the theatrical
quality of Goncharov's writings of the forties and of other prose of the
decade.

completely loyal, takes the form of an accusation that Oblomov knows nothing but words: "You talk nonsense! You are only a master at speaking odd and pathetic words . . ." (*zhalkie slova*).[6] While Zakhar trips over things, Oblomov tries to evade them through language.

Thus, Zakhar opens each of their major comic encounters with a reminder of some tangible need that is pressing in upon them from the world beyond the dusty windows—bills to be paid, a landlord to be dealt with—to which the master responds with ever mounting rhetorical outbursts of indignation, concluding at one point in a characteristic lament: "Oh my God! Life touches one; it reaches everywhere."[7] However, Oblomov not only employs words for the purpose of procrastination; he reifies language so that the word becomes the equivalent of an act. The comedy reaches an apex with Zakhar's modest rebuke in the form of a suggestion that "other people" would encounter no special difficulty in handling the latest crisis, the necessity of moving to a new apartment. Though the comparison to "others" wounds Oblomov's personal and class pride, he also feels it unjust because he has already "acted." He has a "plan" to resolve their difficulties, and for Oblomov a plan, a verbal construct, is equal to an act. The master chides his servant for ingratitude:

> How did your tongue manage that? . . . And I had already assigned him in my plan a special house and a kitchen garden, a regular measure of grain, and I had fixed a salary! You are my steward and major-domo and my special assistant! Peasants bow to you from the waist; everyone calls you Zakhar Trofimych, yes, Zakhar Trofimych! And he is still not content, compares me to "the others"! That's my reward! A fine way to honor his master!

Oblomov finally exhausts his reserves of verbal eloquence, and Zakhar, after dutifully tucking the master into bed, returns to his own concrete and tangible reality. " 'May you choke, you demon! . . . Really, a demon. A special house, a kitchen garden, a salary! . . . An expert at speaking pathetic words. . . . Well, here is both my

---

[6] *Ibid.*, p. 15.
[7] *Ibid.*, pp. 17-18, 82-86, 89-98.

house and my kitchen garden and here I'll breathe my last!' he said, striking the stove with fury."[8]

A clash of perspectives also forms the basis of the comedy Oblomov plays out with the world at large—"the others." The demands of ordinary life penetrate Oblomov's retreat from the outside. Letters arrive announcing that he must vacate his apartment and that some action is required to save his foundering estate. A string of casual visitors drops in "from the cold" and tempts him into the world of action and responsibility.[9] The intrusion of necessity rouses Oblomov to action. But his sphere of action is immediately reduced to an extremely narrow range: setting his world right becomes a question of finding paper and ink in order to write a letter, or getting his relative pronouns straight, and even these small obstacles prove overwhelming. Faced with a double dispossession—an imminent loss of his ancestral home and the retreat he has found on Gorokhovaya Street (and it is the threat of such dispossessions that hounds him through the novel)—Oblomov is reduced to problems of syntax. Alexander Aduev had bemoaned "the Lilliputian comedy" his life had become, and Oblomov likewise finds himself drowning in trivia: "The events of his life had dwindled to microscopic proportions. . . ."[10]

To the trivia of actual life Oblomov opposes a world of dreams. The dimensions of his dreams stand in inverse proportion to those of his waking life: they are expansive and grandiose.

> He sometimes loved to imagine himself as some invincible commander before whom not only Napoleon but even Eruslan Lazarevich means nothing; he invents a war and a cause for it: for instance, he has the people of Africa pouring into Europe, or he

[8] *Ibid.*, pp. 97-98. Poggioli, pp. 42-43, distinguishes the relation between Oblomov and Zakhar from that of Don Quixote and Sancho Panza in seeing Zakhar as "an Oblomov on a lower scale, thus acting as his caricature." The "lower scale" is, however, the concrete and prosaic world—Goncharov's usual lower scale—and the relationship resembles that of Cervantes' famous duo.

[9] Robie Macauley, "The Superfluous Man," *Partisan Review*, XIX, No. 2 (March-April 1952), 172, reads this section as "a mock morality play."

[10] *Sobr. soch.*, IV, 101. Alexander's phrase is literally "pygmy-like comedy." *Ibid.*, I, 143. Earlier (p. 82) Pyotr had suggested that he employ a "minimizing glass" for his feelings, an accurate description of that comedy's instrument.

organizes new crusades and wages war, decides the fate of nations, ravages cities, shows mercy, wreaks vengeance, performs deeds of virtue and magnanimity.

Or he chooses the part of a thinker or a great artist: everyone pays homage to him; he gathers laurels; crowds pursue him, exclaiming, "Look, look, there goes Oblomov, our renowned Ilya Ilich!"[11]

The comedy is related to the deflation of "poetic" hyperbole by its juxtaposition to the prosaic that we observed in *A Common Story* and the early tales. Two levels of experience are played off against each other—here, two "heroisms": the heroic efforts required to overcome the slightest obstacles posed by prosaic reality, and the grandiose pretensions of the dreams.[12] However, Oblomov's comedy evolves much differently from Alexander Aduev's. Alexander became so completely identified with a single comic posture, or mannerism, that he lost any potential for depth. The term "deflation," though especially appropriate for a novel in which a single posture is systematically and relentlessly parodied until the protagonist conveniently exchanges one comic mask for another, fails to describe Oblomov's situation adequately. Oblomov conveys a seriousness, a sense of commitment, completely lacking in the earlier novel. Far from constituting a mere posture, the comic aspects of his self are firmly rooted in his character. There are no easy reversals in store for him. Also, while Alexander Aduev fastidiously disdained prosaic reality, Oblomov, for all his elaborate evasions, makes an attempt to cope with the ordinary demands of life. His actions are misdirected and often ludicrous, but the continual effort establishes a basic and important premise upon which a proper reading of the novel depends—namely, that for Oblomov, if not for "the others," writing a letter, moving to a

[11] *Ibid.*, IV, 69. Eruslan Lazarevich (or Ursulan Zalazorevich) was the hero of an oriental fairy tale adapted in Russia toward the end of the sixteenth century or in the early seventeenth.

[12] Kenneth Burke writes of humor: ". . . it takes up the slack between the momentousness of the situation and the feebleness of those in the situation by *dwarfing the situation*. It converts downwards, as the heroic converts upwards." *Attitudes toward History*, I, 54.

new apartment, and, later, marriage are truly heroic undertakings.

Nor are Oblomov's dreams mere posturings presented solely for purposes of comic deflation. Though frequently humorous in their gross exaggerations—a humor that is heightened by our other image of the unheroic, "reduced" Oblomov—the dreams also contribute a serious dimension to a comedy which might otherwise turn into pure farce. In the realm of the ordinary, struggling to get his pronouns right or to maneuver himself successfully into his slippers, Oblomov is a delightful but limited caricature. The dreams, as we shall see later, constitute the most serious commitment of his life. Through them he reveals his inner self and achieves a depth and range beyond the single plane of caricature. They serve to soften Oblomov, to humanize him, for it is in his dreams that he continually touches not only his own secret life but the secret parts of all of us—here, in Part One, our childish fantasies of glory and renown.

Instead of one level of experience existing solely to deflate another, *Oblomov* presents two worlds—the world of dreams and the world of things. The two worlds, though they continually interact with and comment upon one another, remain independent categories of existence. Oblomov lives in each, subject to the claims of necessity and the whims of his imagination. Each realm is extreme. They are, to extend Goncharov's own metaphor, experience viewed through *both* ends of the microscope. In the world of things Oblomov becomes entangled in trivia and appears comically grotesque in his fumbling efforts to extricate himself; in his dreams he is heroic and, later, the world becomes perfect.[13]

[13] The comic level of Part One corresponds to Eykhenbaum's criteria for the grotesque: "The style of the grotesque demands that . . . the described situation or event be enclosed in a world of artificial experiences, which is small to the point of fantasticality . . . , that it be completely fenced off from a large reality, . . . and . . . that this be done with neither a satiric nor a didactic purpose, but with the purpose of giving scope to *a playing with reality*, to break down and freely transfer its elements, so that customary relations and connections (psychological and logical) appear ineffective . . . and any trifle may grow to colossal proportions." B. Eykhenbaum, "Kak sdelana 'Shinel' ' Gogolya," *Literatura: teoriya, kritika, polemika* (Leningrad, 1927), pp. 162-163. Eykhenbaum is discussing Gogol, and E. Krasnoshchekova in her

In defining humor, Coleridge declared that the "one humorific point common to all that can be called humorous" could be found in "a certain reference to the general and the universal, by which the finite great is brought into identity with the little, or the little with the finite great, so as to make both nothing in comparison with the infinite. The little is made great, and the great little, in order to destroy both, because all is equal in contrast with the infinite."[14] The "great"—Oblomov's verbal eloquence, his exaggerated understanding of life's ordinary difficulties—is played off against Zakhar's prosaic obtuseness and the "normal" views of "the others." But the originality of Oblomov's comedy derives from the fact that "the finite great" and "the little," which stand in a dialectical relation, are usually but different aspects of the same hero. Oblomov has two lives: he is "great" in his dreams and "little" in reality. The "infinite" in the novel—that which is greater than Oblomov's dreams and circumstances and has the power to "destroy both"—is, as we shall see shortly, the inevitable progress of time.

RHYTHM AND PATTERN

Oblomov is often called a "plotless" novel. "Plot," in such characterizations, is used not in its Aristotelian sense as the representation of a "complete action" that is "the whole working out of a motive to its end in success or failure," but as conventionally employed to describe a story arranged to arouse curiosity about impending events.[15] *Oblomov* even has a plot in the latter usage, but it plays a minimal role in the "working out" of the motive. Early in the novel two char-

recent intelligent study, *"Oblomov" I. A. Goncharova* (Moscow, 1970), pp. 8-17, correctly, and with some interesting illustrations, compares Part One, which was written mostly in the forties, to the Gogolian manner.

[14] T. M. Raysor (ed), *Coleridge's Miscellaneous Criticism* (Cambridge, Mass., 1936), p. 444.

[15] Francis Fergusson in an introductory essay to *Aristotle's Poetics* (New York, 1961), pp. 7-22, deduces this distinction from the *Poetics*. Also see R. S. Crane, "The Concept of Plot and the Plot of *Tom Jones*," *Critics and Criticism*, ed. R. S. Crane (Chicago, 1952), pp. 617-623. See Tseytlin, *I. A. Goncharov*, p. 189. ". . . Oblomov is one of the most 'plotless' novels in Russian literature."

acters appear at the Gorokhovaya flat and present opposing choices to Oblomov: the petty clerk and petty villain Tarantev offers him the widow's apartment on the distant Vyborg side of the Neva, which becomes the locality of his final isolation; Stolz offers a life of active participation in the world of "the others." Tarantev continues to conspire against Oblomov while Stolz, with the later assistance of Olga, devises stratagems to save him. However, any potential the situation may have for dramatic conflict and tension is never realized— a major cause of the novel's "plotless" character. Tarantev and Stolz are seldom on stage and they meet only momentarily. Also Oblomov, though his fate hinges upon a choice between the alternatives presented by his two visitors, remains largely oblivious of their efforts. He does not participate in the "plot" contrived by his friends and enemies, but instead follows his own pattern of action and thought.

The pattern falls into a rhythmic movement reminiscent of Alexander Aduev's regular turning from withdrawal and dream to an attempt to realize the dream in the world to comic deflation, except that in the absence of significant plot interest it dominates the novel and determines its form. The rhythm in *Oblomov* begins as a movement from passivity to action and back to passivity. Initially it is a mechanical repetition of comedy or farce. Oblomov strains to lift himself out of bed, finally manages to raise himself a bit, and predictably falls back. Visitors arrive and provoke a momentary interest in the outside world, until he once again settles back into his comforting blanket. However, as Part One progresses, the true pattern of the novel is established. Oblomov, stirred by his tempters from outside and by reminders of his obligations, moves to action, or more often to the thought of action, only to fall back into reflection or dream.

> . . . and thoughts are suddenly kindled; they move and rush through his head like waves of the sea. Then they grow into intentions; they set all his blood on fire; his muscles begin to move; his veins tighten; intentions are transformed into strivings. Moved by a moral force, he rapidly changes his position two or three times in one minute; with shining eyes he half sits up in his bed, stretches

out a hand and gazes about inspiredly—a moment and the striving will be realized—and then, O Lord! . . .

But look, the morning flashes by; the day already wanes toward evening and with it Oblomov's exhausted powers decline to rest. . . . Oblomov silently, thoughtfully turns over on his back, and, fixing his sad gaze on the window and toward the sky, his eyes mournfully follow the sun setting magnificently behind a four-storied house.[16]

It is an ironic movement, but only vaguely related to the abrupt tripping-up of Alexander Aduev, which proceeded so predictably and mechanically through *A Common Story*. Oblomov's aborted moral strivings are as earnest as his dreams, and they add another serious dimension to the evolving comedy.

The pattern of the whole recapitulates the pattern of the parts, giving a novel with frequently divergent tendencies an essential unity. The alternation of dream and reality, withdrawal and action, is sustained through the novel, though the dreams diminish in frequency at its center—the Oblomov-Olga romance—and return to gradually obscure reality for Oblomov in the final pages. The total pattern follows a curve similar to that of Oblomov's smaller movements—for as Oblomov turns from dream and reflection to aborted action to a decline back into dream, his book proceeds from the famous chapter "Oblomov's Dream" to a vain attempt to retrieve the dream in reality through Olga's love, to a final decline into dream and death. The novel can be described by the formula stasis-action-stasis, in which the love affair with Olga marks the turning-point in Oblomov's story. Though the sometimes farcical comedy of Part One may seem incongruous with the somber tone of later sections, its interplay of dream and concrete reality anticipates the major design and provides an overture to what follows.[17] The shape of the novel corresponds to

---

[16] *Sobr. soch.*, IV, 69. For other examples, see *ibid.*, pp. 10, 12-16, 16-18, 19-23, 23-27, 27-31, 68-70, 78-81. N. I. Prutskov, in his first-rate *Masterstvo Goncharova-romanista*, p. 91, writes: "The transitions of Oblomov's moods, alternating like an ebb and flow . . . constitute the basic design of the novel."

[17] Prutskov, *ibid.*, p. 224, describes the novel as a circle inscribing a life's

the shape of its smaller units, but its smaller units are determined by the tendencies of Oblomov's thoughts and desires—as they move from dream to action and back to dream. Thus the patterns of the novel are analogous to the patterns created by its hero's mind.

The rhythms of experience are paralleled by the rhythms of nature, endowing the novel with a quality of "felt life," in Henry James's phrase, lacking in Goncharov's first novel. In the above passage Oblomov's decline into reflection is accompanied by the gradual decline of the setting sun. Part One, except for "Oblomov's Dream," is the motion of a day—from morning and awakening to the descent of dusk. Oblomov's love of Olga is the love of a summer. It fades in autumn with the annual death of the green world. Winter witnesses its final extinction as falling snow buries Oblomov's hopes irrevocably. As Oblomov's thought fades from the possibility of action to pure reflection, as his love fades from hope to futility, the natural world declines from bright summer through grey autumn to the lifeless landscapes of winter. Of the two movements, the motion from passivity toward action and the ebb of decline, the latter is the more sustained and decisive.

The paralleling of the rhythms of experience to the rhythms of nature places the novel in time. The movement from aborted action to dream and reflection introduces the perspective of time in yet another manner. Oblomov exists in a kind of zero present without hope or possibility. In the present he is a comic curio clumsily trying to cope with ordinary reality. In dreams he again finds hope, and he also gains a past, for many of Oblomov's dreams recreate his personal history. Through them and especially through the several dreams that make up "Oblomov's Dream," the novel leaves the flat plane of present time and expands into the history of a life as it passes from childhood to death.

---

cycle, which he summarizes in the formula: "sleep [or "dream"—the Russian is ambiguous]—awakening—sleep." "Awakening" is used by Oblomov to describe his experience with Olga: "And do you think it's possible . . . to fall asleep after such an awakening. . . ." *Sobr. soch.*, IV, 362. The correspondence between the smaller rhythms of the novel and its total pattern was first suggested to me in a lecture by Rufus Mathewson of Columbia University. Goncharov referred to Part One as a prologue in *Sbornik*, p. 164.

In its constant shifts to the past the novel acquires a quality of duration absent from the comedy of the present. "[My life] was not like a morning . . . which later turns into day . . . and naturally and gradually sinks into evening. No, as my life began, it was extinguished. Strange, but it's so!"[18] At a cul-de-sac from the very opening of the novel, Oblomov achieves a sense of duration and process for his life largely through his periodic descents into memory. The continual alternation between a zero present beyond process or possibility and a past where both still exist can perhaps best be summarized by a shift of verb aspects that takes place in a single sentence in one of his histories—from imperfective to perfective: "It [his soul] . . . waited . . . and . . . ceased to wait and despaired." (Ona . . . zhdala . . . i . . . perestala zhdat' i otchayalas'.)[19] *Oblomov* has been cited as a prime example of "the 'imperfective' tendency of the Russian novel—the imperfective being that form of the Russian verb which views the action *in the process* of happening."[20] The novel is "imperfective," it conveys a sense of duration and process, mostly in reminiscence and dream.

The rhythms of the novel are not the regular sweeps of a pendulum. Each important section mounts to its own climax, which may be a climax of thought or action. Part Two concludes with Oblomov's proposal of marriage and the kiss that seals it. Part Three ends with the defeat of love. As we shall see shortly, even "Oblomov's Dream," though almost without action, slowly moves to a final scene which illuminates the preceding sections. The comedy of Part One also rises to a climax. The discrepancy between "the great" and "the little" is gradually increased, and, as a result, the pace of the comedy quickens. Once Oblomov's monumental immobility has been established, almost any invitation to action, even of the most innocuous sort, becomes comical. The incongruity reaches an extreme with the appearance of Oblomov's doctor bearing a list of hyperbolic prescrip-

---

[18] *Sobr. soch.*, IV, 190.   [19] *Ibid.*, p. 62.

[20] Mirsky, *A History of Russian Literature*, p. 184. Mirsky is referring to Jane Ellen Harrison's *Aspects, Aorists and the Classical Tripos* (Cambridge, 1919) and her description of the imperfective quality of the Russian novel and, especially, of *Oblomov*.

tions for the restoration of his health—travel to the spas of Europe for mineral waters, to Egypt for dry air, to America for sea air, etc.[21] As Part One progresses, the dimension of dream also enlarges. Oblomov's dreams become more extensive and grandiose as they approach the great dream of chapter nine. The climax of the comedy of Part One, however, is a climax of thought.

The comedy of "I and the Others," or of "Oblomov and the World," depends upon a certain narrowing of character and a consequent avoidance of complexity of motive or thought. Character is reduced to a series of gestures—Zakhar pounding on the stove to remind us of prosaic reality—or to an emblematic representation of a normative world. Oblomov's visitors, each decked out in a uniform indicating his social station—an elegant riding habit, a dark green tailcoat studded with official seals, the artist's "calculated casualness" of dress—embody in turn a single aspect of contemporary life: frivolous high society, careerism in the government service, and the "realistic tendency" in literature.[22] They enter the Gorokhovaya flat to highlight, through their active involvement in a social role, Oblomov's grotesque passivity. Oblomov himself perceives their fragmentation, the total identification of a man with his role, and makes it the center of his argument against joining the world: "Where is man here? Why is he fragmented and scattered about in pieces?" "And how little of man is necessary here: his mind, his will, his feelings—why is this so?" "Man, give me man!"[23]

But in the comedy of the present Oblomov is also a "fragment," a "piece" of a man.[24] The opening page of the novel had presented him as dominated by a single controlling characteristic—"softness"—and through Part One his incapacity, his "softness," is played upon. Oblomov initially displays the self-contained and restricted quality, what Bergson called the "rigidity," of a comic type. Wrapped in the great, enveloping dressing gown, he seems impervious to experience: "Thought flitted like a free bird across his face, fluttered in his eyes, settled on his half-opened lips, concealed itself in the folds of his brow,

---

[21] *Sobr. soch.*, IV, 86-88. [22] *Ibid.*, pp. 19-31.
[23] *Ibid.*, pp. 23, 27, 30.
[24] *Oblomok* in Russian means "a fragment."

then became lost altogether, and, finally, an even light of unconcern shone across his entire face."[25]

At the culmination of the comedy of "I and the Others" a shift in perspective takes place that allows the novel to develop beyond a static interplay of dream and reality. Oblomov converts the opposition of "I and the Others" from a purely comic plane to the category of thought. What had previously been a comic collision of solidified oppositions—Oblomov the inept dreamer versus the normal prosaic world—now becomes internalized into a questioning of the nature of reality: "What is this? *Another* would have done all that. . . . Another, another—what is *another person?*" Oblomov asks himself. The corollary to the question "What is another?" is "What am I?" and Oblomov immediately turns the question inward: "Why am I like this?"[26]

In internalizing the comic opposition of "I and the Others" into a questioning of his own nature and the nature of the world about him Oblomov ceases to be a mere object to be manipulated for humorous effects. The successive encounters with the others have shattered his comic complacency and opened him to the possibility of experience. In doubting himself Oblomov begins to achieve greater complexity. He also becomes capable of having a "story." No longer a comic curio held up for our inspection and entertainment, he now has a motive— to discover the nature of his self and define his relations with the world—the "others."

With Oblomov's questions the novel becomes a quest. Though he will later attempt to transcend his fragmentary nature and join the normal world, the quest is initially for an explanation of the current impasse, for an answer to the question, "Why am I like this?" Oblomov sets out to look for "the something [that] had prevented him from rushing out into the arena of life . . . , the someone [who] had, as it were, stolen and buried the treasures . . . of his soul," for "some secret enemy [who] had laid a heavy hand upon him in the beginning of his journey and had thrown him away from his true human purpose."[27] As is his habit, he begins his search in dream, a dream in which he summarizes his life from childhood through adolescence.

[25] *Ibid.*, pp. 7-8.   [26] *Ibid.*, pp. 99, 101-102.   [27] *Ibid.*, p. 101.

In the process he acquires a personal history and the sense of a past that forever puts him beyond the single dimension of caricature.

"Oblomov's Dream"

Every valley shall be exalted and every mountain and hill shall be made low.

Isaiah XL. 4.

Et in Arcadia ego

The famous chapter nine of Part One, entitled "Oblomov's Dream," includes a history of the hero from childhood through adolescence, an attempt to uncover the causes of his psychic paralysis, a sociological account of primitive, tradition-bound rural Russia, and a series of ironic genre sketches depicting the quaint, if impractical, folkways of its inhabitants. However, the various tendencies of the chapter are all presented in the context of a dream—a circumstance that must serve as the starting point for any analysis that aspires to understand it.

A strangeness suggestive of the world of dreams penetrates much of the chapter. The tones of mystery derive in part from the accounts of local folklore, several examples of which are included in the text— tales of werewolves, wood goblins, corpses risen from the dead; romances of evil robbers, sleeping princesses, cities and men turned to stone. Intimations of the uncanny are not restricted to the tales the young Ilya Ilich eagerly listens to in the Oblomov household. They are part of the very landscape of Oblomovka. With the descent of evening

> objects lost their form; everything merged first into a grey, then into a dark mass. The singing of the birds gradually grew weak; soon they fell silent altogether. . . .
>
> All was still. . . . White mist rose from the ground and spread over the meadow and the river. The river too grew quiet. . . .
>
> . . . It became darker and darker. Trees clustered into the forms of strange monsters; it was fearful in the forest; something began to creak there suddenly, just as if one of the monsters were changing its position. . . .[28]

[28] *Sobr. soch.*, IV, 119-120.

The tones of mystery and dream enter even those "genre" scenes where Goncharov is most evidently ironic in his attitude toward the inhabitants of Oblomovka. The longest of these describes a dark winter evening in the living room of the Oblomovs, a winter evening that characteristically becomes all winter evenings. The scene is set in terms of largeness—"the large dark living room" with a lone flickering tallow candle, "a huge, awkward and stiff sofa," "a large leather armchair"—a largeness that serves to dwarf the Oblomov family circle and especially the observing child. Snatches of conversation drop into this dark empty space and are rhythmically punctuated by the footsteps of Oblomov's pacing father, the clicking of needles, the rustling of thread, the dull beat of a clock's pendulum, and lengthy silences, which combine to lend a hallucinatory quality to the scene.

> Silence. Only the steps of Ilya Ivanovich's heavy home-made boots resound; the wall clock's pendulum beats mutely in its case; a snapping of thread . . . breaks the deep silence.
>
> . . . .
>
> And again they would fall silent.
>
> . . . .
>
> . . . Ilya Ivanovich would fall silent, and again the entire company would sink into drowsiness. . . .
>
> . . . .
>
> . . . Ilya Ivanovich began once again to walk back and forth.
> Again they all fall silent; only the thread, as it is led back and forth by the needle, hisses.
>
> . . . .
>
> . . . and everything sank into silence.
>
> As before only the swaying of the pendulum, the tapping of Oblomov's boots, and the faint snapping of thread . . . were heard.[29]

The "Dream" conveys a sense of timelessness often encountered in dream states and in the literature of dreams.[30] The usual pattern

[29] *Ibid.*, pp. 130-138.

[30] See Hans Meyerhoff, *Time in Literature* (Berkeley and Los Angeles, 1960).

begins with a specific and temporally limited scene—a day, an evening—which is then generalized into all days and evenings of life in
Oblomov's birthplace, Oblomovka.

> After dinner . . . they all go off to their beds and sleep settles
> upon their carefree heads.
> Ilya Ilich dreams not of one, nor two such evenings, but of
> whole weeks, months, and years of days and evenings passed in
> such a way.
>
> . . . .
>
> "My God, what a child you are, what a frisky fellow! Can't
> you sit still, sir? Shameful!" the nurse said.
> And the whole day and all the nurse's days and nights were
> filled . . . with anxiety that the child would fall. . . .[31]

Often the movement from a specific moment to an unlimited duration is accompanied or accomplished by a shifting of verbs from a
more usual narrative past or present tense to a historic present—as
above: "said"—"were filled"—"would fall (*govorila—napolneny
byli—upadyot*).

> He was (*byl*), it seemed, alone in the whole world; he ran
> away (*ubegal*) from the nurse, looked over (*usmatrival*) every-
> body . . . ; he would stop (*ostanovitsya*) and would look (*osmotrit*)
> attentively at how someone would awaken (*ochnyotsya*); . . . he
> sought (*iskal*) . . . the disturber of this silence: he would catch
> (*poymaet*) a dragon-fly, would tear off (*otorvyot*) its wings. . . .
> Then he would climb (*zaberyotsya*) into a ditch. . . .[32]

An investigator of the language employed in the "Dream" has
noticed a prevailing use of imperfective verbs. The verbs of "Oblomov's Dream" "create the impression of immutably repeated actions. . . . The verbs . . . speak . . . not of any one concrete action,

[31] *Sobr. soch.*, IV, 136, 112. For similar patterns, see pp. 114-115, 116-117,
130-144.

[32] *Ibid.*, p. 117. For similar verb changes, see pp. 114, 118-119, 128-129,
130-143.

but of an action constantly repeated from day to day. . . ."[33] At times the verbs are "doubled" as in folklore, enhancing the quality of a "timeless" imperfectivity—of an action constantly repeated and without limit.

And the child looked all the time and observed all the time . . . (*vsyo smotrel i vsyo nablyudal*).

. . . .

And the child observed and observed all the time (*vsyo nablyudal da nablyudal*).

. . . .

And poor Ilyusha goes and goes . . . (*ezdit da ezdit*).[34]

Grammar, however, is only one element, and probably not the most important, contributing to the quality of timelessness—of a moment that is all moments. "Oblomov's Dream" is virtually eventless, and "there is no time outside the events. . . ."[35] It is composed of a series of static scenes depicting life in Oblomovka, interspersed with the narrator's analytic and critical remarks. The scenes do not develop into a story; they are consecutive because language is unavoidably linear, but they are not consecutive in relation to a narrative plot—an action with a beginning, middle, and end. Nor are the scenes referred to specific historical occasions that might localize the description to a definite and circumscribed time period. What the "Dream" describes are typical moments, a day and an evening, which become "all days and evenings passed in such a way."[36] The very subject matter of

[33] A. F. Efremov, "Yazyk i stil' IX glavy romana I. A. Goncharova *Oblomov*," *Russkiy yazyk v shkole*, No. 2 (March-April 1962), p. 29.

[34] *Sobr. soch.*, IV, 115, 117, 142. Folklore is generally a "timeless" category of literature. See D. S. Likhachev, "Time in Russian Folklore," *International Journal of Slavic Linguistics and Poetics*, V (1962), 74-96. Much of "Oblomov's Dream" has a folklore-ish quality, and several actual folk tales are included in the text (see below).

[35] *Ibid.*, p. 79.

[36] My argument here is influenced by Joseph Frank's "Spatial Form in the Modern Novel," in *Critiques and Essays on Modern Fiction*, ed. John W. Aldridge (New York, 1952), pp. 43-66. Likhachev finds that "Naturalism" [the natural school] "attempted to 'arrest' fictional time and create 'daguerreo-

these slices of Oblomovian life is "timeless." The "Dream" presents the unchanging patterns of domestic life—the daily chores of the barnyard and kitchen, careful preparations for annual holidays, the recurrent cycles of human labor and rest.

Conversation in the "Dream" also has a "timeless" quality. Talk does not arise from the demands of a specific situation and is not intended to reflect an individual psyche. Oblomovka's inhabitants give utterance instead to their perpetual preoccupations, so that what is said at any given moment can be generalized into all the moments of their lives. Their exclamations tend to be gratuitous, unrelated to any temporal sequence of events or thoughts. An anonymous woman interrupts an idle evening's gossip with a commentary that has nothing to do with what came before or comes after:

> They sit for a long time, gazing at one another; now and then they sigh deeply about something. Sometimes someone would even begin weeping.
> "What's wrong, mother. . . ."
> "Oh, I'm sad, my dear. . . . We have angered the Lord God, accursed ones that we are. . . ."
> "Oh, don't frighten me, don't terrify me, my dear one! . . ."
> "Yes, Yes. . . . The last days have come: nation will rise against nation, kingdom against kingdom—the Last Judgment is coming!"[37]

"Oblomov's Dream" presents a timeless world, and the citizens of Oblomovka very much want it to remain so. They conceive of time as a cyclical pattern of "eternal returns"—holidays, familial occasions, the returning seasons—through which experience, instead of

---

types' . . . by means of 'physiological sketches,'" *International Journal of Slavic Linguistics and Poetics*, V (1962), 79. "Oblomov's Dream," written in the forties, has its roots in the "natural school" which dominated the decade. Likhachev, *passim*, also makes a lack of "relation to the general flow of historical time" the determining factor in his argument for the timeless quality of folklore. For a fuller and excellent treatment of time in literature, including a discussion of time in *Oblomov*, see Likhachev's *Poetika drevnerusskoy literatury* (Leningrad, 1967), pp. 212-352.

[37] *Sobr. soch.*, IV, 138.

falling into a succession of discrete events, continually reverts to the same "inevitable and rooted occurrences." Nothing has changed in Oblomovka "from time immemorial." If its inhabitants are dimly aware of time as a linear progression, it is a knowledge they fervently resist with the hope and prayer that "every day be like yesterday, every yesterday like tomorrow!"[38]

The intent of Oblomov's dreaming mind is not merely to summon up in memory a provincial backwater, but to displace the historically contingent world of usual experience and present a "marvelous land": "Where are we? To what blessed little corner of the earth has Oblomov's dream borne us? What a marvelous land!" The exceptional moment of uninhibited lyricism and rhetorical expansiveness without deflating irony at the opening of the "Dream" has suggested to at least one reader a basic sympathy on the part of the author for the world he has evoked.[39] Curiously, Goncharov's great lapse into lyricism is of an inverted and negative kind. He sings the praises of what Oblomovka is not: "It is true there is no sea there, no high mountains, no cliffs or precipices, no dense forests—nothing grand, gloomy, and wild." The following section is composed of a string of antithetical parallelisms presenting the novelist's case against sea and mountains and justifying a landscape without them. He argues that the more dramatic configurations of the natural world are inhospitable to the amenities of human life and, in their grandeur and lack of modest proportion, threatening to human personality.

The roar and frenzied roll of the waves do not soothe the feeble ear; they but repeat the same old song, unchanged from the

[38] *Ibid.*, pp. 127-128, 133, 107, 134. See Mircea Eliade, *The Myth of the Eternal Return*, trans. Willard R. Trask (London, 1955). Eliade describes cyclical time as the time of primitive man: "Basically . . . the life of archaic man (a life reduced to the repetition of archetypal acts, that is, to categories and not to events . . .), although it takes place in time, does not bear the burden of time, does not record time's irreversibility; in other words, completely ignores what is especially characteristic and decisive in a consciousness of time. . . . The primitive lives in a continual present" (p. 86).

[39] Adolf Stender-Petersen, *Geschichte der russischen Literatur* (Munich, 1957), p. 236. Desnitsky, *Izbrannye stat'i*, p. 302, is correct in tracing the style of the passage back to Gogol.

world's beginning, gloomy and of inexplicable content. . . .

. . . .

The devil take it, the sea! Its very calm and immobility does not give birth to a joyful feeling; in [it] . . . man only sees the same boundless . . . force which . . . mocks his proud will and so deeply buries his bold plans and all his labor and toil.

Mountains . . . were also not created for the joy of man. They are menacing, terrifying . . . ; they too vividly remind us of our mortality and hold us in terror and anguish for our lives.[40]

Mountains, cliffs, precipices, the tumultuous and unfathomable sea were among the customary landscapes of the romantics, as "grand, gloomy and wild" were characteristic epithets. However, only an extremely shortsighted criticism would refuse to see anything at work here except another example of Goncharov's "anti-romanticism." Where Goncharov had previously introduced the grandiose and grandiloquent into his fiction as objects for parody and burlesque, he now rejects them, not out of a preference for "common" reality, but in order to substitute an imaginary world of his own invention.

He sets out to create his own version of the natural world through another string of carefully elaborated parallelisms, which repeat the images of the opening while depriving them of their intimidating force. Oblomov's dreaming mind "humanizes" an indifferent and formless nature: he levels it to a human scale, animates it with human presences, and imposes a human-like orderliness upon it. The mountains in Oblomovka become "only models of those terrible far-away mountains which terrify the imagination." The great and anonymous sea is reduced to a river that "runs gaily, playing and romping." The sky that had seemed so distant and untouchable now "presses closer to the earth . . . in order to embrace it more firmly and with love. . . ." Oblomovka turns out to be a land of "joyful, smiling *paysages*," of seasons that follow each other "correctly . . . in a prescribed . . . order," of a nature so predictable that storms come only at their "appointed time" and even the force of the raindrops seems to be the same each year. Winters do not freeze nor do summers scorch. The world is joined in perfect harmony: ". . . the sun once again with its clear smile of love scans . . . the fields and hillocks, and the whole land again smiles in happiness in response to the sun."[41]

"Oblomov's Dream" not only presents a perfectly harmonious and timeless world, but strives to envision a human condition without passion, labor, sorrow, sin, knowledge, and perhaps even death. "This spot blessed by God" is unvisited by God's plagues, untouched by violence and crime, and death itself is viewed as an "extraordinary occurrence." Men in their forties, there, look like youths, and when the old finally die, they do so without pain and suffering, but fade away "as if by stealth." Its citizens, we are told, carefully avoid all forms of passion (passion belongs to the stormy sea and menacing mountains), regard work as punishment, never torment themselves with intellectual or moral questions, and "hence always have prospered in health and joy and have lived long. . . ." The central image of this land of perfect peace and repose, besides the loving and benevolent sun, is the peaceful and immutable river of life: "They [the Oblomovians] need nothing: life, like a peaceful river, flows by them; their lot is only to sit on the shore of this river and observe the inevitable phenomena which, in turn, without invitation, appear before each one of them."[42]

"Oblomov's Dream," then, is a dream of paradise. It is a curious and personal version of paradise, though one consistent with Goncharov's distinctive approach to experience. From the earliest stories through *Oblomov* we encountered a pattern of "deflation" or "reduction" of the sublime by its juxtaposition to an ordinary and prosaic reality—a pattern continued by the introduction to the "Dream," where, through a string of antithetical parallelisms, nature's dramatic configurations are reduced to modest proportions. The entire "Dream" displays this scaling downward to the ordinary. Goncharov's paradise is imaged in homely and domestic terms. The kitchen, barnyard, and meadow mark its boundaries; Oblomovka is

---

[41] *Ibid.*, pp. 103-105.

[42] *Ibid.*, pp. 105, 109, 126-127. See Meyerhoff, p. 25. ". . . The symbolism of time and the river has always meant to convey . . . that time as experienced has the quality of 'flowing' and that this quality is an enduring element within the constantly changing and successive moments of time."

populated not by hosts of angels but by indolent peasants and their equally indolent masters; heaven's manna is a seemingly inexhaustible home-baked pie (*pirog*); its air is fragrant not with exotic "lemon and laurel" but with the more prosaic "smells of wormwood, pine, and bird cherry."[43] However, where Goncharov previously introduced the ordinary into his fiction to mock his heroes' dreams, including dreams of an idyllic condition, he now performs a great shift of perspective and turns the realm of the prosaic into an idyllic landscape. Even the irony that does manage to penetrate the idyll, again through the habitual "scaling downward," is of a playful and loving sort: ". . . there are no roaring lions, no howling tigers, not even bears or wolves. . . . Along the fields and through the village wanders only an abundance of cud-chewing cows, bleating lambs and cackling chickens." The Russian conveys a lyric warmth not felt in translation: . . . net ni l'vov rykayushchikh, ni tigrov revushchikh. . . . tol'ko v obilii korovy zhuyushchie, ovtsy bleyushchie i kury kudakhtayushchie.[44]

Oblomovka resembles the "middle landscapes" of a long tradition of pastoral Arcadias—those ideal terrains lying halfway between the forbidding and impersonal realm of raw nature (the sea and mountains) and the overcivilized city, idyllic places that in the Russian novel (Sergey Aksakov, Turgenev, Tolstoy) are so often identified with the estates of the gentry. Through the novel his dream remains for Oblomov the image of a way of life he can oppose to the bustling and "fragmented" world of Stolz and the "others." However, Oblomovka is more a state of mind than an actual social or geographical location, a retreat into fantasy instead of into the countryside. The urban-rural opposition of traditional pastoral is of secondary importance for Goncharov; indeed, Oblomov finally recovers his dream (for a moment) within the limits of a city, though in its suburbs. A longing for a life without work, passion, guilt, and time haunts Oblomov's imagination, and he tries to discover such a situation wherever he finds himself. "Oblomov's Dream" lacks that esthetic contemplation of nature characteristic of conventional pastoral. Goncharov does

---

[43] The image of "lemon and laurel" is from Pushkin's *The Stone Guest*, where it is used to evoke the atmosphere of Spain.

[44] *Sobr. soch.*, IV, 105-106.

not introduce an urbane and civilized mind to admire the beauties of the rural landscape at a comfortable distance. On the contrary, an almost complete identity between subject and object distinguishes Oblomovian life (Oblomov as a child and the narrator are exceptions). The Oblomovians gaze at the peaceful river, not as an object of esthetic contemplation, but because they perceive in it an image of the unchanging and "inevitable" phenomena of their own lives. Oblomovka is a land where the boundaries between nature and man have become blurred, where nature assumes the benevolent aspects projected upon it by the human mind while man submerges himself in the aimless flow of the natural world. It is a mindless and undifferentiated world, an asylum not only from the complexities of modern society, but from consciousness and individuality. Like the imaginative projections of primitive myth, Oblomovka is a land where man and nature have reverted to a single totality.[45]

And as the existence of mythological Edens depends upon an observance of taboos, Oblomovka is similarly surrounded by forbidden areas. A host of prohibitions circumscribes the range of Ilya Ilich's activity: one must not go far from the house; one must not play in the sun; one must not approach the animals of the yard; the dovecote and the rickety porch that encircles the house are off limits. In the forest (the "wilderness" of the pastoral tradition) there are woodgoblins, demons, and phantoms lying in wait for the disobedient child. Most of all, one must never approach the ravine, which becomes a symbol of all that is forbidden, for the smell of death is there.[46]

The introduction of taboos creates a double image in the

[45] Ernst Cassirer calls the harmony of nature and man, "the unity of life, . . . the characteristic and outstanding feature of the mythical world. . . ." *An Essay on Man: An Introduction to a Philosophy of Human Culture* (New Haven, 1944), pp. 79-84. One of the specific images the "Dream" employs to describe the unity of the world, the sky coming close to the earth "to embrace it . . . with love," is an archetypal image of primitive mythology. See Mircea Eliade, *Myths, Dreams and Mysteries,* trans. Philip Mairet (London, 1960), pp. 59-60. Gogol used it in the famous opening passage of "Sorochinsky Fair." Eliade, *ibid.,* pp. 45-48, 59-72, finds the nostalgia for a primordial condition, in which history, death, sexuality (cf. "passion" in "Oblomov's Dream"), and work are unknown, central to mythic thought.

[46] *Sobr. soch.,* IV, 111.

"Dream"—the dream as a pastoral idyll and the dream as an anxious nightmare. This double image appears at a number of points but is highlighted by two fairy tales standing at its center. The first is a promise of paradise. Ilya Ilich's nurse whispers to him of

> some unknown land where there is no night, no cold, where wonders keep happening, where rivers of milk and honey flow, where no one does anything the whole year round, and fine fellows like Ilya Ilich and maidens, more beautiful than the tale can tell or the pen describe, are carefree the livelong day.
>
> And there lives a kind of enchantress, sometimes appearing to us in the form of a pike, who chooses for herself as a favorite some quiet, harmless fellow, in other words, some lazybones whom everyone insults, and she showers him freely with all sorts of good things, and he eats to his heart's content, arrays himself in ready-made clothes, and then marries some incredible beauty, Militrisa Kirbitevna.[47]

The second tale, which sends Ilya Ilich running into the nurse's arms with tears of terror in his eyes, is a familiar Russian legend about the bear who has lost his leg and who roams the earth on a wooden substitute searching for it.[48] For the remainder of the novel Oblomov carries with him this double image of the "Dream"—an incapacitating wound which provokes anxiety and a vision of a world of perfect peace and contentment where he has been chosen and is loved. The bliss that is paradise will continue to be embodied in food and in marriage to a beautiful woman. Unfortunately the beautiful woman and the woman who feeds him "to his heart's content" do not turn out to be one and the same.[49]

[47] *Ibid.*, p. 120. "The tale cannot tell . . ." is a traditional folk tale formula. Yu. M. Sokolov, *Russkiy fol'klor* (Moscow, 1938), p. 323. Militrisa Kirbitevna is a character in the tale *Bova Korolevich*, which came to Russia probably in the sixteenth century and goes back to the *chanson de geste Beuve de Hanstone* (*Beuve d'Antone*). It gradually was incorporated into Russian folklore.

[48] The bear's song, which is quoted in the text, *Sobr. soch.*, IV, 123, may be found in a similar version in Sokolov, p. 333. The bear in Russian folklore, Sokolov states, is always "clumsy and awkward."

[49] In Oblomov's final illness his left leg grows numb, a coincidence that

The folklore and fairy-tale elements in "Oblomov's Dream," its mythic echoes of a paradisiac landscape circled by a haunted forest, turn it away from a mimetic rendering of an actual remembered landscape to the imaginative dreamlike projections of romance—though, perversely, it is a romance of the commonplace, a Platonism stood on its head, so that the prosaic world of concrete things becomes timeless and eternal.[50] The choice of so humble a place for Oblomov's ideal may easily return the text to an ironic mode as we are made aware of the discrepancy between what is presented and the value placed upon it. The narrator, after the lengthy lyrical overture of the opening, soon reasserts his usual ironic tone. As the "Dream" swings back and forth from unconscious wish to unconscious anxiety, his ironic stance acts to keep both the longing and the terror at a distance. In Freudian terms, it is the "Dream's" "censor"; in literary terms, its "point of view." From the narrator's standpoint, which is sociological and psychological, the terror is equated with primitive superstition, the idyll with Russian backwardness. Though we may not accept the explanations, or accept them only partly, without allowing them to detract from the existential longings and terrors the

would undoubtedly delight the psychoanalytically inclined. *Sobr. soch.*, IV, 444. Freudian theory perceives an analogous duality in dreams—the dream as wish fulfillment and as a recapitulation of a trauma. See *The Basic Writings of Sigmund Freud*, Book II: *The Interpretation of Dreams*, trans. and ed. A. A. Brill (New York, 1938), and Sigmund Freud, *Beyond the Pleasure Principle*, trans. and ed. James Strachey (New York, 1961). Levin, *The Gates of Horn*, p. 28, finds the same double tendency at the heart of the literary process: "The literary imagination, as it refracts the real world, is likely to show either a wishful or else an anxious tendency, to emphasize the aspirations or the revulsions of its epoch, to produce an idyll or a satire." *Oblomov* does both.

[50] See V. S. Pritchett, *The Living Novel* (London, 1946), p. 239. "The undertone of dream and fairy tale runs through the book like the murmur of a stream, so that to call Goncharov a realist is misleading." Also Frye, *Anatomy*, p. 186. "The romance is nearest of all literary forms to the wish-fulfillment dream. . . . The perennially childlike quality of romance is marked by its extraordinarily persistent nostalgia, its search for some kind of imaginative golden age in time or space." Frye, pp. 136-137, also notes a tendency of romance "to displace myth in a human direction and . . . to conventionalize content in an idealized direction." For a useful collection of modern definitions of romance, see Eleanor Terry Lincoln (ed.), *Pastoral and Romance* (Englewood Cliffs, N.J., 1969).

179

"Dream" evokes, the irony prepares us to read the "Dream" with critical distance.

The other point of view belongs to the central character of the "Dream"—the young Oblomov. Goncharov constantly reminds the reader that he is viewing the world as perceived through the prism of a child's imagination: "The mind of the child observed. . . ." "The child gazed. . . ." "The child sees. . . ." At times the world is "made strange," as if the child were seeing it "for the first time." Ilyusha has not yet learned to distinguish shadows from substances.

> . . . he sees Antip going for water, and another Antip, ten times the size of the real one, is walking beside him along the earth, and the water barrel seems the size of the house, and the shadow of the house covers the whole meadow; the shadow took only two steps along the meadow and it was already beyond the hill, though Antip had not yet managed to leave the yard.
>
> The child also took two steps; one more step and he too would be beyond the hill.[51]

The child's role of observer "distances" him from the world of his perceptions. He is part of Oblomovka, but he is also on the outside looking in. Also, the young Ilyusha has not yet accepted the conditions upon which Oblomovian paradise depends—its rigid taboos and prohibitions. Oblomov as a child does not display the paralyzing passivity that will characterize the man. On the contrary, he is "a restless boy," "frisky," even a bit of a rebel. Unobserved for a moment, he rushes out into the sun, runs to the forbidden dovecote and porch, eats wild roots, which he prefers to his mother's jam and apples, and even ventures to the ravine, where terror at last overcomes him. Held fast to his mother's side, he feels drawn outside by the fragrance of lilacs—as later he will feel drawn to the lilacs surrounding the image of Olga Ilinskaya.[52]

The separation of the child from the static world surrounding him engenders the possibility of a story—an event in time. It is the child's

---

[51] *Sobr. soch.*, IV, 112, 113, 116. The term "making strange" was made popular by Viktor Shklovsky. See *O teorii prozy* (Moscow-Leningrad, 1925), pp. 12ff.

[52] *Sobr. soch.*, IV, 111-113, 117.

story; the world that is the object of his gaze remains immutable and timeless. Though made possible by the distancing of Ilyusha from Oblomovka, it relates the process of his incorporation into it. After his several abortive efforts to break out of Oblomovka's encircling ring, the child, at the conclusion of the "Dream," concentrates all his energies into one last effort. A demon, we are told, takes hold of him, and he is filled with an irrepressible urge to break all the taboos and cross all the lines. The demon's urgings prove irresistible, and, suddenly, the child bolts. He is out with the peasant children (the "others"), throwing snowballs, with the wind rushing in his face, "his breast seized with joy." It is not for long. Parental authority quickly reasserts itself! ". . . they took possession of the young master, wrapped him up in a sheepskin coat they had grabbed on the way, then in two blankets, and triumphantly carried him home in their arms."[53] The "Dream" ends in a defeat. When we next encounter Oblomov, he will tell us, ". . . as my life began, it was extinguished."

"Oblomov's Dream," though in many ways a self-enclosed piece, is intimately tied to the rest of the novel—not by a narrative plot line, but through certain repeated patterns and images. The sun that "with its clear smile of love" stands sentinel over Oblomovka, the "bright days" that bless its summers, also guard Oblomov's summer love of Olga and return for a last moment to brighten the darkness of his decline. The major movement of the novel is, as we have seen, from light to dark, from summer to winter, a pattern presaged by the "Dream," as a typical day in the life of Oblomovka is traced from sunrise to dusk and the entire dream sequence moves from mid-summer to winter. The image of life as a peaceful, inevitable flow, like that of a river, becomes the usual image in the novel for peace and contentment—curiously, for Stolz as well as Oblomov.[54] As there are lines and boundaries in Oblomovka that it is forbidden to cross, there are lines throughout the novel Oblomov fails to traverse: the line he perceives as separating knowledge from life,[55] the line between "I" and "the others," and, finally, the boundary formed by

[53] *Ibid.*, pp. 146-147.

[54] *Ibid.*, pp. 210, 224, 388, 417, 438, 464, 487. The "peaceful river" is used as a metaphor for the absence of passion as well as the flow of life.

[55] See *ibid.*, p. 66.

the Neva River, for he will be on one side, Olga on the other, and the river will prove uncrossable.

Finally, the child's story recapitulates in miniature the story of the man. Ilyusha's attempt to break through Oblomovka's enclosing circle of taboos constituted the major (and only) action of the "Dream," and the adult Oblomov's similar effort to escape his isolation and join the world of the "others" provides a central action of the novel. The two stories conclude with similar images. The "Dream" ends in winter and with a symbolic death of the spirit—the sheepskin coat thrown in triumph over the mutinous child. At the climax of the novel Zakhar throws the fateful dressing gown over an Oblomov defeated in love, as the snows of another winter cover the earth like a "death shroud." Paradoxically, Oblomov's paradise, the object of his desire, is associated with defeat and death.[56]

THE ROMANCE OF SUMMER

If all time is eternally present
All time is unredeemable.
What might have been is an abstraction
Remaining a perpetual possibility
Only in a world of speculation.
What might have been and what has been
Point to one end, which is always present.
Footfalls echo in the memory
Down the passage which we did not take
Towards the door we never opened
Into the rose garden.
"Burnt Norton," Four Quartets, T. S. Eliot

"I slept."
"Why?"
"So as not to notice time. . . ."[57]

Earlier, following Prutskov, I described the pattern of the novel as forming a circle—from dream to reality and back to dream. In

---

[56] The peace of Oblomovka is constantly compared to death. See *ibid.*, pp. 104, 107, 116: "A sleep like death," "a death-like silence," "an imperturbable peace, as if everything had died," "an all-consuming, insuperable sleep, a true semblance of death."

[57] *Sobr. soch.*, IV, 361.

Part Two Oblomov puts away the dressing gown, abandons the dusty flat on Gorokhovaya Street for a *dacha* outside the city, and enters the world of "the others." In response to Stolz's urgings he attempts to break out of his isolation and find love.

However, in venturing into the world Oblomov brings with him many of the qualities of his dreams. The love story retains the illusory nature and idealizing tendencies of "Oblomov's Dream," though they are idealizations of a different sort. Where "Oblomov's Dream" raised a prosaic reality to a paradisiac condition, the love episode presents an abstract and "poetic" version of the idyll. The "Dream" evoked a preternatural world sometimes resembling and imitating a fairy tale; Oblomov's love story is the kind of romance more readily found in the nineteenth century. Though nothing "unrealistic" occurs, much of the presentation suggests a realm of experience beyond the usual arena of human complication.

The romance is for the most part enacted outside the limits of the social world. Until its conclusion, when social convention and obligation again intrude, the lovers remain alone in the park they have selected for their rendezvous, separated from society by "a magic circle of love." As in Oblomovka, the landscape is bathed in sunlight and nature's menacing aspects, its storms and tempests, have been momentarily shunted to the side: "Hot summer reigns; . . . everything is . . . still, and . . . feeling flows smoothly like a river. . . ."[58] However, the lovers' idyll never acquires a specific and concretely rendered geography like that of Oblomovka. The atmosphere is extremely rarefied. The natural world appears not in its abundance and variety but as abstracted into two images—light and lilacs.

The images are emblematic. Light is a traditional image of grace, and lilac, in the context of the novel, also promises redemption—"the flower of life" Olga calls it.[59] Olga is so closely identified with the two images, especially the light, that at times she stands in danger of losing corporeality and turning into pure symbol. Her face radiates "an even, peaceful light"; "her gaze stands above him [Oblomov] like the sun"; she plays "the role of his guiding star"; "her eyes glow with the triumph of love . . ."; she sees Oblomov as a man who will

---

[58] *Ibid.*, pp. 248, 275.   [59] *Ibid.*, p. 242.

waken to life through "the light of her gaze." Though Olga later touches solid ground in a crucial moment of the romance, for much of its course she is converted into a devotional ikon or the apparition of a dream: "He sees her in the distance rising to the heavens like an angel; she is ascending a hill; her feet touch the ground so lightly; her figure undulates. He sets out after her, but she barely touches the grass, and she actually seems to be flying away."[60]

The discourse of love has an airy and unreal quality about it. Though Oblomov at times displays an engaging frankness, the lovers generally avoid direct expressions of their feelings. They talk around their subject—in "hints" as the narrator puts it.[61] Olga tears off a lilac branch, and later, in "vexation" with Oblomov, throws it away. When Oblomov returns the broken branch, it is a sign, as we learn only after several pages, that he recognizes her feelings for him. A second lilac branch offered by Olga indicates that she has forgiven him for daring to presume about her affections. Nothing is spoken; only hinted.

> "What's that?" he asked in confusion.
> "You see—a branch."
> "What kind of branch?" . . .
> "Lilac."
> "I know, but what does it mean?"
> "It's the flower of life and—" . . .
> "And?"
> "My vexation. . . ."
> "Then I can hope. . . ."
> "For everything! But—"[62]

The repeated imagery imparts a lyrical quality to the story. Lilacs and light and their associations—"flower of life," "triumph of love," etc.—have a certain "poetic" nuance. The terms through which the images are presented may at times strike the reader as strained, but for the moment we are concerned with how they operate in the con-

---

[60] *Ibid.*, pp. 195, 200, 239, 271, 254, 285. The comparison to an angel is made several times (cf. pp. 258, 273, 275).

[61] *Ibid.*, pp. 238, 247.   [62] *Ibid.*, pp. 215-217, 226, 232, 242.

text of the novel. Light and lilacs in their frequent repetition become lyrical refrains through which Goncharov strives to suggest what he calls a "poem of love"[63]—a poem that underlies or complements the story. A lyric, or a song, is also one of the recurrent metaphors of the romance. Oblomov falls in love upon hearing Olga sing "Casta diva" from Bellini's *Norma,* and she is continually associated with the aria and with music.[64] Love eventually takes on the shape of a song in the imaginations of the lovers: "Thus one and the same motif was played between them in a multitude of variations. Their meetings, their conversations were all a single song, a single sound, a single light which burned brightly and whose rays broke up and were refracted into rose, green, and yellow hues and shimmered in the surrounding atmosphere."[65]

The passage can be read as both a description of the artist's technique and an expression of his understanding of Olga's and Oblomov's romance. Like his characters, Goncharov plays upon "one and the same motif"—the love story's images. In continually returning to the images that marked its inception, the romance acquires a double tendency. As the story unfolds, the "poem of love" holds on to the moment when love began—the singing of "Casta diva," the breaking of the lilac branch, and the vision of light. Narrative exists in time; lyricism is directed toward the instant of emotion. In lingering upon several lyrical tokens, Goncharov strives to convey his understanding of Oblomov's love as an attempt to retain a single and unchanging moment. The lovers' meetings and their conversations are not viewed as a number of discrete events forming a sequence in time. They are instead "a single song" which merely appears in "a multitude of variations," "a single light" refracted into the various hues of its spectrum, but nevertheless the same light.[66]

Oblomov's romance revolves around images of permanence and grace similar to those of his dreams. The central images of "Oblo-

---

[63] *Ibid.,* p. 311.

[64] *Ibid.,* pp. 197-204, 216-218, 226, 242-244.

[65] *Ibid.,* p. 253.

[66] Cf. *ibid.,* p. 282. "Notwithstanding the frequent modifications of this rosy atmosphere, the cloudless horizon was its fundamental basis."

mov's Dream" were the "loving" sun and the "peaceful" immutable river. Another dream projected the idyll of childhood into the future. It visualized an estate like Oblomovka of "clear days, clear faces . . . , eternal summer, eternal joy, sweet food, and sweet idleness." A beautiful woman stood at its center. Oblomov envisioned her as "the queen of everything surrounding her, his deity—a woman! a wife!"[67] In the romance Oblomov attempts to recapture in reality the images and conditions of his dreams. Its season, like the season of the dream, is summer; its heroine, a woman endowed with the light of divinity. Olga's light, like Oblomovka's river, is "smooth, peaceful." Living with her, ". . . he would feel life, its quiet flow, its sweet streams. . . ." Like the sun, Olga promises life: ". . . without you there is neither day nor life; at night I dream of flowering valleys."[68]

But the dream was of "eternal summer," and in actuality it proves as short-lived and illusory as the moment of a dream. Oblomov soon perceives its illusory nature: "While love appeared in the form of a light smiling vision, while it sounded in 'Casta diva,' was carried along by the fragrance of a lilac branch, by unspoken sympathy and a shy glance, I did not trust it, taking it for a play of the imagination. . . ."[69] The very vehicles of the romance—the images that give it its tone and imply its significance, the shy hints of "unspoken sympathy" that constitute its discourse—are ultimately viewed as something insubstantial and unreal. The play of imagery was merely "a play of the imagination." The world within the magic circle turns out to be a "fairy-tale land." The "flowering summer poem" must come to an end because ". . . it lacked sufficient content." The choice of images underlines the momentary and fragile nature of the experience: a summer sun, lilacs that fade, and a brief but compelling song—images in which "there was reflected but one moment, one ephemeral breath of love, its one morning, one fanciful pattern."[70] Goncharov creates "a poem" only to reject and finally destroy it.

He destroys it through the operation of the same images that convey its insubstantiality. The images of the romance serve a double

---

[67] *Ibid.*, pp. 79-80. [68] *Ibid.*, pp. 195, 253, 224, 286.
[69] *Ibid.*, p. 258. The comparison to a dream is made in the text (p. 282).
[70] *Ibid.*, pp. 282, 311, 254.

function. They express "the poem of love," but they also operate within the narrative. As metaphors they imply a redemptive grace that will transcend time by containing it in a recurring and inextinguishable "poetic moment";[71] like leitmotifs they indicate to what point the story has progressed. Earlier, we saw how a play with lilacs "hints" at the state of Olga's and Oblomov's affections. However, at that point love was still "one and the same motif" played, if not in "a multitude," then in several variations. Later, a shift in imagery—from light to dark, from bright summer to gray autumn, and a fading of lilacs—indicates that the romance has run its course in time.

The narrative of *A Common Story* also hinged on the repetition of several leitmotifs. A number of key verbal signs and images, functioning as the mechanical repetitions of comedy rather than as lyrical tokens, paralleled the central action of the novel. The leitmotifs of *Oblomov* are not parallel but oblique to the action; they anticipate rather than signal events. In telling Stolz of his ideal of life, Oblomov uses "Casta diva" as an emblem of cultural refinement, and moments later Olga is introduced and the song sung. Lilacs fade, skies cloud over, and the "fairy-tale world of love [turns] into an autumn day" even before Oblomov has managed to screw up his courage, cross his "Rubicon," and propose marriage. The autumn rains darken the deserted dachas and park before the final defeat of love and its burial under the snows of winter.[72]

The anticipation of event by image engenders a strong sense of predetermination and inevitability in the novel. It also establishes its major ironic pattern. Where irony in *A Common Story* depended upon the protagonists' differing opinions concerning the nature of reality, in *Oblomov* it derives from a persistent incongruity between the tendencies of the hero's thoughts and the movements of nature. As action grows out of the germ of Oblomov's dreams—the vision of "eternal summer," it is nullified by a process beyond his control—the turn from light to gray, from summer to autumn. In *A Common Story* action and leitmotif stood in perfect consonance, giving that novel an excessively tidy and calculated symmetry. In *Oblomov* they appear in a subtle and complex counterpoint. Love at one point is

[71] *Ibid.*, p. 330.　　[72] *Ibid.*, pp. 186, 203, 282, 239, 311.

called "a music of the nerves" and "a music of the spheres."[73] The
lovers' nerves and the spheres do not play the same melody. Nor are
there any abrupt reversals waiting to rescue Oblomov from the logic
of his life. Unlike his somewhat contrived and abstract fictional ante-
cedent, Oblomov lives in the grip of nature—a nature oblivious of
his dreams.

More precisely, the major tension of the novel results from a clash
between Oblomov's imaginative projections of a timeless condition
and the inevitable movement of time. To escape history is Oblomov's
central ambition.

> And history itself only plunged him into melancholy: you learn
> and read that now years of calamity had come, that man was un-
> happy; or that now he musters his powers, works, struggles, labors,
> and bears terrible hardships, constantly preparing the coming of the
> bright days. And now they have come—here at least history should
> take a rest: no, again clouds appear; once again the structure
> crumbles; again man has to work and struggle. The bright days
> do not come to a standstill; they run on and all life only flows and
> flows, and everything crumbles and breaks.[74]

Thus far we have witnessed two attempts to hold on to the "bright
days"—"Oblomov's Dream" and the love story. In the first instance
the novel evoked a world where time moved in a cyclical pattern, eternally returning to the same, and thereby preserving the sunny landscapes of childhood from change. The summer romance attempted to
concentrate time in an imperishable moment, again emblematized by
images of bright sunlight. In each instance time as a linear or "historical" progression negates Oblomov's effort to hold on to the bright
days. The present circumstances of the dreamer—the dark flat on
Gorokhovaya Street that the sun of May first cannot penetrate—
point to his separation in time from the protective sun of the childhood home. In the romance the movement of time turns the dream
of love's "eternal summer" into a gray autumn. When the skies
darken Oblomov is, as usual, penetrating in his anguish: "What does
it mean? . . . And—love also—love? But I thought it would hang

---

[73] *Ibid.*, p. 244. [74] *Ibid.*, pp. 64-65.

over lovers like a hot noon and nothing would move or breathe in its atmosphere: but there is no peace in love either; it too constantly keeps moving forward—'like all life,' Stolz says. And there has not yet been born the Joshua who would tell it, 'Stand still and do not move!' "[75]

Besides indicating the passage of time, the shift in imagery parallels a change in Oblomov's perception of the nature of love, which further implements the destruction of the "poem." The first indication that "the moment of symbolic hints, significant smiles, and lilac branches has passed irrevocably" is Olga's transformation from the embodiment of the light of love into an incarnation of the principle of duty. Oblomov's Beatrice now appears as his "Cordelia."[76] The relationship, like so many human relationships in Goncharov's fiction, becomes pedagogical, as Olga, exercising a series of calculated wiles and stratagems, attempts to draw Oblomov into the routines of normal social life and an acceptance of its responsibilities. It is this didactic level of their story—Olga's attempted education of Oblomov and his failure to pass the course—that has gained the almost exclusive attention of criticism. However, aside from Oblomov's all-too-evident failure to assume the responsibilities of participation in the adult world, he experiences a second crisis that seems more decisive.

The darkening of the summer sky, the turn to autumn, and the withering of lilacs marks the intrusion of sexual passion into the idyll. Late in the romance Oblomov dares to ask for a kiss. Olga has just appeared to him "in brightness, in radiance . . . , her eyes [glowing] with the triumph of love. . . ." She steps back at Oblomov's attempt to kiss her; the radiance disappears from her eyes and is replaced by an image of storm. Olga, "the angel" of purity and light, becomes "a goddess of pride and wrath." It is the moment in the progress of love when lilacs fade.[77]

The next encroachment of desire upon the idyll occurs, surprisingly, through Olga. Besides her radiant eyes, her other distinguishing physical feature is her eyebrows. They do not lie evenly; one is always raised slightly above the other as if to mark her complication—the woman behind the icon. Suddenly, during one of their encounters, "a

[75] *Ibid.*, p. 273.   [76] *Ibid.*, pp. 247, 251.   [77] *Ibid.*, pp. 271-273.

lunacy of love" overcomes her, and she appears to Oblomov in "a new light." Everything about her "burns" as if there were "a fire" in her—her breast, her breath, her smile, "her burning tears." Oblomov feels paralyzed: "He did not move a finger, did not breathe. And her head lay on his shoulder, her breath covered his cheek with a wave of heat. He also trembled, but did not dare to touch her cheek with his lips." He departs with the thought that he has come across a new image of Olga: whoever she is now, she is not Cordelia. It is their first encounter that does not take place beneath the bright summer sun. Heavy clouds have suddenly covered the sky and plunged trees and bushes into a black, gloomy, and indistinguishable mass. A moment later and we learn that summer is departing, and that not only have the lilacs faded, but the lime trees are withered and the berries gone.[78]

Goncharov's paralleling of the eruption of desire with nature's annual death in autumn reverses traditional associations of passion with the flowering of the green world. It is consistent, however, with the tendencies of Oblomov's dreams. In the "Dream," metaphors of passion—the turbulent sea, the terrible mountains—were systematically deprived of their potency and replaced by homely, unintimidating images of playful streams and gently rolling hills. In still another dream Oblomov envisioned a perfect woman—perfect, above all, because she did not know desire. The woman appeared to him as "an ideal . . . of triumphant peace . . . ; her smile was not passionate, her eyes not moist with desire. . . ." The metaphors of the river and the mountains reappeared. He hoped to discover in her "an immutable physiognomy of peace, an eternal and even flow of feeling." Passion must be contained in an "orderly flow" like that of a river: ". . . passion is a misfortune, like happening to find oneself on a rough, unbearable mountain road where horses stumble and the rider becomes exhausted. But the native village is already in view; one must not lose sight of it, and quickly, quickly get out of the dangerous spot."[79] In the "native village," in Oblomovka, there are no mountains.

Physical desire corrupts the dream. It is the snake in Oblomov's

---

[78] *Ibid.*, pp. 277-281.   [79] *Ibid.*, pp. 210-211.

Garden of Eden.[80] It turns love from a decorous play of light and lilac into an illness, "a gangrene of the soul." "I have become sick with love; I have felt the symptoms of passion," Oblomov writes to Olga, when he would break off the relation before it is too late and "the abyss" envelops him. When he reverses himself and sets out to propose marriage, the meanings implied by the darkening skies and the nature of the abyss become explicit: "You are young and don't know all the dangers, Olga. Sometimes a man has no control over himself; some sort of demonic force takes root in him, darkness descends into his heart and lightning flashes in his eyes. His mind darkens; respect for purity, for innocence, is carried away by the whirlwind; a man forgets himself; passion breathes upon him; he loses control—and then an abyss opens beneath his feet."[81]

Darkening also marks the intrusion of "the others"—the conventional social world—into the "magic circle." The entrance of Olga's gossipy friend Sonechka and her entourage of carefree gentlemen and ladies is, like the eruption of desire, imaged in cloud. They gaze at Oblomov and Olga inquisitively, rumor spreads, Olga's aunt joins the growing ranks of the curious, and the lovers are no longer alone. Before the gaze of the others Oblomov is consumed by guilt: "I presumed to ask for a kiss, . . . and that's a capital crime in the moral code. . . . I'm a seducer, a lady-killer!"[82]

Part Three relates the story of Oblomov's mounting guilt. Necessity returns with autumn: "the poem passes and stern history commences."[83] Oblomov makes a vain attempt to deal with the ordinary demands of life, as usual exaggerates the difficulties, and falls back into the kind of comedy that characterized Part One. But the distorted perspective of the normal world, which previously provided occasions for humorous incidents, now gives rise to a story more grim

---

[80] When Olga saw Oblomov's "fixed passionate gaze . . . something cold, like a snake, crawled into her heart, sobered her from the dream, and the warm fairy-tale world turned into an autumn day when all objects appear gray." *Ibid.*, p. 282.

[81] *Ibid.*, pp. 258-260, 289.   [82] *Ibid.*, pp. 283-284.

[83] *Ibid.*, p. 302.

than humorous. The comedy of "I and the Others" turns into a portrayal of Oblomov's obsessive guilt before the world. At his insistence the engagement has remained a secret and everywhere—on the street, at the opera, in the Summer Garden—Oblomov sees "strange, cold, inquisitive faces" who stare at him as if they know his secret. When the "coarse, slovenly Zakhar" becomes aware of the engagement, "the colors [of the poem of love] are no longer the same"— a kind of ironic contrast we witnessed in Part One. After his encounters with the anonymous crowd, however, Oblomov "long afterwards kept dreaming of something dreary and terrible."[84] When Oblomov finally enters the world of "the others," his existential mode becomes one of guilt and terror.

Terror is generally submerged in the novel, or, as in "Oblomov's Dream," at its edges—in the sinister forest. Out in the world, confounded by obligations and tormented by guilt, Oblomov leaves the sunny landscapes of his "Dream" and enters its nightmare terrains: "He found himself in a forest at night, when in every bush and tree there seems to be a robber, a corpse, a wild beast."[85] When the dream of love finally fails and Olga's tears flow "like the autumn rain" for what is already a memory—"It is not I who weep; memory weeps!"—his guilt before her is indeed terrible: "I am small, pitiful, beggarly—beat me, beat me!"[86]

In a novel where the shape of experience constantly recapitulates and realizes the shape of previous dreams, the love episode constitutes one of the major returns. It marks Oblomov's first attempt to recapture the salient components of his dreams: timelessness, a sunny noontime peace undisturbed by "dark" passion, and a woman with the visage of divinity. It repeats not only the vision of paradise—the eternal summer of bright days—but the images of nightmare that encircled Oblomovka. On the edges of love's idyll, as well as on the edges of the idyll of childhood, stand prohibitive and inhibiting sentinels.

[84] *Ibid.*, p. 330. For the sections of Part Three described here, see pp. 327-345, 358-360, 365-367, 376-377.

[85] *Ibid.*, p. 368. Eliade, *Myths, Dreams and Mysteries*, p. 197, finds the forest an archetypal symbolization of death.

[86] *Sobr. soch.*, IV, 381-382.

In each case they inhibit an assertion of the self. The child's brave attempt to break out beyond the limits imposed by parental authority saw him carried home in triumphant arms wrapped in a sheepskin coat; the adult's effort to break out of "the magic circle of love" and cross "that line where," as Oblomov puts it, "tenderness and grace lose their rights and the realm of manhood begins," ends with a return to the dressing gown.[87] In the first instance external force led to the child's defeat; in the second attempt Oblomov's sense of guilt keeps him from reaching the "realm of manhood." Around the sunny garden of his romance lies the grey world of "the others," the world of adult social relations—work, marriage, the responsibilities of family life. Tempted to join "the others," Oblomov guiltily withdraws. For him they are not his fellow-men but his judges.

Mirsky, who had excellent taste, found the love story of the novel "inadequate" and the heroine "unconvincing."[88] It is a judgment that probably has been passed by many a modern reader. In a novel that is in many ways extremely contemporary to us, the refinements and sentiments of Oblomov's romance may seem dated. Though not without a certain charm and delicacy, the love by "hints" is a bit too chaste, the lyricism too rarefied and self-conscious for modern appetites. Olga as an angel strains our credulity; as a schoolmistress lecturing Oblomov on the virtues of duty and responsibility, our patience.

However, a part of a work of art is ultimately "adequate" or "inadequate" only to the whole that contains it. The romance, whatever its limitations, serves an important function. Of Goncharov's three novels *Oblomov* comes closest to his ideal of a literature that would portray a life that has settled and become fixed in time. Its hero is predetermined by events that took place before the moment of the novel's opening. Much of the work consists of a presentation of Oblomov's successive states of mind as he seeks out the roots of his current impasse. It is this static interplay of dream and reality that undoubtedly provoked Dobrolyubov's sensitive description. "He [Goncharov] reflects every phenomenon of life like a magic mirror; at any given

[87] *Ibid.*, p. 364.
[88] *A History of Russian Literature*, p. 183.

moment, and in obedience to his will, they halt, congeal, and are molded into rigid immobile forms. He can, it seems, halt life itself, fix its most elusive moment forever, and place it before us, so that we may eternally gaze upon it for our instruction or enjoyment."[89] But *Oblomov* is not merely an accumulation of static pictures and "elusive moments." As it attempts to halt time, to "congeal" the phenomena of life into "rigid immobile forms," it also displays a countertendency which places experience into narrative time. "Oblomov's Dream" evoked a timeless world outside of history and causality, but in the larger context of the novel its effect was to grant Oblomov a past and a causal history. It was a dream of paradise regained, but it was also a dream recapitulating Oblomov's childhood. Oblomov's love, in spite of his effort to turn it into an eternal moment, is yet in time. The love is a summer poem, but it is a poem contained in a story. It proceeds from late spring to its full flowering in midsummer to eventual decline. In its passage love moves through crisis and a peripety.

The effect of the story of love as distinct from the poem of love is to inform the tale of Oblomov's life with pathos. In his passivity Oblomov stood in danger of remaining a pathological specimen or a comic object held up "for our instruction or enjoyment." Through the love story Goncharov, in the description of one critic, transplants his hero to a "human level."[90] Oblomov's life may be prefigured by the dream that dominates his mind, but for the moment he has refused to accept its inevitability. In putting away the dressing gown and attempting to reach another human being, he becomes a man, like other men, struggling with his fate. Goncharov abandons the extreme detachment, the comic aloofness, that had characterized earlier sections and moves closer to the hero's interior conflicts. The

[89] N. A. Dobrolyubov, "Chto takoe oblomovshchina," *Izbrannye sochineniya,* ed. A. Lavretsky (Moscow-Leningrad, 1947), p. 78. Also see Stender-Petersen, *Geschichte der Russischen Literatur,* p. 229. ". . . each of his characters is, as it were, poured into its immutable, single form. His method consists . . . of moving his figures, slowly and consistently, in the light of various reflectors. Their human natures are, so to speak, predetermined (*Präexistierendes*), and it is only a question of showing them from all sides and from various angles of vision."

[90] Macauley, *Partisan Review,* xix, No. 2, 177.

novel opens with a somewhat one-dimensional caricature and, as it evolves, Goncharov progressively broadens his initial presentation. Previous glimpses of Oblomov's inner world appeared in dream; in the love story they enter his consciousness. Oblomov begins to achieve a measure of self-awareness. If the romance is "inadequate," it also includes a critique of that inadequacy, formulated by its protagonist. It is Oblomov who defines the play of light and lilac as "a play of the imagination." He fails to break out of his isolation, but in the attempt he becomes aware of the limitations of his own view of experience.

Finally, Goncharov maintains the essentially ironic view of experience that informs the novel through the romance, despite its occasional lapses into sentimentality and an excessive sweetness of tone. Mirsky, while dismissing the love story, praised Parts Three and Four as "unquestionably the highest achievement of Goncharov," an achievement he attributed to the "atmosphere of inevitable doom." The sense of inevitable doom first appears, however, in Part Two, for it is here that the movement of time becomes an active and decisive force in the affairs of the novel. Oblomov is doomed because he cannot live in a world of change. In the romance he tries to realize his dream of permanence, a dream made impossible by the progress of time. The central ironic tension of the novel—the discrepancy between Oblomov's grandiose effort to have the sun "stand still and not move" and the ineluctable forward motion of historical time—is retained to its conclusion but first manifests itself in the story of his summer romance.

CONTRAST AND ALLEGORY

Sometimes I fear that I do not have a single type, but only ideals. . . .
In a letter to I. I. Lkhovsky, August 2, 1857[91]

Andrey Stolz, when he enters the novel, is described in terms designed to present an image of Oblomov's polar opposite. Oblomov is round and soft; Stolz is lean and wiry—"all bone, muscles, and nerves. . . ." Stolz lives in "constant movement" and exercises perfect "unslumbering control over his expended time, labor, spiritual pow-

[91] *Sobr. soch.*, VIII, 291.

ers, and his heart." To achieve self-control he has had to "budget" his emotions and deny the imagination: "There was no room in his soul for the enigmatic, the mysterious, the dream." Oblomov controls nothing: thoughts flit like birds across his smooth unruffled brow; time eludes him; he never finds his labor. While Andrey's life proceeds "stubbornly along a chosen path," Ilya Ilich's turns in circles from dream to dream.[92]

The diametrical opposition of the two friends has given rise to a persistent tendency of criticism to allegorize the novel. Stolz and Oblomov cease to be important, and an idea, or in Oblomov's case a condition, Oblomovism, takes precedence. Stolz is treated as an emblem of the progress- and achievement-oriented West; Oblomov incarnates the "indolence" of the gentry, or in some versions the Russian temperament.[93] Such a reading finds support in the text. Stolz's description concludes with one of Goncharov's rare and oft-quoted asides to the reader, pointing to both his Western origins and his didactic function as an embodiment of Russia's promise: "How many Stolzes must soon appear with Russian names!" Not only Andrey's ancestry, but his education as well, is non-Russian. His father, an industrious German burgher, personally undertook the son's education and instilled in him the virtues of self-discipline and practicality—virtues he exemplifies for Oblomov and implicitly for everyone with a "Russian name." Oblomov, we are constantly reminded, is a *barin*—a master—and ". . . he can do nothing and does nothing; others do everything for him—he has a Zakhar and [at home] still another 300 Zakhars. . . ." Goncharov identifies Ilya Ilich—the

[92] *Ibid.*, IV, 167-171.

[93] Both readings can be traced back to Dobrolyubov's influential (and perceptive) article, "Chto takoe oblomovshchina," though it gave greater emphasis to Oblomov's social status. See *Izbrannye sochineniya*, pp. 79, 82. "The story [of Oblomov] . . . is not . . . such an important story. But Russian life is reflected in it; the living contemporary Russian type stands before us. . . . The main thing here is not Oblomov but Oblomovism." Though an allegorization of the novel is implicit in such a reading and in most subsequent Russian criticism, which proceeds from Dobrolyubov, the term is not usually employed. However, see Tseytlin, *I. A. Goncharov*, p. 173. "This [Oblomov] is more than a type; it is an allegorical portrait of a whole way of life. . . ."

name is typically Russian—with at least one aspect of Russia: its "Asiatic" backwardness. Through much of the novel Stolz, away on business, beckons Oblomov to Europe, but Oblomov prefers to dream of Oblomovka, which, we are told, lies somewhere on the edges of Asiatic Russia. Oblivious to history and progress, he wraps himself in "an Eastern dressing gown of Persian cloth without the slightest suggestion of Europe about it. . . ."[94]

However, a reading limited to expounding Oblomov's and Stolz's antithetical opposition not only fails to do justice to the novel's intricacies of thought and experience; it does not even accurately describe what we may call its surface schema—an ideological framework to which experience is occasionally referred but that proves unable to contain it. Stolz does tend toward the unitary condition of an allegorical agent: he becomes identified with an idea. But the idea differs from the common description and proves unable completely to obscure Stolz's existence as a fairly complex, if not altogether successful, novelistic character.

Stolz, despite his dedication to an ethos of work and activity, is ultimately conceived of as an emblem of synthesis—a figure who will mediate the moral extremes of the novel. As in *A Common Story*, where Goncharov posited ethical opposites and then proceeded to bring them together, the major tendency of *Oblomov* is toward unity and reconciliation. Stolz, we learn in the opening sentence of his biography, was "only half German"; his mother was Russian, a circumstance to which Goncharov grants particular emphasis. He describes her reading to the young Andryusha from the lives of the Russian saints, acquainting him with Russian literature, relating the epic tales of Russia's heroic past—tales like those Ilya Ilich heard from his mother at Oblomovka. Her capacity for sentiment—she weeps easily—is viewed as a distinctly Russian quality as compared to the father's Germanic severity. Goncharov presents her values not only as Russian but as the special property of one class of Russians, the aristocracy. Stolz's mother envisions her son as an "ideal gentleman" (*ideal barina*) and strives to cultivate in him a delicacy of sentiment

[94] *Sobr. soch.*, IV, 392-393, 8. *Khalat*, "dressing gown," has the derivative *khalatnost'* (adjective, *khalatnyy*), which means "carelessness," "negligence."

and sensitivity to art that his "bourgeois" father lacks. Like Olga, she is associated with music. We encounter her at a piano playing Herz's variations,[95] singing to her son of flowers and "the poetry of life." Andrey, we are told, spent his life shuttling between two extremities: his mother's fragrant room, her piano, the portrait gallery of a neighboring prince where he views the delicate profiles and white hands of a noble lineage and, at the other pole, the bare, severe, workaday office of his father.[96]

Stolz's spiritual legacy, then, is twofold. When he left his native village to make his way in the world, unlike Oblomov with his one dressing gown, Andrey bore two coats—his father's rude oilskin mackintosh and an elegant frock coat the mother had bequeathed her son. But the second side, the mother's, remains a potential to be realized. For much of the novel Stolz is entirely his father's son—all "bone, muscles, and nerves." Only in the success of his marriage to Olga does he recover the maternal images. The recently married couple surround themselves with tokens of memory, among them the father's oilskin coat. The place of honor is given to a piano. It was the mother, we are told, "with her songs and tender whispers, then the prince's variegated household, then the university, books, and society [that] led Andrey away from the narrow rut his father had traced out for him; Russian life had drawn its invisible patterns and had turned a colorless sketch into a broad and bright portrait."[97]

At the conclusion of the novel Stolz combines his father's and mother's spiritual inheritances into a perfect unity of self, into one "broad portrait."[98] He fuses discipline and sensibility, action and sentiment, practicality and art—values that in the context of the novel are perceived as respectively Western and Russian, bourgeois and aristocratic, paternal and maternal. If *Oblomov* was indeed the swan song of the Russian gentry, it was the second set of values, the mother's, that Goncharov would preserve. But in the process of achieving

---

[95] Henri (Heinrich) Herz (1803-1888), a popular German pianist and composer. Goncharov obviously chose him for the implications of his surname, i.e., "heart."

[96] *Sobr. soch.*, IV, 158-164.   [97] *Ibid.*, pp. 460-461.

[98] See Mazon, *Ivan Gontcharov*, p. 133.

perfection as opposed to its final consummation, Stolz, contrary to what might be expected, loses some of his allegorical rigidity and comes closer to the more usual condition of a novelistic character—someone "as we are."[99]

Allegory is the most intellectual of fictional modes.[100] The allegorical agent stands in a one-to-one relation to a single idea or moral concept. He is Good Deeds or Indolence, Hope or Despair, Truth or Falsity and not a blend of several qualities. ". . . the particular effect at any given moment is one of discrete particularity: the Ideas are presented . . . as entities capable of the most refined and narrow delineation."[101] The power of allegory hinges on unequivocal moral conviction; it founders, or turns into something other than allegory, with excessive ambiguity.[102] When Stolz tenaciously holds to his father's ideal of practical activity, he is all of a piece. But the achievement of unity through a synthesis of *opposed* value systems proves incompatible with allegory. It stretches "the refined and narrow delineation" of ideas to encompass differing moral concepts. Stolz acquires a second dimension, his mother's side. More importantly, Goncharov presents the final unity as the result of a process. Stolz is not made perfect by fiat; it is something he comes to through experience. Whatever we may think of his ultimate perfection, the requirement that he must discover it presupposes a measure of incompleteness in him, aspects of the self that remain to be fulfilled and reconciled. Stolz also has a story—the retrieval of his mother's legacy of sentiment and sensibility.

The story hinges on moments of pathos rather than intellectual argument, further mitigating Stolz's "mechanistic" rigidity.[103] Its opening describes a loss; its resolution, a recovery; in both instances

[99] See above, chap. five.

[100] Coleridge, *Miscellaneous Criticism*, p. 99. ". . . [allegory] cannot be other than spoken consciously."

[101] Angus Fletcher, *Allegory: The Theory of a Symbolic Mode* (Ithaca, 1964), p. 30.

[102] Coleridge, p. 30, speaks of allegory's "unmixed effect."

[103] See Fletcher, p. 55. "Constriction of meaning . . . causes that personification [of an idea] to act somewhat mechanistically. The perfect allegorical agent is . . . a robot. . . ."

Goncharov indicates Andrey's longing for completion, not merely the result. When the boy took leave of his father (the mother had died) to seek his fortune in the world, the two were surrounded by their Russian neighbors, who expressed dismay at the absence of any display of affection or feeling. Finally one old woman, unable to bear it any longer, emitted a loud cry of lamentation and rushed forward to embrace and bless the departing youth. Andrey burst into tears and heard in the simple woman's warm speech "the voice of his mother," saw before him "her tender image." Toward the end of the novel, when Stolz realizes the image of his love in Olga, we are told that "the office, his father's cart, the leather gloves, the greasy accounts, his entire workaday life were now obscured by his happiness. There rose in his memory only the fragrant room of his mother, Herz's variations, the prince's gallery, blue eyes, powdered chestnut hair—all this was in Olga's tender voice. . . ."[104] Through Olga, Stolz retrieves the lost images of childhood and finds his ideal unity. But the effect is not "unmixed." At a level of abstraction Stolz becomes a perfect man. Reading the novel as experience, however, we are given a momentary glimpse of his all-too-human deprivation— the music, the fragrance, the tenderness (the "tender voice," the "tender image") that was lost in all these years of "budgeting" his emotions, "steeling himself," and "puritanical fanaticism."[105]

Comparing Stolz's and Oblomov's stories we discover a similar procedure. In both instances Goncharov, perhaps because of his belief that a writer should restrict himself to "a dominant element" of character,[106] started out with a somewhat one-dimensional or "flat" conception of his protagonist. Oblomov begins the novel as a comic caricature; Stolz often displays "the compartmentalizing of function"—the acting out of a single rigid idea or habit—that characterizes allegorical agents.[107] Both go back in memory to childhood in

---

[104] *Sobr. soch.*, IV, 167, 435.

[105] *Ibid.*, pp. 469, 170. See Coleridge, p. 31. ". . . if the allegoric personage be strongly individualized so as to interest us, we cease to think of it as allegory. . . ."

[106] See *Sobr. soch.*, VIII, 291.

[107] Fletcher, p. 40. Fletcher, pp. 33-34, also argues "that caricature is allegorical in essence . . . ," having in common with it an abstraction of a con-

order to retrieve a lost dimension of their lives, and in the process acquire the complexity and depth engendered by a historical perspective. In addition, pathos and irony enter the novel as the characters' unitary present condition is set against values and potentials that existed in past time—specifically, in childhood. Childhood in *Oblomov* is the crucial experience of man's life; memory, his most important mental faculty.

What ultimately overcomes the "discrete particularity" of the allegorical opposition is the intricate relation that exists between the apparent ethical opposites of the novel. Stolz's and Oblomov's ties of experience and spiritual affinities run much deeper than the momentary historical squabble that has enveloped them. What binds them and makes them inseparable in spirit if not person—they are rarely together and yet are constantly in one another's thoughts—is presented so emphatically as to make it all the more incomprehensible why the bulk of criticism has concentrated its energies on their ideological opposition.[108]

Their ties are also rooted in the experience of childhood. Oblomov and Stolz are of the same age; they come from the same locality; they grew up and studied together. When Oblomov's indolent nature led him to difficulties with his studies, as it invariably did, it was young Andrey who helped him. Nor were the needs that sought fulfillment all Oblomov's. Stolz regularly visited Oblomovka to find a momentary respite from his harsh Spartan education in "the kind, bountiful Russian caresses" that awaited him there. Twice in the novel Oblomov rouses himself to an act of self-assertion, each time to defend Andrey's integrity. "Closer than any relation," he cries out to Tarantev, when the latter challenges him about his friendship with "the German." "I grew up with him, studied together with him. . . ."[109]

---

cept. E. M. Forster implies the same by including caricatures and people who are converted into an idea in his famous definition of "flat" (vs. "round") characters. *Aspects of the Novel* (New York, 1927), 103-104.

[108] Notable exceptions are Macauley, *Partisan Review*, XIX, No. 2, 169-182, to whom I am indebted for pointing out "the most subtle sympathy" that exists between Stolz and Oblomov, and Stilman, *American Slavic and East European Review*, VII, 59, who notes that "the two characters are complementary."

[109] *Sobr. soch.*, IV, 171, 54, 457-459.

Verkhlyovo, Stolz's native village, though a separate entity when the novel opens, was originally a part of Oblomovka. The two friends, "closer than any relations," move through their fictional lives conscious of a lost unity of self analogous to their former unity of place—a unity they seek to restore.

Each seeks it in the other. When Olga defines "the poem of love" as only "half" of life and sets Oblomov the task of searching out the missing half, he immediately thinks of Andrey: "What other sort of life does Andrey want of me?" The thought of Stolz acts as a constant reproach to Oblomov's conscience and provides an image of that part of life—"the realm of manhood"—he feels destined never to attain. Stolz would know how to talk to Olga, how to reach her and lead her to happiness; Stolz would unravel all his entangled affairs and set his disjointed world straight. "Give me some of your will and intelligence and lead me where you wish," he had implored Andrey, and, trapped in the complexities of love, Oblomov turns in thought to his absent friend for those qualities of manliness he lacks.[110]

But Stolz for much of the novel is also "half" a man—his father's side. He needed "the tender image" to complete himself, an image that, whomever else it may touch, is Oblomov's special property. Olga tells us that she had loved him for his tenderness, a tenderness she had never before seen in any man. "Tender, tender, tender!" she sighs ruefully, though not without irony, when Oblomov's failure to achieve the missing half of his self becomes evident.[111] As Oblomov in love was obsessed by thoughts of Stolz, Andrey and Olga, through their courtship and marriage, continually recall their absent friend. The chapter devoted to a description of their married life even concludes with an oft-quoted eulogy to Oblomov. It is spoken by Andrey, who characteristically gets caught up in his own rhetoric and exaggerates. However, the last virtue he ascribes to Oblomov is said as an afterthought and set off from all the others. The mention of Ilya Ilich's "dove-like tenderness" not only has the power to recall him to their memories but provokes Andrey to pledge never to desert his friend, unless some unforeseen "abyss" opens between them.[112] Stolz

---

[110] *Ibid.*, pp. 242-243, 248, 189.   [111] *Ibid.*, pp. 247, 282, 363.
[112] *Ibid.*, p. 481. Also see p. 431.

turns back in memory to childhood for "the tender image," and he, as well as Olga, seeks it in Oblomov.

Oblomov comes to feel that he had played a crucial role in Olga's and Stolz's happy marriage. He perceives his own love as a sacrificial act. Informed by Andrey of the marriage, he is completely without rancor: ". . . tell her, remember, that I met her in order to lead her to this path. . . . I am not ashamed of my role; I do not repent. . . ." It is a surprising statement, one unexpected of a character criticism has taught us to regard incapable of any role, but nevertheless something more than a chance remark. Oblomov has had premonitions that he would play a part in the destiny of his friends. He begins to conceive of his relations with Olga as merely "a preparation for love," for "another." Later, Andrey wonders who could have been responsible for Olga's sudden transformation into a mature woman and immediately thinks of Ilya Ilich.[113] As Olga passes on to Andrey his mother's "tender image," she also conveys something that Oblomov gave her.

What Oblomov passes on to the lovers is never made explicit, but he can only give what he has—his "half of life." In a novel that tends to separate human faculties into discrete antinomies, in the case of the male protagonists the active self versus the passive self, Oblomov is given all the passive virtues—tenderness, repose, imagination. If his "role" in Stolz's success is not specified, he does assert his larger human role: ". . . he finally decides that his life not only took shape [as it did] but was created, even predestined . . . in order to express the possibility of an ideally peaceful side of human life."[114] Goncharov, as usual, treats his hero's claim with irony and qualifies it with an important reminder that he expresses only "one side" of life. However, each vision, Stolz's (before the proclaimed synthesis) as well as Oblomov's, is but half the story. When Andrey through Olga recovers maternal images of tenderness and grace, he also touches Oblomov's world—"the peaceful side"—even to the extent of acquiring the central metaphor of that peace. Life for Stolz had previously resembled "a broad loudly rushing river with seething waves . . ."; in marriage "the rushing subsides . . . [and] both

[113] *Ibid.*, pp. 445, 257-260, 412.   [114] *Ibid.*, pp. 487-488.

their existences, hers and Andrey's, flow together in one river-bed
. . . ; everything was peace and harmony, . . . even as Oblomov had
dreamed."[115]

Stolz, in recovering his mother's spiritual inheritance, had returned
in memory to the world of childhood. In touching Oblomov's part of
life, he again restores contact with childhood, for Oblomov's virtues,
as well as his visions, derive from the unextinguished child in his
nature. Oblomov fails in life because he cannot cross "that line where
tenderness and grace lose their rights and the realm of manhood begins," but Stolz, if not everyone else, turns to him from the other side
of the line for those same virtues. Earlier, Oblomov had accused the
emblematic representatives of the workaday world who attempted to
entice him into action—Stolz was the last in the line—of fragmenting
life in their exclusive concentration upon a social role. As the novel
progresses, social man's fragmentation is seen as resulting from the
loss of a condition that existed in childhood. Stolz, we were told, when
weary with his business affairs and varied social activities, would always come to Oblomov, drawn to him by his "bright childlike soul."
In the presence of Ilya Ilich, in indolent conversation with him on his
wide sofa, his troubled and weary mind would feel calmed and at
peace, as if he had returned "to the birch grove where he had roamed
when still a child."[116]

Stolz's attitude toward Oblomov—not to speak of Goncharov's—
is much more ambivalent than the previous discussion has permitted
me to indicate. As Olga and Stolz in memory and thought turn to
their absent friend, they simultaneously pull away from him, until

[115] *Ibid.*, pp. 348, 465. Macauley, *Partisan Review*, XIX, No. 2, 179, writes:
". . . the memory of Oblomov seems to make a gentle ghostly third with them;
it seems to temper their nervous vitality with a reminder of something else."
Oblomov's ability to affect the lives of those around him is more explicit in the
instance of Agafya Matveevna, the dull widow who through him feels alive
for the first time. See *Sobr. soch.*, IV, 440-441, 485-486.

[116] *Ibid.*, pp. 171-172. Druzhinin noted the fact that everyone in the novel
is drawn to Oblomov and defined his attractive qualities as those of the child—
"qualities which in their own right, in the midst of great practical intricacies,
often open for us a region of truth. . . ." A. V. Druzhinin, "*Oblomov*, roman
I. A. Goncharova," *Goncharov v russkoy kritike*, ed. Polyakov, pp. 176, 180.

Stolz finally feels that the "abyss" has indeed opened and abandons him altogether. The rejection of Oblomov, a character whose entire mental life is directed backward in time, is ultimately a rejection of the past, of everything it signifies except "the tender image." Through their entire courtship the two lovers speak of little else save Ilya Ilich and the past he represents. The courtship turns into a confession in which Olga tells all that occurred between her and Oblomov, and a dispute in which Stolz dissolves the bonds of love and guilt that still bind her to Oblomov's memory.[117] Stolz's attempt to absolve Olga of memory does not stem from a natural impulse to have his fiancée forget her former alliance; that Olga remain without a past is instead a fundamental premise upon which the didacticism of the novel depends. Goncharov presents her as an orphan who, unlike Oblomov or Stolz, has no history to contend with and no entanglements of tradition or family to bind her. Emancipated by Stolz from her nostalgia for Oblomov, that insinuating specter of human frailty, she becomes for Andrey a *tabula rasa* upon which he can write his testament to the future. Olga is a promise, not only for the men who love her, but for her nation: "He dreamed of a mother-creator and a participant in the moral and social life of an entire happy generation."[118] In a novel where character acquires a shadow through descents into memory, only Olga retains "the single light" of allegory.

What it is that Stolz rejects in Oblomov becomes clear only at the moment of his ultimate success in marriage to Olga. Stolz "feared the imagination above all," and imagination means Oblomov. Oblomov's imagination is also directed toward childhood, to a child's timeless Arcadia, but he projects his vision of paradise upon the future, so that his beginnings become his desired end. Earlier he made explicit for Stolz the issues that underlie the argument of the novel. "Doesn't everyone strive for the very same things I dream of?" he asked; ". . . isn't the goal of all your running about, your passions, of wars, trade, politics . . . this ideal of a lost paradise?"[119] Having achieved a final happiness—like that of which "Oblomov had dreamed"—

---

[117] The courtship is described in Part Four, chap. four (*Sobr. soch.*, IV, 409-436).

[118] *Ibid.*, p. 468.   [119] *Ibid.*, p. 187.

Andrey again confronts the same questions, now posed by Olga. Her brief bout with "Oblomovism," the terror of "Oblomovian apathy" and "a slumber of the soul" that inexplicably overcomes her, often baselessly interpreted as a symptom of dissatisfaction with her "bourgeois" husband, results instead from an existential dread of the timeless and immutable condition for which Oblomov longs. In her happiness Olga suddenly realizes that there is nothing left to strive or hope for, that "the circle of life" is complete, that "the road goes no further." Nature speaks to her, and its message is of "a monotonous flow of life without beginning or end." Anxious at her discovery, she turns to her husband "as a sick person to a doctor." His diagnosis confirms her intuition: ". . . you have come to that point when growth in life ceases—when there are no mysteries, when everything is laid bare."[120] In his success Stolz is again asked to confront the paradox implicit in his own purposiveness—the goal achieved, doesn't life stop?

His answers are not answers at all, but therapies. Such questions, he tells Olga, lead one "beyond life's limits" to an "abyss" where there are no solutions, only a nameless melancholy. However, the experience is its own reward. It brings out the best in a man, encourages him to test his powers; life becomes even more attractive after a return from the verge of the abyss to solid ground. If the questions continue to gnaw at the soul, there is always stoicism. The metaphors of Stolz's rhetoric become characteristically those of struggle or economy: ". . . arm yourself with firmness . . . ," "preserve your powers!" for the real issues of life—illness, labor, and the deprivations wrought by time. As paradise totally possesses Oblomov's imagination, Stolz's is entirely circumscribed within images of the fall: "This is the price for Prometheus' fire!" "This is not your sorrow; this is the sorrow of all mankind." In response to Oblomov's earlier questions, Stolz had denied life ultimate meaning, defining it as work "for the sake of work and not for anything else," and his position stays unchanged through the novel. Intellectually, the two friends remain opposites.

[120] *Ibid.*, pp. 469, 472-473. The interpretation of Olga's *Angst* as a symptom of her dissatisfaction with Stolz also derives from Dobrolyubov. Olga, in his view, holds "the portent of a new life" in which Stolz has no part. *Izbrannye sochineniya*, pp. 94-95.

Where one would seduce us into dreaming only of final ends, the other would limit us to stoically and unquestionably bearing the passing minutes of daily existence.[121]

But the situation is ultimately too complex and fluid to be consigned to the rigid compartments of allegory. The tendencies of the heroes' thought constantly break through the enclosing symmetry provided by their ideological opposition. The novel does not merely oppose two ideas; it presents two closely implicated lives. From either side of the line that separates maturity from childhood, Stolz and Oblomov look longingly to each other for the qualities and values they lack—the former for what he has left behind, the latter for what he has not yet achieved. Goncharov saw fit to grant Stolz a final unity that he denied his friend, but Andrey also fails to incorporate the missing half. What evades him is that which Oblomov has too much of—imagination. In a novel like *Oblomov* it is a serious deficiency. Imagination and dream in the novel form the road not only to the unconscious, but to the past. Stolz in narrowing his imaginative life simultaneously severs connections with his personal history. All we get are momentary glimpses, enough to save him from the single dimension of allegory, but insufficient to endow him with the fullness of life. But the sense of life that informs the novel, as we shall see shortly, is also connected with the world of childhood—a world the novel restores largely through Oblomov's imaginative faculties.

With the marriages that conclude the novel Oblomov and Stolz finally step into differing worlds. Stolz's practical talents are wedded to Olga's spiritual refinement in an ideal union. Oblomov sinks back into a prosaic realm of mute things. The two women who hold their destinies emblematize the differing worlds. Agafya Matveevna's description is as carefully pointed against Olga's as Stolz's was against Oblomov's. Where Olga's constantly moving brows indicate her vivacity and her luminous eyes promised spiritual grace, Agafya's face is blank and expressionless. She has no brows, only faint strips of sparse hair; her eyes are a dull gray. The kitchen forms the center

---

[121] *Sobr. soch.*, IV, 474-475, 189. See Milton A. Mays, "Oblomov as Anti-Faust," *Western Humanities Review*, XXI, No. 2 (Spring 1967), 141-152, for a thoughtful and somewhat different discussion of these issues.

of her world; its outer reaches extend no farther than the vegetable patch or the barnyard. Her appearances provide occasions for lengthy catalogues of the varied fixtures and provisions of hearth and home. The images that accrue to her person all suggest physical labor or domestic comfort. The shawl she wears is like a horse-cloth; she stands "erect and immobile like a horse having its collar put on." Her bountiful and imperturbable breasts are like sofa cushions. Approaching her is like coming close to a warm fire. As simile associates her with domestic life, a series of recurring synecdoches totally identifies her with household tasks. The woman disappears and the function takes over. Now she is but a bare arm extended from the kitchen offering Oblomov a steaming pie; now a huge back and bared nape of the neck bent over the stove; and finally, of course, those round and dimpled elbows, "good enough to belong to a countess . . . ," Oblomov exclaims in rapture, elbows constantly in movement— cleaning, sewing, darning, and preparing abundant and interminable meals.[122] As Olga's image dissolves into a ray of spiritual light or the redemptive promise of a sprig of lilac, Agafya is reduced to the status of a kitchen utensil, a domestic beast of burden, or a household furnishing.

The significance of the opposition is evident. Oblomov's entry into the concrete world of Agafya Matveevna marks his fall from grace, while Stolz discovers through Olga a higher realm of spirit and art.[123] Through Part Three the images of the two women contend for Oblomov's soul, as his two countrymen, Stolz and Tarantev, had competed for it earlier. Music, light, and lilac are pitted against casseroles, elbows, and a homely geranium plant.[124] Eventually Agafya triumphs, and if we are are at all in doubt what her triumph means,

---

[122] *Sobr. soch.*, IV, 306-307, 314-315, 324-325, 328, 346-347, 350-351, 394-396, 485. Agafya's family name, Pshenitsyna, comes from the Russian word for "wheat" (*pshenitsa*).

[123] Northrop Frye, in "Nature and Homer," *Fables of Identity: Studies in Poetic Mythology* (New York, 1963), pp. 39-41, gives a brief history of literary divisions of nature into two levels—"the ordinary physical world, which is . . . 'fallen,' " and "the upper world . . . of 'art.' "

[124] See especially *Sobr. soch.*, IV, 308, 324-328, 350-351.

Goncharov makes it clear by having her retrieve from storage that recurrent emblem of Oblomov's doom—the now frayed dressing gown—and restore it to the declining hero. However, even at the moment when Stolz and Oblomov find themselves furthest apart, the situation remains ambiguous. More than one reader has felt uneasy about Stolz's proclaimed salvation and Oblomov's apparent doom[125]—an ambivalence that results, I would suggest, from the differing manners in which Goncharov chose to render their destinies.

The presentation of Stolz's courtship and marriage provides an exceptional moment in Goncharov's fictional corpus. Throughout his career the novelist usually preferred "scenic" narration and restricted the narrative voice to a minimum.[126] *A Common Story* consisted largely of a string of dialogues between uncle and nephew, and Alexander's several love scenes. In *Oblomov* the omniscient narrator has a greater role, but he usually relinquishes the "point of view" to the mind of the dreaming hero. Much of Stolz's love story is *told* rather than *seen*. The narrative is introduced as past experience, but while Oblomov's past achieved immediacy through presentation as his personal dreams—dreams that visualize a recollected reality—the omniscient narrator now immediately betrays the summary tone he sustains for much of the story:

> It is now necessary to go somewhat back to a time before Stolz's arrival at Oblomov's name-day party and to another place far from

[125] The pro-Oblomov argument goes back to Druzhinin, *Goncharov v russkoy kritike*, ed. Polyakov, pp. 161-183, and Apollon Grigor'ev, *Sochineniya*, I, 423.

[126] Both Belinsky and Dobrolyubov commented upon the reticence of the narrator's voice (identified with that of the author) in *A Common Story* and *Oblomov* respectively, and the observation has become a commonplace of criticism. Belinsky, III, 830. Dobrolyubov, p. 76. The distinction between "scenic" narration and narration by a narrator is often associated in English and American criticism with Percy Lubbock, *The Craft of Fiction* (New York, 1921), but is as old as Plato. For a summary of its history and a bibliography, see Norman Friedman, "Point of View in Fiction," in *The Theory of the Novel*, ed. Philip Stevick (New York, 1967), pp. 108-117.

the Vyborg side. There we shall meet characters familiar to the reader. . . .

.   .   .   .

And what about Olga? Didn't she notice his situation or was she indifferent to him?

.   .   .   .

Here is the reason why Stolz. . . .[127]

A conspicuous number of the paragraphs of the summation open with the same personal pronoun (sometimes preceded by a conjunction or adverb), a procedure that not only imparts an extremely logical character to the prose but also suggests a perfunctory interest on the part of the writer: "He immediately saw that it was impossible to amuse her. . . ." "He sometimes came home at the end of the day exhausted from this struggle. . . ." "And he could not understand Olga. . . ." "He with the flame of experience [*sic*] in his hands. . . ." "And he was so completely happy when. . . ." "He reflected about Olga as he had never reflected about anything. . . ." "He approached it slowly. . . ." "He even knew. . . ." "He of course was proud. . . ."[128]

The summary manner of narration, besides falling into a monotonous repetitiveness, lends an abstract and discursive quality to the Olga-Stolz love story.[129] Its abstractness is magnified by the almost total absence of a setting. The lovers meet in Paris, fall in love in Switzerland, but neither location is described. They finally take up residence on the shores of the Black Sea in a cottage crammed with *objets d'art* that are the tokens of their spiritual refinement but that cause the cottage to resemble more a museum that a home.[130]

Though much of the narrative is expository, Goncharov tries to introduce an element of dramatic tension and suspense into Stolz's love story absent from other sections of the novel—presumably to support a view of Stolz as a dynamic personality. Oblomov's and

[127] *Sobr. soch.*, IV, 409, 418, 420.

[128] *Ibid.*, pp. 412-415. Cf. *ibid.*, pp. 416-423, 467-470.

[129] Pisarev noted the summary manner of Stolz's presentation and commented upon its incongruity for a character conceived as a man of action. *Goncharov v russkoy kritike*, ed. Polyakov, p. 128.

[130] *Sobr. soch.*, IV, 459-460.

Olga's love is quickly established as a *fait accompli* whose illusoriness is then exposed; the entire novel in a sense begins with a *fait accompli* (". . . my life began, as it was extinguished"). However, Stolz's love is blocked by an obstacle that must be overcome through action— Olga's emotional attachment to Oblomov. The previous episodes of the novel describe a complex interplay between illusion and reality, past and present, dreaming and wakefulness in a narrative time that is either suspended or considerably slowed. The Stolz-Olga story proceeds in a tidy, linear fashion from a fairly recent past to the "fictive present" of its scenes, from apprehension to dramatic confrontation to successful resolution.[131]

In trying to impart dramatic tension to the Stolz-Olga love story, Goncharov came up against the limitations of his prose style. V. K. Favorin, in an interesting study of the novelist's language, demonstrated Goncharov's inability to distinguish the various forms of his characters' "speech"—dialogue as well as interior monologue—from his own style. Favorin found their speech "weakly individualized and marked by a high degree of smoothness, regularity, and composure . . . ," generally characteristic of the author's own style. The characters' thoughts fall into "a smooth, logical and orderly flow . . . even though this may contradict the conditions of the plot and the experience of the character."[132] Artists, however, frequently turn their limitations into assets. A language characterized by "smoothness, regularity, and composure," by an "orderly flow," can prove eminently suitable for a character whose mode of being is purely reflective and passive. The smooth flow of language, the regular and unvarying phrases of Oblomov's dreams, contributed to the sense of timelessness, of "a dream-like *durée*," in Jane Harrison's phrase, in which nothing happens to alter or disturb the ceaseless flow of life. If the style is passionless, so is the world of Oblomov's dreams. A sub-

[131] A. A. Mendilow, *Time and the Novel* (London-New York, 1952), p. 94. "Mostly the past tense in which the events [of novels] are narrated are [*sic*] transposed by the reader into a fictive present, while any expository material is felt as a past in relation to that present."

[132] Favorin, *Izvestiya Akademii nauk SSSR: otdelenie literatury i yazyka,* IX, No. 5, 352-357. (Author's italics omitted.)

dued nostalgia makes up the larger part of Oblomov's emotional life, and the muted leisurely rhythms of the prose often express an appropriate quality of evocation, as Oblomov tries to summon up in memory his lost paradise.

> . . . a ona nashoptyvaet emu o kakoy-to nevedomoy storone, gde net ni nochey, ni kholoda, gde vsyo sovershayutsya chudesa, gde tekut reki myodu i moloka, gde nikto nichego kruglyy god ne delaet, a den'-den'skoy tol'ko i znayut, chto gulyayut vsyo dobrye molodtsy, takie, kak Il'ya Il'ich, da krasavitsy, chto ni v skazke skazat', ni perom opisat'.[133]
>
> (. . . and she whispers to him of some unknown land where there is no night, no cold, where wonders keep happening, where rivers of milk and honey flow, where no one does anything the whole year round, and fine fellows like Ilya Ilich and maidens, more beautiful than the tale can tell or the pen describe, are carefree the livelong day.)

A prose style distinguished by regularity and smoothness is a liability for a character whose literary mode is active and dramatic. The novelist takes us into Andrey's inner world in a moment of crisis in the following manner:

> On chuvstvoval, chto i ego zdorovyy organizm ne ustoit, esli prodlyatsya eshcho mesyatsy etogo napryazheniya uma, voli, nerv. On ponyal—chto bylo chuzhdo emu dosele—kak tratyatsya sily v etikh skrytykh ot glaz bor'bakh dushi so strast'yu, kak lozhatsya na serdtse neizlechimye rany bez krovi, no porozhdayut stony, kak ukhodit i zhizn'.[134]
>
> (He felt that even his healthy constitution would give way if this strain of his mind, will, and nerves continued for months more. He understood—what had until now been alien to him—how one's powers are lost in these secret struggles of the soul with passion, how incurable wounds cover the heart, which, though bloodless, give rise to moans, how even life fades away.)

[133] Harrison, *Aspects, Aorists and the Classical Tripos*, p. 27. *Sobr. soch.*, IV, 120. The diction here is of course strongly folkloric.

[134] *Sobr. soch.*, IV, 418.

The paragraph's verbal symmetry, which recalls Goncharov's earlier symmetries of structure, is striking. The independent clauses that open the two sentences form a tidy syntactical parallel—a repeated subject (*on*) plus a single verb. The subordinate clauses that follow immediately upon them are fairly even in length (14 and 10 syllables respectively); the second subordinate clause of the initial sentence and the second and third of the following sentence vary no more than five syllables (23, 19, and 18). Two brief clauses of almost identical length (7 and 6 syllables), commencing with the conjunction *no*, form a tidy coda at the paragraph's conclusion. The methodical regularity of the prose can hardly convey "all the torments and tortures of love" Stolz is supposedly experiencing at the moment.

The logical, emotionless tone continues when Olga and Stolz finally get to speak in the brief scenes that decide their fate. The love story acquires an extremely didactic character, as Stolz sets out, in accents as studied as those employed to present his inner thoughts, to instruct Olga concerning "what has been and even perhaps what would be." His prose becomes an exercise in definition—of friendship, love, life, of Olga's experiences and feelings. The copula "to be," often omitted in Russian but nevertheless implied, is his favorite means of joining sentences: "Friendship is a good thing, Olga Sergevna, when it is love between a young man and woman. . . . But God spare us, if it is. . . ." "I know that love is less exacting than friendship, . . . that it is often blind. . . . But for love something is necessary. . . ." "This is not love, this is. . . ." ". . . this is an excess of imagination." ". . . if this is not a sign of some disorder, if you are entirely healthy, then. . . ." "If this is so, then this is not foolishness."[135]

Attempts to inject emotional force into the neutral expository prose or the dry didacticism result either in an exaggerated rhetoric— "That unfading and imperishable love lay mightily, like the power of life, upon their countenances . . ."—or in melodrama—"Judgment has come!" (*Sud nastal!*) introduces the long awaited confrontation that will decide the outcome of the courtship. "The conversation has come!" (*Razgovor nastal!*) inaugurates the interview

---

[135] *Ibid.*, pp. 426-428, 473-474.

that resolves the crisis in their marriage with a repetition of the same verb and the same portentous inflection.[136]

The summary manner of narration, its emotional coldness and abstractness give credence to the critical view that detects an underlying sympathy for Oblomov and coolness toward his ethical antagonist. Goncharov generally appears reluctant to get close to Olga and Stolz, especially in Stolz's maturity, and the consequence is conceptualization instead of rendered experience, "composition" for "creation."[137] Their story also reveals a fundamental limitation of his art that was to have disastrous consequences in his next novel. The narrow range of his style, his view of character as fixed and stable, and his mistrust of sharp emotions made it extremely difficult for him to render dramatic modes of experience. The controlling emotion of *Oblomov* is nostalgia; the pathos the novel communicates derives not from confrontation of character but from the private memories of its protagonists. Even in Oblomov's romance, which is enacted by two characters in present time, emotive function accrued to several fleeting images which quickly passed into tokens of memory.

The artifacts of domestic life also acquire an emotive function, but even here, as we shall see, memory plays a decisive role. The very objects intended to denote Oblomov's fall from grace are often treated in a manner subversive of the intention. Oblomov himself wavers: when his thoughts turn to Stolz and Olga he is consumed by guilt and remorse; confronted with Agafya's domestic and culinary skills he falls into raptures of appreciation. The narrative voice frequently shares his enthusiasm. "And, my God, what a wealth of domestic knowledge they [Agafya and her servant girl] exchanged, not only about culinary matters, but about cloth, thread, sewing, washing linen, dresses, cleaning silks, lace, gloves, taking stains out of various materials, the use of various home-made medical concoctions, herbs—about everything. . . ."[138] The focus is entirely upon concrete nouns, upon things. The passage includes only one verb and

---

[136] *Ibid.*, pp. 476, 424, 470.

[137] Druzhinin observed that "Mr. Goncharov, describing for us Stolz's childhood in great detail and very poetically, . . . cools toward the period of his maturity. . . ." *Goncharov v russkoy kritike*, ed. Polyakov, p. 175.

[138] *Sobr. soch.*, IV, 323.

few adjectives—none to qualify the specific household items that constitute the list. The central catalogue in the Russian—*kholsta, nitok, shit'ya, myt'ya bel'ya, plat'ev, chistki blond, kruzhev, perchatok*—is a list of short nouns, all disyllabic except the monosyllabic *blond,* and *perchatok.* The brevity of the nouns (for Russian), the stress on almost every other syllable, the natural pauses, marked by commas, between substantives without intervening verbs or modifiers make it virtually impossible to read without strong emphasis on practically each word. Where the prose of Stolz's world glides smoothly, evenly, and indiscriminately from abstraction to abstraction, from one rhetorical disquisition to another, Oblomov's frequently stops short upon the things that nurture human existence.

A lyrical apprehension of the things of domesticity is pervasive. Another passage, extending over several pages of which I quote only part, merits attention.

> Kukhnya, chulani, bufet—vsyo bylo ustanovleno postavtsami s posudoy, bol'shimi i nebol'shimi, kruglymi i oval'nymi blyudami, sousnikami, chashkami, grudami tarelok, gorshkami, chugunnymi, mednymi i glynyanymi.
>
> . . . .
>
> Tselye ryady ogromnykh, puzatykh i min'yatyurnykh chaynikov i neskol'ko ryadov farforovykh chashek, prostykh, s zhivopis'yu, s pozolotoy, s devizami, s pylayushchimi serdtsami, s kitaytsami. Bol'shie steklyannye banki s kofe, koritsey, vanil'yu, khrustal'nye chaynitsy, sudki s maslom, s uksusom.
>
> Potom tselye polki zagromozhdeny byli pachkami, sklyankami, korobochkami s domashnimi lekarstvami, s travami, primochkami, plastyryami, spirtami, kamfaroy, s poroshkami, s kuren'yami; tut zhe bylo mylo, snadob'ya dlya chishchen'ya kruzhev, vyvedeniya pyaten i prochee, i prochee. . . .
>
> . . . .
>
> Na polu stoyali kadki masla, bol'shie krytye korchagi s smetanoy, korziny s yaytsami—i chego-chego ne bylo![139]

(The kitchen, the pantries, the sideboard were lined with shelves

[139] *Ibid.,* pp. 482-484.

215

of crockery, with large and small, round and oval dishes, sauce-boats, cups, piles of plates, iron, brass, and earthenware pots.

. . . .

There were whole rows of huge round-bellied, and miniature, teapots and several rows of china cups, plain ones, and others with paintings, gilding, mottoes, flaming hearts, Chinamen. There were large glass jars of coffee, cinnamon, vanilla, crystal tea caddies, cruets of oil, of vinegar.

Then entire shelves were piled with packets, phials, boxes of household remedies, with herbs, lotions, plasters, spirits, camphor, with powders, with incense; there were also soap, fluids for cleaning lace, removing stains, and so on, and so on. . . .

. . . .

On the floor stood tubs of butter, large covered earthen pots of sour cream, baskets of eggs—and what, what was not there!)

This is again prose designed to call attention to itself. It displays an emphatic rhythmic quality, deriving largely from syntactical parallelisms and parallel orders of grammatical forms.[140] The several sentences have a somewhat similar shape, as subject, compound subject, or subject and verb are followed by strings of words and phrases performing the same grammatical function (modification) and in the same grammatical case—often the instrumental plural. Within sentences, in a group of isolated words—*kukhnya, chulani, bufet* (incidentally, a dactylic line)—each word of course balances the other. Successions of words or phrases governed by an identical word form similar parallel groups: *s zhivopis'yu, s pozolotoy, s devizami, s kitaytsami / s poroshkami, s kuren'yami / dlya chishchen'ya kruzhev, vyvedeniya pyaten,* etc. Compound subjects and the phrases joined to them also contribute parallel clusters: *bol'shie steklyannye banki s kofe, koritsey, vanil'yu, . . . sudki s maslom, s uksusom / bol'shie krytye korchagi s smetanoy, korziny s yaytsami / tselye ryady ogrom-*

[140] See V. M. Žirmunskij, "On Rhythmic Prose," in *To Honor Roman Jakobson: Essays on the Occasion of his Seventieth Birthday* (The Hague-Paris, 1967), III, 2376-2388.

*nykh, puzatykh i min'yatyurnykh chaynikov i neskol'ko ryadov far-
forovykh chashek.* In addition, there are pairings of adjectives—
bol'shimi i nebol'shimi, kruglymi i oval'nymi—word repetitions (excluding the pervasive "*s*")within a sentence—*ryady . . . ryadov / i
prochee i prochee / chego-chego*—as well as a repetition that in one
instance helps establish a parallel between sentences, *Tselye ryady . . .
Potom tselye polki. . . .*

Finally, the accumulation of words in the instrumental plural
heightens the rhythmic quality of the prose by creating auditory resonances through the passage (in one instance given added emphasis
by inversion—*gorshkami chugunnymi, mednymi, glinyanymi*) and
strings of words with a similar falling intonation at their endings.
However, though a patterned prose, it is again not a prose that slides
smoothly over its constituent parts, but one that, because of the brevity of its phrases (often consisting of a single nominal), its auditory
resonances, and the fact that it is a static catalogue (in two sentences
even omitting verbs), focuses upon the word or, to be more precise,
the noun—the thing. The cumulative effect is celebrative and lyrical—"and what, what was not there!"—a modest "prose poem"
that is at once a poetry of the prosaic. As Alexander Aduev returned
home at the end of his novel to rediscover the poetry of prose, "a
poetry of a grey sky, a broken fence, wicket gates, and a muddy
pond," Oblomov finds it in the household on the Vyborg side of the
Neva.[141]

"Enter the courtyard [of Agafya's home] and you are enveloped
by a living idyll,"[142] the narrator tells us, and there is indeed a quality
of the idyllic about the interminable catalogues of casseroles, pots, and
pans, of jugs brimming with butter and cream, of pantries stuffed with
hams, cheeses, smoked fish, sacks of mushrooms. The lengthy descriptions of the appurtenances of hearth and home do not merely serve
as a setting, though they contribute importantly to making Oblomov

---

[141] The poet Innokenty Annensky spoke of Goncharov's "incomparable
ability to poeticize the most simple and uncomely thing." "Goncharov i ego
Oblomov," *Russkaya shkola*, No. 4 (April 1892), p. 90.

[142] *Sobr. soch.*, IV, 482.

a convincing inhabitant of an experienced reality, a dweller in "imaginary gardens with real toads in them," as Stolz rarely is. Ultimately they transcend their function as emblems of Oblomov's spiritual defeat. At one point in his portrayal of the bounty and munificence of the Agafya Matveevna kitchen and pantry, the narrator invokes Homer as his muse, and, as in epic literature, the artifacts of daily life and the rich accumulation of concrete detail are indulged in and enjoyed as ends in themselves.[143]

The novel had previously lingered upon scenes of domestic life in "Oblomov's Dream," and the "imperfective" quality of the "Dream" also returns in the Agafya Matveevna episode. The narrative again proceeds from mealtime to mealtime, holiday to holiday, season to season in a continuous flow uninterrupted by "events" that might separate experience into discrete categories of "before and after." As in the "Dream" certain regular repetitions—the turning of a coffee mill, the snapping of thread, the swing of a clock's pendulum, a canary's chirping, Agafya's constantly moving elbows—combine to evoke the eternal rhythms of domestic life.[144] Earlier I described this kind of presentation as an attempt to convey a sense of permanence, but it is a distinctive kind of permanence—not the imperishable "poetic moment" of the romance, but the permanence of an unlimited and immutable process. The process leads nowhere, but it exists in the same durative condition through which all human experience unfolds. While Stolz's story summarizes and conceptualizes, Oblomov's renders mimetically the aimless flow of life as it is being lived.

Ilya Ilich would get up at about nine; sometimes he would catch a fleeting glimpse through the fence-grating of the paper parcel of [Agafya's] brother on his way to the office; then he would take up his coffee. The coffee is, as always, excellent; the cream is thick; the rolls rich and crumbly.

Then he would take up a cigar and listen carefully to the broodhen cackling, the chicks squeaking, the canaries and siskins chirp-

---

[143] *Ibid.*, p. 483. D. S. Merezhkovsky makes some comparisons to Homer, in "I. A. Goncharov, kriticheskiy etyud," *Trud*, VIII (October-December 1890), 594.

[144] See especially *Sobr. soch.*, IV, 323-326, 345-349, 394-397, 488-494.

ing. He did not ask that they be taken away: "They remind me of Oblomovka," he said.[145]

It is certainly the most perplexing aspect of the novel that Oblomov in his apparent spiritual defeat seems very much alive and real while Stolz in his success is a lifeless abstraction. The difficulty diminishes, however, once we realize that the ambiguous treatment, instead of resulting from a momentary indecisiveness on the part of the author, is consistent with a paradox at the heart of *Oblomov*. We have several times noticed a double tendency of wish and anxiety, idyll and nightmare. In each instance the conflicting tendencies resided in an ambiguous vision of childhood. "Oblomov's Dream" presented a child's Arcadia, and yet equated that paradise with death. In the love story Oblomov's attempt to achieve manhood resulted in defeat, but his "bright childlike soul" proved to be the source of his unique and compelling attraction. This ambiguous perception of the world of childhood persists through the Agafya Matveevna episode, for in entering the widow's domain Oblomov fails to discover his human completeness and, as I have already implied and shall make more explicit in the following section, succeeds in regaining the idyllic condition of childhood. The rich feeling for the rhythms and things of domesticity found on the Vyborg side of the Neva is, like almost all the richness of the novel, a product of things remembered. If Stolz seems less alive after his final "success," it is because the price of that success had been a denial, or at least a devaluation, of the dreams of childhood, just as Oblomov's "failure" allows him to retain its tokens and memories. Childhood in *Oblomov* is concurrently a standard of all value and a source of defeat, a realm of absolute freedom and a confinement of the spirit, a condition one longs for and seeks to escape. This double vision finds an analogue in modern psychoanalytic theory whose "wisdom directs us to childhood—not only to the immortal wishes of childhood for the substance of things hoped for, but also to the failure of childhood for the cause of our disease."[146]

---

[145] *Ibid.*, p. 323. Krasnoshchekova, whose *Oblomov I. A. Goncharova* came to my attention after this book was completed, makes some of the same points in comparing the Olga-Stolz and Agafya Matveevna episodes (pp. 66–71).

[146] Norman O. Brown, *Life Against Death: The Psychoanalytical Meaning of History* (New York, 1959), p. 110.

RESOLUTION

The general basis of comedy is . . . a world in which man has made himself, in his conscious activity, complete master of all that otherwise passes as the essential content of his knowledge and achievement; a world whose ends are consequently thrown awry on account of their own lack of substance.

Hegel[147]

Sometimes you look for one thing and you find another.

Sancho Panza

At the opening of Part Four Goncharov introduces a new conception of time, one that dominates the final phase of the novel. Its image is repeated four times—thrice at the opening as an overture to the work's conclusion, a last time to introduce the story of Oblomov's death. The passage of time was previously mirrored in the sun setting to bring a single day in a man's life to a close, or in a fading of lilacs which conclude a season in a man's life; it is now presented in terms of geological changes over the entire planet.

> . . . life did not stand still; its phenomena were constantly changing, but they were changing as gradually and as slowly as the geological transformations of our planet: here a mountain was slowly crumbling away; there the sea was running up onto the shore or receding as it had for centuries and was forming new land.
>
> . . . .
>
> The gradual settling or raising of the bottom of the sea and the crumbling away of mountains took place everywhere. . . .[148]

This new conception presents time as an impersonal and inevitable force, but not as a malevolent one. Previously, a linear or historical time, a time that "constantly keeps moving forward," had intruded into the novel to destroy Oblomov's dreams. "Geological time," the time of Goncharov's planet, though it does not preserve a permanent state of "eternal returns," yet describes patterns that are cyclical instead of linear. The world maintains a perpetual balance. The phe-

[147] *The Philosophy of Fine Art*, trans. F.P.B. Osmaston (London, 1920), IV, 301.
[148] *Sobr. soch.*, IV, 385-386, 388, 488.

nomena of life may be irreversible; they are "constantly changing," but what is brought down in one corner of the universe is restored in another. A mountain crumbles away, and elsewhere the sea forms new land. The oceans carry alluvial silt from one part of the earth only to deposit it in another. Time in Goncharov's new formulation does not proceed in a straight line of successive instances in which every new moment immediately annuls its predecessor, but instead follows the arc of a pendulum, abolishing creation in one sweep, renewing it with another.[149] Though Oblomov had resisted the forward movement of time with dreams of permanence, he now resigns himself to the world's inevitable drift. In Part Four the tension between time and timelessness that dominated the earlier sections of the novel disappears, as the patterns of the hero's life fall into harmony with the cycles of the natural world.

The first swing of time's new pendulum is toward restoration and regeneration. Part Three ended with a symbolic death: the dressing gown Zakhar throws over a defeated Oblomov, the snows that cover the earth until "everything died and was wrapped up in a winding sheet." Oblomov returns to life by submitting to the cycles of "geological time": "But the mountain crumbled a bit more, the sea receded from the shore or flowed onto it, and Oblomov gradually returned to his previous normal life."[150] The narrative resumes the "eventless" imperfective flow described in the previous section, proceeding leisurely from season to season and holiday to holiday, and lingering over the details of domestic life. The image of peace and immutability returns once more, as life "flowed like a river." Apparently the tides of geological change allow for temporary streams of stability.[151]

The next cycle swings downward into decay and disintegration. The final movement of the novel is also one of decline, as Oblomov

---

[149] A time intermediate to timelessness and succession may seem an illogical category, but the literary, as well as philosophical, imagination has often attempted to conceive of such an order. For a brief history, see Frank Kermode, *The Sense of an Ending: Studies in the Theory of Fiction* (New York, 1967), pp. 67-89.

[150] *Sobr. soch.*, IV, 383-386.

[151] See *ibid.*, pp. 385-397 (Part Four, chap. one).

slides into death and Zakhar, in the epilogue, into penury and beggardom.[152] Oblomov's death marks not only a personal extinction but the death of a dream and a way of life as well. Stolz had earlier assumed control of Oblomov's childhood home, and a moment before Ilya Ilich's death he announces the end of "old Oblomovka": railroads, piers for river boats, and other artifacts of modern civilization have finally reached that isolated corner of Russia. Soon after, we learn that Agafya Matveevna has been supplanted as mistress of the now decrepit house on the Vyborg side.[153] At his death Oblomov is dispossessed of two idylls—that of memory and of the attempted retrieval.

The dispossession is effected through an erosion of the same images and tokens that marked the idyll. Oblomov understood his dream of a land of "milk and honey" literally; an abundance of food was one of his major conditions for paradise. In his decline the cupboards are empty; ordinary horseradish and onions replace the more delectable cinnamon and almonds; Agafya's once constantly busy arms with their dimpled elbows hang idly over empty pots and pans. The bright and benevolent sun that guarded Oblomov's several idylls disappears, as the landscape of decline becomes enveloped in darkness: "My God! how dark everything . . . appeared . . ." opens the first downward cycle, and in the final descending arc the once bright and solitary house on the Vyborg side is forever cut off from the rays of the sun by newly constructed summer cottages and a tall stone government building. Finally, the once magnificent Asian dressing gown—the emblem of Oblomov's isolation and defeat and yet the envelope of his repose—is now worn, tattered, and in patches.[154]

Between the two downward sweeps the pendulum swings momentarily toward a restoration of the idyll. The interlude provides a respite before the collapse of Oblomov's world, but it also constitutes the resolution of the novel. Parallel to the intensifying tempo of dis-

[152] See *ibid.*, pp. 436-452 (Part Four, chaps. five and six); and pp. 498-507 (ten and eleven).

[153] *Ibid.*, pp. 497-500. ". . . the gentry is vanishing!" Zakhar laments in the epilogue (p. 505).

[154] *Ibid.*, pp. 436-438, 498-499. The coming of the summer cottages foreshadows the conclusion of Chekhov's *Cherry Orchard.*

integration, Part Four witnesses a concurrent cycle of integration— a building up of mountains. At the end of the novel the stage is filled, as in the final acts of classical comedies, with married couples: Stolz and Olga in their world; Oblomov and Agafya, Zakhar and Anisya (Oblomov's maid), Agafya's brother and his bride in theirs. The unification of Oblomov's world manifests itself not only through the somewhat casual announcements of the successive marriages; it is also realized through a decisive action. Earlier Anisya and Agafya—they are cut out of the same cloth—had merged their kitchens to form the new locus of Oblomov's universe, and Ilya Ilich, the putative "master" of this tiny realm, begins to assume at least some of the responsibilities of a *paterfamilias*. He adopts Agafya's children, personally tends to their education, touches his new-found family with a tenderness that seems to have grown through defeat, and finally rouses himself to action. When Tarantev, the only villain in the novel and the only important character not eventually married off, threatens the tranquility of his domestic nest, Oblomov physically assaults the usurper of his peace and banishes him from his realm, as Zakhar and Agafya close ranks to support him. In the context of Oblomov's usual immobility, it is perhaps a heroic act. Ilya Ilich—the name carries heroic overtones for Russians—has through his own efforts resolved the novel's intrigue, driven out his enemy, and preserved the integrity of his home.[155]

But Oblomov never conceived of the integration of his world in terms of physical action. Throughout the novel he sought domestic peace, but a peace that would recapitulate the perfect repose of childhood and which seemed attainable only in dream. He identified his image of peace with a woman and long remained confused as to what kind of woman would prove able to provide the conditions for the retrieval of the dream. Oblomovka's Militrisa Kirbitevna, the legendary woman who promises perfect contentment, would appear to him in a dual aspect. Several times he envisioned her surrounded by tokens that spoke of art, culture, and spiritual refinement—flowers, books, a piano, elegant furniture,

---

[155] *Ibid.*, pp. 458-459. Oblomov's namesake is Ilya Muromets, the best-known hero of Russian epic literature.

the aria "Casta diva"—only to discern a decidedly more prosaic woman intruding into his dreams—a red-cheeked servant girl "with bare, round, and soft elbows" who brings him his meals as he sits idly contemplating the sun. Failing to find the idyll in one woman, Oblomov recovers it in the other.

Silence descended. The housekeeper [Agafya] brought in her needlework and began to move her needle to and fro, glancing from time to time at Ilya Ilich. . . .

Oblomov imperceptibly sank into silence and reverie . . . , into a vague, mysterious condition, a kind of hallucination.

. . . .

. . . a silence which had already existed somewhere engulfed him; the familiar pendulum swung to and fro, he heard the snapping of thread . . . ; familiar words and whispers were repeated.
. . .

Indolently, absentmindedly, as if unconscious, he gazed into the housekeeper's face and a familiar image he had seen some place emerged from the depths of his memories. . . .

And there appeared before him the large dark drawing room lit by a tallow candle in the home of his parents; his dead mother and her guests are sitting at the round table sewing; they sew in silence; his father paces in silence. Past and present had merged and intermingled.

He dreams that he has reached that promised land where rivers of milk and honey flow, where people eat bread they have not labored for and go clothed in gold and silver.

He listens to the tales of his dreams, their tokens, the rattle of plates and the clatter of knives; he presses close to his nurse, listens attentively to her ancient quavering voice: "Militrisa Kirbitevna!" she says, pointing to the image of the housekeeper.[156]

The novel has described a complete circle, from dream to dream, from idyll to idyll, from the momentary vision of a lost paradise to

[156] *Ibid.*, pp. 79-80, 186, 492-493.

its momentary realization.[157] Oblomov starts his book in a quest for the past and at the end retrieves it. Olga represented a false and illusory idyll; the discovery of the idyll in Agafya Matveevna is the true "working out of the motive" of the novel. The resolution, when it comes, has a quality of inevitability about it. Earlier we saw a pattern or rhythm of experience proceeding from dream (or repose) to aborted action and back to dream, and through repetition the smaller circles of the novel become predictive. Even in the opening pages the pattern defines Oblomov as a man who, when he tries to act in the world, declines into dream, and the overarching pattern of the novel recapitulates that customary decline. When, in the romance with Olga, Oblomov takes his dreams with him into the "real world," he confirms our estimation of him as a character who cannot escape the pull of his private visions.

Does *Oblomov*, then, present a completely closed and determined world? Are its only alternatives a passive submission to the cycles of nature and the dreaming mind or, as Stolz argues, a stoic resignation to a meaningless succession of events without end? Is the resolution of Oblomov's story in any sense "an achievement?" Frank Kermode, in a book concerned with the function of endings, talks about "the conflict between the deterministic pattern any plot suggests, and the freedom of persons within that plot to choose and so to alter the structure, the relations of beginning, middle, and end."[158] *Oblomov* displays something of the kind—a freedom exercised within a deterministic pattern. We have already noted Oblomov's act of will in resolving the mechanical plot of the novel—the intrigues posed by Tarantev. But even in terms of its decisive rhythms, the patterns imposed by his dreaming mind, Oblomov evinces a capacity to affect the nature of experience and, if not evade, then "alter the structure." The novel traces the

[157] "Oblomov's Dream" is in Part One, chap. nine; its recovery in Part Four, and again chap. nine, providing, as in *A Common Story*, a purely arithmetical symmetry to supplement the esthetic symmetry.

[158] *The Sense of an Ending*, p. 30.

severe limitations of a life lived almost totally in imagination, but it also bestows upon the human imagination a power to bring coherence to life and even transform it. In connecting past and present, Oblomov's mind stamps a final confirmation upon the novel's logic of inevitability and unifies beginnings and ends in a concordance of necessity—a necessity whose recognition, it is true, may provide the reader with a sense of freedom denied the hero. But in converting the widow's modest suburban home into a miniature of paradise, Oblomov transforms his necessary end into his desired one. Unable to escape his fate, he learns to live with it, and his defeat becomes a simultaneous success.

The conception of time introduced in Part Four also serves to free the novel of its enclosing circles. "The crumbling away of mountains took place everywhere," and Oblomov's idyll soon disintegrates under the pressure of time. But the final downward movement includes suggestions of both a new regenerative cycle— "the forming of new land"—and continuity with the dying phase. *Oblomov* ends not with Oblomov's death but with the introduction of his son, who is an image of the father's delicacy, and as we might have expected in a novel that turns upon memory, with the reminiscences of the mourners. We have seen how the memory of Oblomov affects Stolz's and Olga's lives. In Agafya's case the gift of memory turns her from a mute thing into a person conscious of a past, as it allows her to preserve "the soft light of seven years which had flown by like a single moment . . . for a lifetime. . . ." As time in *Oblomov* reduces experience to a fleeting moment, memory retains what has been lost and grants man a permanence of the unforgetful imagination—the only kind of permanence the novel allows.[159]

By making time Oblomov's greatest enemy, Goncharov points to the essential limitation of his imagination. It is not what Oblomov dreams about—the Arcadia of childhood, full satisfaction of the oral appetites—that the novel ultimately holds up to criticism. Nor does it at all reject the passive reflective life. What limits Oblomov's

---

[159] *Sobr. soch.*, IV, 499-503. Branches of lilac and the more prosaic wormwood commemorate Oblomov's grave.

mind is the *form* his thought takes. The absolutism of his imagination, its complete absorption in a single ("half") view of life, its tendency to rigidify vision into the unalterable patterns of myth, render him incapable of dealing with a world in constant flux.[160]

CONCLUSION: THE TWO WORLDS

We have seen a series of oppositions running through the novel —the heroic and the ordinary, the ideal and the prosaic, paradise and the temporal, dream and "reality"—of which the former belong to the world of romance, the latter to the "normal" world, which is literary realism's more usual domain. In previous works Goncharov had employed a similar opposition of two orders of existence to parody romantic conventions or burlesque a romantic attitude, and many critics perceive a similar intent in *Oblomov*. Thus F. D. Reeve finds the purpose of the novel in a discrediting of romantic (as well as classical) notions of the hero; Soviet criticism in a satire of "gentry romanticism"—a blanket term employed to cover Oblomov's life of dream and illusion.[161]

A parodic element, if we include under "parody" the deflation of a literary sensibility or state of mind, finds its way into *Oblomov*, as into almost everything Goncharov wrote, providing some justification for a reading of the novel as an ironic commentary upon the "romance imagination"—a kind of "anti-romance."[162] Oblomov's

---

[160] See Leonida Gančikov, "In tema di 'Oblomovismo,' " *Ricerche slavistiche*, IV (1955-1956), p. 175. "It is the torment of consciousness, which in its recognized insufficiency to impress upon life truly absolute significance, does not succeed in contenting itself simultaneously with solutions of relative value. . . ."

[161] F. D. Reeve, "Oblomov Revisited," *American Slavic and East European Review*, XV (1956), 113. Prutskov, *Masterstvo*, pp. 98-108, 122, gives the most extended version of the usual Soviet argument. Again, the view goes back to Dobrolyubov, who placed Oblomov in a line of romantic heroes. See *Izbrannye sochineniya*, pp. 82ff.

[162] Maurice Z. Shroder, "The Novel as Genre," in *The Theory of the Novel*, ed. Stevick, pp. 17-18, defines the novel generically as an "anti-romance"—an exposure of the illusoriness not of another genre or mode but of the "romance sensibility." The view is widespread in modern critical theory.

ineptitude and the decline in his circumstances are, as we saw, played off against heroic longings sometimes associated with Russia's heroic past and its epic heroes, among them his namesake Ilya Muromets,[163] but more often with chivalric notions of the hero. *Barin*—"lord," "gentlemen," "master"—is Ilya Ilich's usual epithet, and the novel makes much of its genteel implications. His face, we are told, is not coarse but pale and delicate; his hands are white and small; he treats his person with careful delicacy, speaks "cleverly, beautifully, unusually," for "he is a *barin*, he is radiant; he sparkles!" But Oblomov's station in life becomes either a subject for this sort of gentle mockery or a reminder of the discrepancy between his ideals of heroism, poetry, honor and the actual state of affairs—the dusty city flat where he plays out a grotesque comedy with a stubborn and refractory "servant-knight," who, unlike his distant ancestors, "those Russian knights of the servants' quarters, without fear and reproach . . . ," is, like his master, "a knight with both fear and reproach." Oblomov, dispossessed of his crumbling estate by a changing world, finds that his title has become the mark of his superfluousness: "Who am I? What am I? . . . I am a *barin*, and I don't know how to do anything."[164]

As the novel juxtaposes Oblomov's unheroic circumstances with heroic memories, it also sets the prosaic landscapes of his modest estate against grander, more "poetic" and "romantic" versions of the manor of the gentry. Poets and dreamers, we are told, would find Oblomov's and Zakhar's birthplace uncongenial for elevated sentiments. Oblomovka's nights are illuminated not by a "lunar orb" but simply by a moon that resembles a very ordinary copper basin. Oblomovka has no nightingales, but only quails; no purple evenings "in the Swiss or Scottish style"; no cavalcades of gentlemen escorting their "ladies" (English in the original) to gloomy ruins where they may sup on wild goat and listen to ballads of ancient battles

[163] *Sobr. soch.*, IV, 121.

[164] *Ibid.*, pp. 392-393, 70-77, 367-372. He is a Prince Hamlet for whom "To be or not to be" resolves itself into the question of how to maneuver from bed into slippers (p. 193).

sung to the accompaniment of a lyre.[165] Instead of "gloomy ruins," Goncharov presents an estate of dilapidated peasant huts and a manorial house whose porch constantly threatens to fall apart and miraculously never does. Oblomovka's ladies and gentlemen are but idle country folk blissfully unaware of a world of great and heroic deeds.

Finally, the story of Oblomov's two loves describes a downward movement from the ideal to the prosaic, from a world of spirit and art to a realm of things and appetites, from an idealized garden to a busy kitchen. Like that other deluded and visionary nobleman with whom he and his story have much in common, Oblomov sets out to find his Dulcinea and discovers instead a rude and homely housekeeper, his Aldonza.

However, it is doubtful that Goncharov set out to mock a style of the imagination or satirize a social class in *Oblomov*, though the novel does some of both. A novel built upon contrast may compel readers to choose sides, but *Oblomov* in the long run does not. Dorothy Van Ghent, in a discussion of *Don Quixote*, reminds us that the word "parody" is formed from a prefix meaning "beside" or "contrary to" and a root meaning "song" or "poem" and "referred originally to a song or poem placed in sequence with ('beside') another song or poem." The word "paradox" denotes a closly related concept; instead of a song or poem, "one thought, opinion, or interpretation . . . is set up 'beside' . . . another different, even opposing, interpretation." Neither paradox nor parody requires preferential judgments or offers moral examples. Paradox refers to "a concentrated opposition of two outlooks or views both of which had to be held in the mind at once without a discarding of either one . . . and which are both 'real'. . . ." Parody, often loosely used to describe a burlesque imitation showing the weakness or falsehood of the object imitated, instead is able, in its more vital forms, "to intertwine many feelings and attitudes in such a way that they do not merely grapple with each other antagonistically but act creatively on each other, establishing new syntheses of feel-

---

[165] *Ibid.*, pp. 106-107. The references are, of course, to Sir Walter Scott.

ing and stimulating comprehensive and more subtle perceptions. . . . It is a technique of *presentation*."[166]

Goncharov's progress from the earlier works to *Oblomov* can be summarized as an advance from burlesque to parody (in Van Ghent's definition), from debate to paradox. Over the course of this essay I have argued the integrity of the differing worlds and visions of the novel and their ambiguous interrelationship. *Oblomov* presents an ideal garden of love, opposes it to commonplace kitchens and barnyards, only to preserve the ideal in Stolz's marriage, and, more convincingly, eventually to idealize the concrete world of Oblomov's fall from grace. Conversely, it offers a highly individual version of romance's golden age, a paradise of those same kitchens and barnyards, grants it a seductive power that transcends any satiric intention, and then proceeds to demonstrate its fragility by confronting it with the exigencies of history and time. It juxtaposes heroic longings and dreams with the fumbling of what in the jargon of our day is called an "anti-hero," places its chivalric *barin* and his rude squire in most ungenteel circumstances, but ends by bestowing upon its protagonist, if not heroism, then dignity. Oblomov fails to enter Stolz's world, but he acts decisively to preserve his own. As he achieves a degree of success in action, he also comes to a success of the mind, again within his limited sphere. His novel does not follow the usual nineteenth-century route of *illusions perdues*— what Harry Levin has called realism's technique of systematic disillusionment—but ends with a (partial) affirmation of the powers of the illusion-making imagination.[167] *Oblomov* offers two "songs" or "views," limits each by its juxtaposition with the other, and strives to preserve both.

What, then, holds the differing aspects of the novel together, or is *Oblomov* merely a "plotless" accumulation of "elusive moments" —an aimless alternation of dream and "reality," lyricism and genre scenes, romance and ironic commentary? I have several times described a rhythmic presentation of experience, rising from dream

[166] Dorothy Van Ghent, *The English Novel: Form and Function* (New York, 1953), pp. 11-13.

[167] Levin, *The Gates of Horn*, p. 48.

230

to action and subsiding into dream again—a pattern recapitulated by the whole, whose resolution ties together beginnings and ends. But the beginnings and ends of the central action of the novel—the recovery of the dream—are also the beginnings and ends of Oblomov's life. *Oblomov* tells the story of a man who wishes to escape history in the form of a history, a fictional biography that proceeds from early childhood to death and in which the overarching pattern of ascent and decline imitates the inevitable pattern of human life. It is this historical sweep of the novel, reinforced by its acute consciousness of the passage of time, that provides a context for its diverse modalities of thought and manner. It takes up the visions of paradise, the heroic memories, and "poetic" interludes and converts them into moments on the parabola of Oblomov's journey through the world.[168] Instead of ideas to be attacked or defended, literary positions that must be held to or derided, they become fictional parts of the total fiction that is Oblomov's life story. The world of romance is largely a projection of its hero's mind; it exists not as an object for ridicule, but to express the wishful tendencies of his thought. Similarly, the "normal" world—Stolz's world, because of its fragmented character, fails to provide a comprehensive framework of reality, a "reality principle," as the psychoanalysts put it—in terms of which Oblomov's illusions are to be judged. It carries no absolute value but also exists in relation to Oblomov's fictional life. Limited itself, the normal world in turn circumscribes Oblomov's desires with limiting factors.

[168] Criticism has habitually resorted to analogies to the epic in order to describe the sense of magnitude *Oblomov* conveys. Poggioli, *The Phoenix and the Spider*, pp. 47-48, e.g., calls it "a great cyclic poem, . . . a vast epos in prose." I would suggest that the novel's quality of "epicality" derives from its formal inclusiveness—the mixture of genres—and its historical dimension. W. P. Ker writes of the epic: "It is exposed to the attractions of all kinds of subordinate and partial literatures—the fairy story, the conventional romance, the pathetic legend,—and it escapes them all by taking them all up as moments, as episodes and points of view, governed by the conception, or the comprehension, of some of the possibilities of human character in a certain form of society." *Epic and Romance: Essays on Medieval Literature* (London, 1931), p. 175. Novels, of course, often display an analogous inclusiveness and historical breadth.

Stolz and Oblomov had attempted to merge their differing worlds into a single harmony, but the resolutions of their stories take place in separate spheres of existence: Andrey's in the "real" world of work and activity that has received the illumination of Olga's spirituality and whose rigors have been softened somewhat by the "tender image"; Oblomov's in a world of dreams that transform the widow's kitchen into a simulacrum of paradise. *Oblomov* is ultimately an irreconcilable comedy; it strives for total unity, but its two "halves," though they inform each other, fail to combine. In an article entitled "The Argument of Comedy," Northrop Frye describes a similar comic pattern, which he calls a comedy of "the green world" and "the normal world." The normal world is problematic, in history, and takes its conventions from Menandrine or New Comedy. The green world suggests an original golden age, has the feel of something maternal about it, and derives from the dramas of folk ritual. Frye takes his example from Shakespeare, who "brings the two worlds opposite one another, and makes each world seem unreal when seen by the light of the other . . . . his distinctive comic resolution . . . is a detachment of the spirit born of this reciprocal reflection of two illusory realities."[169] In the case of *Oblomov*, at least, "unreal" and "illusory" are a bit too strong. Goncharov was too much a man of his age to deny the claims of society and history, too captivated by the dream of a golden age to relinquish it altogether. "Detachment of spirit" is right, but it is a detachment born of the reflection of two partial realities—the two halves of life as the novel described it.

[169] Frye, in *Theories of Comedy*, ed. Lauter, pp. 459-460.

CHAPTER VIII

The Ravine

WHERE the oppositions of Goncharov's previous fiction were between certain absolute moral positions or modes of existence—practicality versus idealism, active work versus the passive imagination, the "real" world versus the world of dreams—the conflicts of *The Ravine* are explicitly political. *A Common Story* told of Alexander Aduev's journey to make his way in the great city of Petersburg; *Oblomov* recounted its hero's failure to adjust to urban life; *The Ravine* picks up the story with Boris Raysky's flight home from the city to his ancestral estate, Malinovka. Raysky, yet another impractical and idealistic dreamer, like Alexander Aduev tries and fails to find himself through artistic activity, and like Alexander and Oblomov seeks salvation in the love of a woman—with as little success. Politically, Raysky is a well-intentioned liberal of the kind commonly associated with the generation of the forties. Disappointed in his attraction to a Petersburg society coquette, Sofya Belovodova, whom he cannot arouse to concern for the suffering masses of Russia, he turns his attention to his two cousins at Malinovka—briefly to Marfenka, who proves too conventional and ordinary, with somewhat greater persistence to her intense and mysterious sister, Vera.[1] Vera, however, prefers a "nihilist" who has been exiled to the vicinity of Malinovka; after interminable arguments over their differing views of morality she finally yields to him at the bottom of the slope (or ravine) from which the novel takes its name. Raysky, who also argues much, at first leans toward the nihilist Mark Volokhov's "new morality"; traditional morality is represented by the crusty

---

[1] Goncharov said that Marfenka and Vera were patterned after Olga and Tatyana, respectively, of Pushkin's *Eugene Onegin. Sobr. soch.*, VIII, 77-78.

matriarch of Malinovka, Tatyana Markovna, affectionately called "grandmother." Later he and everyone else turn against the nihilist; Volokhov is roundly condemned for his perfidy; Vera is forgiven by her great-aunt, the "grandmother"; and the novel ends with the expectation that the fallen Vera will find resurrection in the strong arms of the sound, reliable, and practical neighbor of Malinovka, Ivan Tushin—the Stolz of this novel.

Evgenev-Maksimov, writing in 1925, developed a view of the genesis of *The Ravine* that persists in Soviet criticism to this day. He maintained that in the sixties Goncharov's political opinions underwent a severe change from "moderate liberalism" to an extreme conservatism and even a "reactionary ideology." The novel had been conceived in 1849—twenty years before its publication—and to accommodate it to his newly acquired political faith Goncharov revised his original intentions, whatever they were, and in midstream turned the work into a polemic against the nihilists. The artistic consequence of this sudden shift in political philosophy and literary intention is a series of ideological inconsistencies and historical anachronisms. Goncharov's earlier liberal views stand side by side with his newly acquired opinions of the sixties; the rendering of Russian social life under serfdom is incongruously mixed with a depiction of the post-emancipation situation; Raysky and Mark Volokhov, the idealist of the forties and the "new man" of the sixties, though they seem to belong to different epochs, are presented as members of the same generation.[2]

Maksimov was right about the inconsistencies, but his explanation rests upon the assumption that to have opposed the nihilists is to be a reactionary, which, if true, would place the likes of Turgenev and Tolstoy, along with a more promising candidate like Dostoevsky, in the reactionary camp. In an earlier chapter, using the same material employed by Maksimov, we found Goncharov's politics liberal in regard to the expression of opinion and conservative in the defense of certain fundamental institutions, notably the family, and we shall discover the same mixture in *The Ravine*.[3] Moreover, the quality

[2] *I. A. Goncharov*, pp. 92-133.

[3] See above, chap. one. In 1939, when it had become less acceptable in the

of the knowledge we achieve depends above all on the questions we ask, and we may wonder why a writer whom everyone, including Maksimov,[4] describes as indifferent to politics suddenly undertook a political novel.

It may very well have been that artistic rather than ideological considerations prompted the introduction of the anti-nihilist theme in the sixties. The work in progress bore the title *Raysky, the Artist* or simply *The Artist* from its conception in 1849 until at least the winter of 1857-1858.[5] At the turn of the decade Goncharov, as we saw in chapter three, experienced a crisis of confidence provoked by a failure to find a means to tie his work together and decided to start over from the beginning. He invariably associated his difficulties in locating a principle of unity for the novel with the problem posed by the hero of the original conception. The problem of the novel became the problem of what to do with Boris Raysky. Thus a paragraph in a letter complaining of an inability "to clarify the goal of the creation, its *necessity* upon which the whole creation must hinge," opens with a recurrent expression of despair over the nature of Raysky "Who is the hero, what is he, how may I express him. . . ." The decision to start over again from scratch likewise appears in the context of a discussion about Raysky, who is "still not entirely clear." In August of 1860, while giving vent to his persistent dismay over the character of Raysky, Goncharov indicated his original intention: "The hero is not coming out at all or is coming out odd, unformed, and incomplete. It seems I took upon myself an impossible task: to portray the insides, the heart of an artist and the backstages of art."[6]

USSR to denigrate the reputations of the major Russian writers, the same Evgen'ev-Maksimov on the basis of the same censorship material found Goncharov's censorship activity in the period under discussion to be "the sole ray of light on a gloomy censorship horizon. . . ." *Poslednie gody "Sovremennika": 1863-1866* (Leningrad, 1939), p. 68.

[4] *I. A. Goncharov*, p. 98.

[5] See *Sobr. soch.*, VIII, 72; Mazon, *Ivan Gontcharov*, pp. 440-441.

[6] From letters of the summer of 1860 to E. A. and S. A. Nikitenko, in *Sobr. soch.*, VIII, 340-341, and *Literaturnyy arkhiv*, IV, 139; and to V. N. and E. P. Maykov, in *Sobr. soch.*, VIII, 350.

The nature of the artist, Goncharov's original subject, though not entirely absent from the completed novel, is pushed to the side and obscured by the emerging theme of the sixties, the nihilist question. Goncharov never said why he suddenly changed his subject after a decade of preoccupation with *Raysky, the Artist*, but in all likelihood technical problems dictated the shift, and the turn to the nihilist theme, instead of indicating a dubious ideological conversion, marked an attempt to solve (or evade) the overriding question of 1859-1860: what to do with Boris Raysky? It seems more than coincidental that the first indication of the new nihilist topic, Goncharov's oft-cited discovery in June of 1860 of "the significance of a second hero—Vera's lover" and his "whole new side," occurred simultaneously with the finding of "a way to lead the hero through the whole novel. . . ."[7] More importantly, a comparison of *The Ravine* with Goncharov's previous fiction, though evincing no significant modifications of the author's *Weltanschauung*, will reveal instead a decisive change in his approach to the writing of novels.

Despite huge differences of scope and complexity, there are several important similarities between *A Common Story* and *Oblomov*. Character in both novels, in conformity with Goncharov's stated view of a literary type, displays a stable and unitary quality—sometimes resembling the condition of an allegorical emblem or a comic humor. The novelist's view of character was complemented by (and perhaps even dictated) a literary structure that placed the protagonists, each identified to varying degrees and extents of time with a single trait or value, into diametrical opposition: Alexander Aduev against Pyotr Ivanych, Oblomov against Stolz. However, the former member of each pair dominates the stage, while his antagonist is relegated for much of the action to the role of an ironic commentator (Pyotr Ivanych) or an emblem of a moral alternative

---

[7] To E. A. and S. A. Nikitenko, *ibid.*, pp. 329, 340. Goncharov later dated Volokhov's transformation into a nihilist to 1862. In an earlier version he was merely a "freethinker," and the novel was to end with Vera following him to Siberia. *Sbornik*, p. 15. Goncharov had visited some of the exiled Decembrists on his way through Siberia from Japan, and this version probably arose after his return in 1855. Most likely, the changes in conception that turned *The Ravine* into a political novel evolved over a period of years.

(Stolz). The first two novels are biographical, narrating the lives of Alexander Aduev from adolescence to maturity, of Oblomov from childhood through death, though in *A Common Story* Goncharov failed to convey a sense of an unfolding life. In each novel a solitary hero moves through a fictional world he is unable either to influence or to join, seldom confronting or engaging his antagonists; "the others" exist primarily to deflate his excesses of rhetoric or fantasy, provide ethical contrasts, or, in the case of women, to pose a test. Wayne Booth has made a helpful distinction between "dramatic situation," which gives "the impression that the story is taking place by itself . . . unmediated by a narrator" (i.e., scenic narration), and "dramatic manner," which shows "characters dramatically engaged with each other, motive clashing with motive, the outcome depending on the resolution of motives . . . ."[8] Goncharov's previous fiction, though dramatic in representation, was undramatic in manner. Avoiding confrontation and conflict, almost eventless, his art tended instead toward the pictorial. To recall Dobrolyubov's famous description, life seemed to "halt" and "congeal," become "molded into rigid immobile forms," as, in Stender-Petersen's elaboration of Dobrolyubov, a central character, "poured into its immutable, single form," was moved "slowly and consistently, in the light of various reflectors" and was viewed "from various angles of vision."

In *The Ravine* Goncharov reversed the pattern of his previous fiction and wrote a novel extremely dramatic in manner. Instead of a central hero, *The Ravine* focuses upon a central conflict—the competition of Raysky, Volokhov, and Tushin for the love of the dark and mysterious Vera. Where the action in *A Common Story* covered fourteen years of Alexander Aduev's life, in *Oblomov* approximately thirty-seven years, *The Ravine's* "drama of passion," as Vera calls it, is compressed into a brief half-year, from spring to autumn.[9] In its course the story evolves through a long period of

---

[8] Wayne C. Booth, "Distance and Point-of-View: An Essay in Classification," in *The Theory of the Novel*, ed. Stevick, pp. 103-104.

[9] *Sobr. soch.*, VI, 35. The time computations are Tseytlin's, *I. A. Goncharov*, pp. 64-65, 163.

suspense, engendered by the mystery veiling Vera's true intentions, and a series of tense confrontations during which the characters explore each other's motives. A single crisis—Vera's seduction by the nihilist—forms the climax of the novel, and Raysky's voluntary withdrawal from the competition and Tushin's triumph over the nihilist resolves the conflict.

In addition to a climate of suspense, tension, and dramatic confrontation atypical of Goncharov's earlier fiction, *The Ravine* displays a higher degree of plot complexity. Several sub-plots gradually appear and multiply the dramatic entanglements. Some are related to the major plot: thus Marfenka's and the equally conventional Nikolay Vikentev's love story, sanctioned as it is by familial authority, serves as a contrast to Vera's "fall"; the promiscuous activities of the servant girl Marina, and Ulyana, the wife of Raysky's school friend Leonty, provide another contrasting pole of complete abandonment to animal passion; finally, Tatyana Markovna— the sisters' guardian or "grandmother"—has her own secret love story which is revealed with the disclosure of Vera's seduction, providing an opportunity for a double repentance and a reconciliation of the divided family.[10] Unrelated to the central conflict is a large share of Raysky's story: his search for love in a succession of women besides Vera, and his quest for fulfillment as an artist—a story that was very probably Goncharov's original intention and to which we shall return.

Conflict in *The Ravine* is also internalized to an extent unknown in Goncharov's earlier fiction. Where Alexander Aduev and Oblomov, one in his romantic posture, the other in his total dedication to a dream, were "molded into rigid immobile forms" and then brought into ironic contact with a refractory reality, the protagonists of *The Ravine* are beset by internal contradictions of personality or motive. A comparison of the descriptions that introduce Oblomov

---

[10] In "Namereniya, zadachi i idei romana *Obryv*," Goncharov declared his subject to be "the varied appearances of passion" and went on to describe the characters of the novel according to the degrees and kinds of passion they experience. *Sobr. soch.*, VIII, 208-210. Prutskov, in *Masterstvo*, pp. 154-155, notes Goncharov's shift from a single character to an "event" and also the relative plot complexity of *The Ravine*.

and Raysky to the reader is illustrative of Goncharov's new approach to the novel. Oblomov's description begins as a portrait of a somewhat nondescript individual with a singularly inexpressive face, and then, in accordance with the novelist's stated approach to the depiction of character, focuses upon a single dominant trait—"softness."

> He was a man of about thirty-two or thirty-three, of medium height, pleasant appearance, and with dark grey eyes, but with an absence of any definite idea, of any sign of concentration in the features of his face. . . .
>
> At times his gaze was darkened by an expression as if of weariness or boredom, but neither weariness nor boredom could banish the softness which was the dominant and fundamental expression, not only of his face, but of his entire being. . . .[11]

Before the description finally concludes, "soft" or "softness" is repeated another four times—twice for Oblomov's person, twice for the two objects closely identified with him—his slippers and his dressing gown. On the other hand, "changeability" (*izmenchivost'*), the potentiality for alternative possibilities, is presented as the essence of Raysky's character.

> It would have been difficult for a physiognomist to determine his traits, inclinations, and character by his face, because it was subtly changeable.
>
> Sometimes he would seem so happy; his eyes would brighten, and an observer who was on the verge of surmising an open character, communicativeness, and even garrulity, would, if he looked at him again in an hour or two, be struck by the paleness of his face, by some inner and perhaps incurable suffering, as if he had in all his life never once smiled.
>
> He seemed ugly in these moments. Discord showed in the lines of his face; a sickly hue replaced the lively color of his brow and cheeks.
>
> But if a peaceful breath of life blew over him or if he simply

[11] *Sobr. soch.*, IV, 7.

"came across a happy line of verse," his face reflected reserves of strength and will, inner harmony and self-possession, and at times a capacity for unrestrained reverie, a suggestion of dreaminess, which lay now in his dark eyes, now in a slight trembling of the lips, and which suited his face so well.

His moral nature was even more elusive. . . .[12]

Similarly, Vera's description suggests inner contradiction: there is "some sort of mystery" about her; like Raysky, she is "elusive"; her face displays "a double expression." Even Tatyana Markovna, though she possesses a moral certitude and solidity most of the other characters lack, is granted a measure of duality: her bearing reflects "strength, imperiousness, and pride" and yet in unguarded moments something "dreamy" and "sad."[13]

In endowing his characters with a measure of duality Goncharov may have wished to write a more conventionally "realistic" novel— one that would avoid the idealizations of romance and allegory and the extremes of comic caricature that had entered his previous fiction (whether he succeeded is another question). Not only has the novelist's concept of character become more conventional, but the procedures employed in presenting his protagonists are closer to the norm of nineteenth-century fiction. Apparently impelled by his new concept of a fluid and "changeable" type, Goncharov abandoned that earliest and most persistent of his literary devices, the identification of a character with a significant gesture or (in *Oblomov*) a metaphoric image—light, lilacs, etc.—that is then threaded through the fiction like a leitmotif. Instead, the presentation in *The Ravine* proceeds from a detailed and "rounded" description (as in the above example) to a scene through which the author strives to reveal the psychology of his characters in collision with others. Even the most incidental characters receive this full portraiture. The comic play of *A Common Story* and *Oblomov*, which resulted from the rigidity of a hero tied to a single aspect of personality, is largely absent from *The Ravine*, as are the lyricism and the atmosphere of dream and fancy of *Oblomov*.

[12] *Ibid.*, v, 44-45.
[13] *Ibid.*, pp. 294-295, 73.

Also, the characters of *The Ravine* are more firmly anchored in contemporary social reality than the people of Goncharov's previous fiction. Where Alexander and Pyotr Aduev had argued over the abstract values of practicality and sentiment on an empty stage in what seemed like a timeless comedy of "the way of the world," where the estate of "Oblomov's Dream" was transmuted into an Arcadia of the imagination, which turned the novel from social satire (which it in part is) into an ironic commentary upon the chronically human nostalgia for paradise, the arguments of *The Ravine* center upon what Goncharov said literature should avoid—the "topical." Its characters talk at length, and often anachronistically, about such issues as serfdom, the nihilists, Russia's economic and social progress, and, most of all, about the "woman question," which is equated with what later generations called "free love." Except perhaps for Vera and Marfenka, they are not polarized into the customary pairs of ethical opposites but are distributed along a wider range of contemporary social relations. Nor do the oppositions of *The Ravine* evolve into a contrast of a world of dreams and the "real" world, a realm of spirit and art and the concrete "fallen" world. Though many of the old antagonisms persist, they are presented entirely in the context of a specific society located in the historical arena of usual experience. Place acquires much greater importance in this final novel. A character's moral worth is to a large extent determined by his geographical location and the social entity it signifies. Conversely, the protagonists' conflicts, in addition to whatever psychological import they may have, become representative (or "typical") of larger social divisions.[14]

[14] Roman Jakobson, "O khudozhestvennom realizme," in *Michigan Slavic Materials*, No. 2 (Ann Arbor, December 1962), pp. 29-36, notes that nineteenth-century realism avoided metaphor and that its distinctive techniques were instead metonymic. René Wellek, *Concepts of Criticism*, pp. 240-241, offers " 'the objective representation of contemporary social reality' " as a working definition of realism. I would still call Goncharov's earlier novels "realistic" for their ironic conception of experience, their frequent renderings of ordinary life, and, especially in *Oblomov*, the presentation of psychological and social causality. But their realism, like that of much Russian fiction, is of a mixed kind, veering in *A Common Story* to the forms of classical comedy,

Malinovka, the estate managed by Tatyana Markovna, serves as the novel's moral frame of reference. Like Oblomovka and Alexander Aduev's ancestral Grachi, it constitutes a repository of traditional values and an idyllic community—the explicit "Eden" of this novel.[15] However, unlike Goncharov's earlier paradises, Malinovka is treated largely without irony (or lyricism) and *all* the characters are measured against its values. The "grandmother" represents its authority, Marfenka accepts it, Vera rebels. Raysky is a visitor, neither completely part of the domestic idyll nor able to separate himself.[16] Beyond Malinovka lies Petersburg, with its frivolous Europeanized "high society" (French is the language of discourse) as represented largely by two characters: Ayanov, a card-playing government official and "man about town" ("high rank and salary and no work"), and Sofya Belovodova, the pampered and shallow coquette. Sofya's social pretensions—she derives all her values from the notions of "ancestry" and "lineage"—are perceived as the cause of her isolation from the broad currents of Russian life, its suffering poor and its "passions."[17]

Closer to Malinovka but not part of it lies the provincial town, an epitome of Russian backwardness and stagnation: "this is not a town but a graveyard like all these towns."[18] Its locus of authority is a benighted reactionary and pompous hypocrite, Nil Andreich Tychkov, the only complete villain of this ostensibly "reactionary" novel. His true moral antagonist turns out to be not the nihilist but Tatyana Markovna, the defender of Malinovka and of the honor of the gentry. When that imposing matriarch finally loses patience and drives the local official, Tychkov, from her realm, she displays a consciousness of her role in denouncing him as a traitor to his class:

---

in *Oblomov* to the symbolic landscapes and idealized types of romance, while also continuing a purely comic tradition.

[15] "What an Eden opened up before him [Raysky] in this small corner of the world. . . ." *Sobr. soch.*, V, 61. Also see V, 160, 289-290; VI, 47.

[16] Though Raysky is the legal heir to Malinovka, he considers himself a guest. See *ibid.*, V, 170.

[17] *Ibid.*, pp. 8-10, 28-37, 105-110.

[18] *Ibid.*, V, 187-189. Also *ibid.*, p. 336, where "the whole town and all the towns of this broad kingdom" are said to labor solely under "the whip."

". . . you do not act like a member of the gentry! . . . you are a lowly clerk, a *parvenu.* . . ."[19]

Two characters, the nihilist and the "positive hero," reside outside the established societies of the novel. Mark Volokhov is "homeless," "without a 'nest,' a hearth, property," and finally "outside of life." Tushin, Goncharov's answer to the nihilists ("our true party of action, our sound future"), makes his home in the great Russian forest. This is but one of several allusions to his authentic Russian character: in addition, his baptismal name and patronymic are Ivan Ivanych; he is regularly compared to a bear (Mark Volokhov is the "wolf" of the novel); he possesses "a simple, practical Russian nature."[20] Despite Tushin's function as an alternative to the nihilists, we find him strangely enough putting into practice one of their favorite ideas. Following the example of Robert Owen—also a major source of Nikolay Chernyshevsky, the radicals' leading theoretician—Tushin has established an industrial commune in the forest, as well as schools, hospitals, and banks for the peasants. His community bears "no traces of a poor serf economy"; its manager is but "a first . . . worker among his workers. . . ."[21]

Actually, Tushin and Mark Volokhov are radically opposed on only one issue of the period, the "woman question." Sexual morality furnishes the real subject of contention in the novel. Mark denies the authority of marriage (it is the only specific institution this nihilist negates) and appeals instead to the authority of nature: "I want your love," he tells Vera, "and I shall give you my own; here is the one 'rule' of love—the rule of free exchange as shown

[19] *Ibid.,* VI, 25-26.

[20] *Ibid.,* V, 167; VI, 359, 265, 394-395. Comparisons to animals recur through the novel; one of the major themes is the consequence of "animal passion."

[21] *Ibid.,* VI, 394-396. For a summary of Chernyshevsky's views on the communal organization of industry, see E. Lampert, *Sons against Fathers: Studies in Russian Radicalism and Revolution* (Oxford, 1965), pp. 194-204. The search for a practical and efficient hero who would rescue Russia from its backwardness was widespread in Russian fiction of the nineteenth century, though especially intense in Goncharov's work. For an excellent study, see Rufus W. Mathewson, Jr., *The Positive Hero in Russian Literature* (New York, 1958).

us by nature." Tushin, whom Vera learns to love with "human feeling"—Mark had cited animals as models of behavior—and "not with passion, that is, not physically," fully accepts society's conventions of courtship and marriage.[22]

The crucial boundary, "the Rubicon,"[23] of the topography of the novel is formed by the wooded slope or ravine (the *obryv*) that separates Malinovka from the rest of the world. Like the ravine bordering Oblomovka it is taboo, though not everyone observes the prohibition. Its associations are with passion and death: a crime of passion, a double murder and a suicide, once occurred there, and legend maintains that the aggrieved husband, who took vengeance upon his wife and her lover and then destroyed himself, still wanders its forests. Tatyana Markovna, who defends the sacraments of marriage and the primacy of the family—"let her marry and then fall in love"—never enters the forbidden terrain; nor does her dutiful ward Marfenka. At the opposite pole, the nihilist habitually makes his appearances in the ravine. Raysky is ambivalent; he fears it and yet is attracted to its "mysterious darkness." Vera's "fall," her seduction by the nihilist, takes place at its bottom. With the seduction the two associations tied to the place—passion and death—merge, for Vera perceives her fall as a spiritual death: "Your 'pure' Vera is buried there; she no longer exists; she is at the bottom of that ravine."[24]

The estate itself includes further key distinctions of place. There are two houses at Malinovka: a "new" house that is a beehive of domestic activity, "comfortable and full of life," and a gloomy, decaying older building abandoned by all save Vera, who still lives there among the portraits of her aristocratic ancestors—the rebellious daughter and the emblems of traditional authority. Vera regularly repairs to a small chapel, which contains a solitary icon of Christ, in a vain quest for strength against the enticements of the nihilist—"Truth and light . . . , where are you? There, where he claims, where my heart draws me [the ravine]? . . . Or is truth here [the chapel] . . .?"[25]

---

[22] *Sobr. soch.*, VI, 262, 179-181, 259-260, 390.   [23] *Ibid.*, p. 336.
[24] *Ibid.*, V, 178; VI, 417; V, 76; VI, 305.   [25] *Ibid.*, V, 227; VI, 182.

The novel concludes with the most extensive, if not the most convincing, synthesis in Goncharov's fiction. In the previous novels the artist had set up antithetical moral poles and then proceeded to bring them together. However, a fine sense of irony and critical detachment had kept him from too-easy solutions of the antagonisms of motive and value his characters presented. Alexander and Pyotr Aduev finally meet in the epilogue to their novel, but their coming together is only a momentary "uncommon incident" on the descending curves of their sterile lives. Stolz and Oblomov seek each other out, occasionally come close, but never really find one another. Goncharov's true subject had been the impossible discrepancies in human life and the yearnings of men to overcome them. In *The Ravine* the final resolution is total and almost everyone is included.

A series of changes in place, a general moving day at Malinovka, marks the resolution. The movement is from the surrounding localities of the novel to its central community, the family of the gentry. Vera confesses her sin to Tatyana Markovna, is forgiven, and abandons her seclusion in the old house to rejoin the domestic nest. Her rebellion, which lay in a refusal to abide by the claims of the family —". . . I forgot all of you, you [Raysky], grandmother, sister, the whole house . . ."—is resolved by a submission to familial authority, as Vera becomes like her dutiful sister, the Martha of the novel: "Take me out of here; Vera no longer exists. I shall be your Marfenka. . . ."[26] Simultaneously Tushin comes in from the forest to assume the management of Malinovka, as Stolz had taken over Oblomovka before him, though this estate is from all appearances a thriving establishment. Marfenka and her fiancé Vikentev return to be married. Even several minor characters, unrelated by blood to the Malinovka family, are brought into its fold. Leonty, abandoned by his promiscuous wife, finds a home at Malinovka; Tit Nikonych, the secret lover of Tatyana Markovna's past, returns from a temporary seclusion necessitated by the rumors that Vera's adventure had aroused.

Significantly, two characters are excluded from this expanding community, the reactionary Nil Andreich and of course the nihilist.

[26] *Ibid.*, VI, 293, 333-334. See also VI, 296.

However, the latter's ostracism from society is not final. If the others in returning to Malinovka recover "Eden," Mark is condemned to a purgatory from which redemption is still possible. At the conclusion of the novel he repents of his evil and decides to re-assume his former position in the officer corps of the Russian army.

Raysky the artist, who was never completely a part of Malinovka and yet was unable to separate himself entirely, is reunited with the family, not in fact, but in imagination and sentiment. On the final pages of the novel the family is associated with Russia.

> And everywhere, amidst this feverish artist's life, he did not betray his family, his group; he did not grow roots in a foreign soil but always felt himself a guest and stranger. Often . . . he felt drawn back home. He wanted to absorb the eternal beauty of nature and art . . . and bring it back there, to his Malinovka.
>
> Three figures always stood behind him and fervently called to him—his Vera, his Marfenka, and the grandmother. And behind them always stood yet another gigantic figure, another great "grandmother," who beckoned him even more intensely —Russia.[27]

The resolution witnesses not only a return to the family (Russia) but the family's consolidation against the forces of both the left and the right (the two excluded parties) who would undermine its vitality. Earlier, during one of the recurring debates between Mark and Vera over the issue of "free love," the nihilist had perceived several forces lurking behind her and thwarting his arguments: ". . . her faith [*vera* is Russian for "faith"], . . . Raysky with his poetry, the grandmother with her morality . . . were bolstering her strength and supplying her with weapons against his truth."[28] Faith (the chapel that survives when the summer cottage in the ravine is destroyed), Raysky's gift of art, and Tatyana Markovna's "old morality" combine forces at the conclusion of the novel to resist the nihilist threat. To these we may add Tushin's contribution: a promise of the modernization of old Russia (one of the last scenes in the novel shows him planning "radical transformations"

---

[27] *Ibid.*, p. 430.   [28] *Ibid.*, p. 270.

for Malinovka) and a vague hint at greater social equality ("the first worker among his workers"). Also, Vera's abandonment of "the old house" with its portrait galleries of her aristocratic ancestry in order to move into "the new house," where she will soon become Tushin's bride, provides another suggestion that Russia's "sound future" will be unlike her "feudal" past.[29]

The politics of *The Ravine* are hardly reactionary or even especially conservative. They are instead a politics of compromise and consensus. The novel seeks to locate a middle position that will bridge the gap between the radicals and traditional Russia. Through Tushin, Malinovka accepts a program of economic and social reform, which, though left vague and undefined, suggests by its source (Robert Owen) that it may have been designed to placate the very nihilists who are under attack. The other characters, in rallying around Malinovka, reaffirm the traditional values of religious faith, art, and the family. An attempt to mediate or synthesize opposed positions is typical of Raysky, Goncharov's frequent mouthpiece in the novel. Raysky considers himself neither "a new man" nor "backward." He denounces "the uncompromising past, the despotism of arbitrariness, and the greed of the landowners" and welcomes "new revelations, discoveries, and changes," but changes that occur "naturally" and are not "forced." He greets the coming of the new as he greets the arrival of spring—without "enmity for the departing order and its outlived principles" but in recognition of "their historical inevitability" and "their ties of continuity with the verdure of the new spring. . . ."[30]

If all this reads like an attempt to mute real antagonisms instead of resolving them, there is another sense in which Goncharov's novel is emphatically "conservative"—though not at all so in the usual political sense of the term. In *The Ravine* that persistent tension of Goncharov's fiction between the individual's dreams, illusions, or desires and society's ("the others'") demands is finally resolved with

[29] *Ibid.*, VI, 415. See V, 61. "She [the grandmother] ran [Malinovka] . . . despotically and upon feudal principles."

[30] *Ibid.*, VI, 7-8. Raysky's politics here closely resemble Goncharov's. Cf. *ibid.*, VIII, 87-89, 148-158.

the triumph of the latter. The integration of society, which proved to be ironic in *A Common Story* and partial in *Oblomov*, is now total and unequivocal. The novel in its major argument and action grants precedence to the claims of an institution (the family) over the assertions of individuals (here of their passions instead of their dreams). Goncharov's idyllic community, though inclusive and tolerant in its standards of admission, has its distinct limitations. What is excluded, however, are largely not dissenting political opinions, but the impulses and uncertainties of the passionate life—the ravine. It is of more than passing interest that the two characters most representative of the values and vitality of that community—Tatyana Markovna, the defender of its "old morality," and Tushin, its reformer—both conform, as the others generally do not, to Goncharov's view of a literary type as extremely stable and fixed, with the difference that what was perceived to be a comic vice in the instances of Alexander Aduev and Oblomov is now a virtue. Tatyana Markovna, despite her momentary inner turmoil over the indiscretions of her youth, is ultimately conceived as "a finished (*gotovyy*) formed human being," who recognizes neither "contradiction" nor "division." She confines her life within "a simplicity of form," "a definite tight frame," in which one lives by the repetitions of domestic and agrarian life. Tushin is altogether unambiguous. He stands like "a firm mountain" against the "infections of passion"; he also knows no internal "division" but has been "created by nature . . . such as he is . . ." into "finished solid forms."[31] Passion disrupts the stability of this "solid" world and its outburst affects everyone in varying degrees of intensity. However, once its perturbations have subsided, an image already familiar to us from *Oblomov* returns, as ". . . peace hung over Malinovka [and] life, held back by catastrophe, once again, like a river, . . . flowed on more smoothly."[32]

The integration of society is the theme of comedy, but *The Ravine* is instead a melodrama—what Frye has aptly called "comedy without humor."[33] Mark Volokhov, despite early intimations of "a

[31] *Ibid.*, VI, 80; V, 228-229; VI, 391-392.

[32] *Ibid.*, VI, 347. Also see V, 228.

[33] He finds two themes that are important to it, "the triumph of moral virtue

mystery" in his past and attributions of "great talent and knowledge," turns out to be a stock villain of the period, which saw a flood of anti-nihilist novels. He is presented through certain melodramatic gestures—shooting off a rifle to announce his presence in the ravine, crawling over fences and through windows to make sudden (nocturnal) appearances; or through indecorous mannerisms—cleaning his ears with the pages of Raysky's rare books, unceremoniously putting his feet on a table "in the American fashion." If Malinovka represents the family, Mark Volokhov is little more than its *enfant terrible*.[34]

The problem with Vera is even more serious. She is the central figure of "the drama of passion," if not of the entire novel (after *Raysky, The Artist* was abandoned, the work in progress bore the title *Vera* virtually until its completion in the summer of 1868).[35] If Mark can remain a conventional villain, the reader expects of Vera, who rebels against her family, tradition, and an idyllic community—"this paradise," as she herself called it—a motive for her actions. Vera's plot is a "plot of character"; the change she experiences is a change of the self; and for the transformation from rebellious to dutiful daughter to be believable, it must be felt as a result of an inner process.[36]

---

over villainy, and the consequent idealizing of the moral views assumed to be held by the audience." *Anatomy*, pp. 40, 47.

[34] *Sobr. soch.*, V, 222; VI, 258. Charles A. Moser, *Antinihilism in the Russian Novel of the 1860's* (The Hague, 1964), pp. 137-180, itemizes common traits of the nihilists in the literature of the sixties. Volokhov shares his fictional semblances' careless dress, long hair, disorderly rooms, and fondness for Proudhon's "la propriété—c'est le vol." *Sobr. soch.*, V, 269, 343-345; VI, 170. It seems that Goncharov initially intended to grant even Volokhov a more "rounded" presentation: an excluded section described his background in length and attempted to provide psychological motivation. See Tseytlin, *I. A. Goncharov*, pp. 473-476.

[35] See Mazon, *Ivan Gontcharov*, pp. 440-441.

[36] *Sobr. soch.*, VI, 47. R. S. Crane, in *Critics and Criticism*, pp. 616-623, divides plots into plots of action, character, and thought, according to the nature of "the completed process of change." For an elaboration of Crane's definitions, see Norman Friedman, "Forms of the Plot," in *The Theory of the Novel*, ed. Stevick, pp. 145-166.

Goncharov promises much, but delivers woefully little. We are told that there is "something uncontainable hiding in her soul . . . ," that "her gaze beckoned and drew one into depths . . . ," that "she is all glimmer and mystery like the night. . . ." "What is she?" "Who is she?" are the questions posed after her appearance. They are never satisfactorily answered—simply because the melodramatic urge to keep good and evil strictly apart will not permit it. The work aims at the final vindication of Malinovka and the apotheosis of its women, a purpose that can tolerate little moral ambiguity. Vera's first dramatized descent into the ravine in response to Mark's rifle shot coincides with a question that has been nagging at the reader for some time: "And how is it that Vera, this refined creature, . . . this beautiful pearl of the entire region, whom the finest eligible bachelors regarded timidly, before whom even bold men turned shy, not daring to cast an immodest glance at her or risk a compliment, Vera, upon whom even the breeze did not dare breathe, was suddenly going to a secret rendezvous with a dangerous suspect!" The question of Vera's motive, posed once again, remains unanswered, so that we are left with a discrepancy between the rhetoric of the novel—here, as it points to Vera's chastity—and her real actions.[37] This discrepancy is never bridged. The psychological complexity that Goncharov initially promised and that appeared to be his intention in this novel remains on the level of a verbal gloss—"double expression," "depths," "glimmer and mystery," "impenetrability," "mermaid," "enchantress," "alluring, mysteriously beautiful"—designed to suggest levels and depths never actualized in experience.[38]

The artist's failure to go beyond "suggestive" epithets in exploring Vera's personality may have compelled him to develop his story as he did, with almost exclusive attention to its machinery. The "drama of passion" turns out to be a detective story. Having evaded the earlier question—"what is she?"—the novelist becomes engrossed with the mystery of "who?": who wrote to Vera on blue stationery? who fired the shots in the ravine? who met her there in

[37] *Sobr. soch.*, V, 294-295, 349, 358; VI, 169. Vera and Tatyana Markovna are eventually perceived to be "saints" (VI, 338-339).

[38] *Ibid.*, V, 294-295; VI, 76; V, 363; VI, 56, 76, 200, 226; V, 300.

secret rendezvous? who has told her about the "new ideas"?[39] In the tradition of the mystery story, false leads are strewn about the landscape as Raysky, the novel's "detective," is confronted with several innocent letters devised to throw him off the track of "the blue letter" (the nihilist's) and a false suspect, Tushin. As a contriver of mysteries Goncharov, it must be said, proves inept. If the mystery of motive remains unexplored, the mystery of discovery becomes tedious and obvious. For most of the novel Mark Volokhov furnishes the only available suspect and Tushin, otherwise an unlikely villain, appears when the secret has already been revealed to the reader. As a result, we are placed in the position of waiting for a solution we already possess.

Should the reader lose interest or even question the importance of knowing what is happening in the ravine, the prose would convince him that it is indeed of the greatest import. The melodramatic heightening, the exaggerated emphases and portentousness that we observed in Goncharov's other attempt to write in a dramatic manner (the Stolz-Olga romance) run rampant in this final novel. A scene depicting one of Vera's several descents into the ravine is not atypical:

> She fell to her knees at the threshold to the chapel, covered her face with her hands and froze into immobility. Raysky silently approached her from behind. "Don't go, Vera," he whispered.
>
> She trembled but looked intensely at the icon. . . . In terror she drew herself up, rising slowly from her knees. She did not seem to note Boris.
>
> A second shot resounded. She rushed headlong across the meadow to the ravine.
>
> "What if he is returning—if my 'truth' has triumphed? Why else would he call?—O God!" she thought, rushing toward the shot.
>
> "Vera! Vera!" Raysky spoke in terror, stretching out his arm to prevent her.

[39] *Ibid.*, VI, 34, 41-47, 53, 58, 64, 76, 113, 152-155, 189, 273. See Tseytlin, *I. A. Goncharov*, p. 258.

Without looking back she removed his hand and barely touching the grass with her feet, not looking back, flew across the meadow and disappeared behind the trees of the garden into the path leading to the ravine.

Raysky froze on the spot. "What is this, a fateful mystery or passion? Or one and the other?" he asked himself.[40]

When the prose is not melodramatic, it is polemical and didactic. In this novel whose acknowledged subject is "the varied appearances of passion," virtually the only passions its characters can muster are those of the pedagogue or preacher. I take my example from Raysky, *The Ravine's* most indefatigable didact.

> Do not laugh Vera; yes, I am its [freedom's] worthy knight! Not permit you to love! I even bring you a sermon precisely about that freedom! Love openly, publicly, don't hide; don't fear your grandmother or anybody! The old world is decaying; life's new shoots have broken into leaf; life beckons, it opens its embraces to all. You see—you are young, you have never been away from here, and the spirit of freedom has already wafted over you; you already possess a consciousness of your rights, healthy ideas. If the dawn of freedom rises for all, shall one woman remain a slave? You love? Speak boldly: passion is happiness![41]

The Olga-Stolz love story taught us that Goncharov's even, measured prose, though consistent with Oblomov's reflective mode of being and with a novel that to a great extent consisted of the dreams and reminiscences of a single hero, was incompatible with a more dramatic manner of presentation. The discrepancy between the experience conveyed and the language employed to convey it is felt everywhere in this final novel. When Vera received another letter from the nihilist to precipitate yet another crisis after the fateful "fall," her "thoughts didn't tie together, she felt confused; anguish and the beating of her heart disturbed her." Her confused thoughts are presented in carefully ordered phrases and clauses of almost equal length.

[40] *Sobr. soch.*, VI, 186-187.
[41] *Ibid.*, V, 357. The abundance of exclamation points is typical.

Ne mogu, sil net, zadykhayus'! . . . Ne mogu, ne znayu, s chego
nachat', chto pisat'? Ya ne pomnyu, kak ya pisala emu, chto govorila
prezhde, kakim tonom—Vsyo zabyla!

(I cannot, I have no strength, I am suffocating! . . . I cannot, I don't know how to start, what to write? I don't remember,
how I wrote to him, what I said to him previously, in what tone—
I have forgotten everything!)

As we move from Vera's interior monologue to the narrative voice
—at first continuing the presentation of her thoughts in "quoted
speech" (*erlebte Rede*) and then resuming the narration proper—
the prose maintains the same even phrasing, so that stylistically the
two are virtually indistinguishable.

Vsyo eto neslos' u ney v golove, i ona to khvatalas' opyat' za
pero i brosala, to dumala poyti sama, otyskat' ego, skazat' emu
vsyo eto, otvernut'sya i uyti—i ona bralas' za mantil'yu, za
kosynku, kak byvalo, kogda toropilas' k obryvu.

(All this rushed through her head, and now she again seized
the pen and threw it away, now she thought she would go herself, seek him out, tell him all this, turn away and leave—and she
grabbed at her cloak, at her kerchief, as then, when she had
rushed to the ravine.)

Vera's articulated speech, when she tells "grandmother" of this
latest dilemma, becomes so regular as to suggest that she may be
speaking verse.

Ya nichego ne khochu, ya edva xozhu—i esli dyshu svobodno i
nadeyus' ozhit', tak eto pri odnom uslovii—*chtob mne nichego ne
znat', ne slykhat', zabyt' navsegda—A on napomnil! zovyot tuda,
manit schast'em, khochet venchat'sya! Bozhe moy!* (Italics
mine.)[42]

(I don't want anything, I can barely walk—and if I breathe
freely and hope to come to life, it is under one condition—that
I may not know anything, not hear, forget forever—but he re-

---

[42] *Ibid.*, VI, 360-364.

minded me! He calls me there, entices me with happiness, wants to marry me! My God!)

The frequent incompatibility of language and experience results in something akin to what psychologists call "dissociation." The characters of *The Ravine* are constantly trying to persuade us and each other that they suffer the most violent emotions. But their agitations either are submerged in a smooth logical flow of symmetrical phrases indistinguishable from the narrator's usually dispassionate voice, or else are contained in a rhetoric so inflated and overblown—though syntactically regular—as to be hardly believable. ". . . all our endless arguments were merely the mask of passion," Mark Volokhov remarks in a singular moment of insight, and the novel's incessant harangues, its intense urgencies, instead of communicating deep conviction, leave the reader with a sense of emptiness, of passion that is only a façade or a mask.[43] *The Ravine* for the most part lacks a personal tone, a suggestion of intimacy and of private areas of sentiment. Virtually all its emotions are those of the public arena—of the orator and the debater. Goncharov had achieved a personal tone in *Oblomov*, but there had been little need in that novel to individualize the voices of his characters, and even less to find a diction capable of suggesting violent emotion. *Oblomov* was dominated by one character, and one stylistic voice was largely sufficient. Its pathos did not depend upon passionate conflict and drama but derived from dream-like reminiscences and the muted aches of nostalgia—modes of experience that harmonized with the artist's gifts and did not contradict his temperamental mistrust of sharp emotions.

If the novel's "drama of passion," or its "melodrama," is contrived and artificial, it may very well be because Goncharov's true interests lay elsewhere. Upon publication of *The Ravine* he wrote Ekaterina Maykova that ". . . Raysky [was] my major concern . . . [and] Mark fell in by chance," and several years later in "Better Late Than Never" he again cited Raysky as his main interest.[44] What then has become of Raysky the artist—Goncharov's original subject and "major concern"? It will be recalled that the first hint of the theme

<hr/>

[43] *Ibid.*, p. 358.   [44] *Ibid.*, VIII, 397-398, 402, 71.

of the nihilist occurred simultaneously with a discovery of "a way to lead the hero through the whole novel." In the completed work Raysky is "led through" by becoming, besides the *raisonneur* of the novel, its observing eye: much of the action and a number of descriptions of place are presented through his perceptions.

However, the novel begins as Raysky's story—more precisely, as the story of his life. Part One, completed in 1858 and *before* the introduction of the nihilist, opens with an episode from Raysky's life (his love of Sofya Belovodova), and proceeds through eight chapters that recount his childhood and youth.[45] Raysky also remains in the foreground through Part Two, most of which was completed in 1860 when the new theme was just emerging. Half way through Part Two Vera's mystery is introduced.[46] Part Three, begun in the mid-sixties and well *after* the discovery of the theme of the nihilist, opens with what reads like a herald of the shifting locus of interest— a discussion of Raysky's politics followed by a political discussion among the local gentry. In Part Three the nihilist makes his entrance and the drama of the ravine, the competition of the several men for Vera, commences. Raysky, initially a participant, recedes from center stage to become an observer and occasional commentator upon the action until the last few pages, when he is again the focus of interest. *The Ravine*, then, started out with the promise of becoming, like Goncharov's other novels, a fictional biography. It also had the potential to be the distinctively ironic kind of fictional life the novelist had given us before. That central problem of his fiction, the discrepancy between a solitary hero's illusions and a refractory reality upon which he futilely tries to enforce his desires, is translated in this final novel into a study of the relations between art and life. According to his own testimony Goncharov wished to observe in the charac-

---

[45] Chaps. six–thirteen. For details of the novel's history, see above, chap. three.

[46] In Part Two, Malinovka, its environs, and inhabitants are described largely through Raysky's eyes. He goes through a succession of encounters with the "grandmother," Marfenka, and Leonty (including a lengthy flashback describing their student years—chaps. five and six). Vera's "mystery" is first mentioned in chap. eleven.

ter of Boris Raysky "the curious psychological . . . process . . . , namely, how the power of imagination in artistic natures, when it is not applied to vital work, plunges into life itself, and clothes the trivial appearances of the latter in its own colors and hues, producing those extravagances, eccentricities, and deformities that frequently abound in the lives of artists everywhere."[47]

Raysky dabbles in painting and music; his major artistic project, however, is the writing of a novel that, as it turns out, has the same subject matter as the novel we are reading. The device of a novel-within-a-novel may be employed for several ends, but a major use, especially for modern artists, has been to achieve irony. The protagonist's novel conflicts with the actual novel, which is granted the authority of "true" experience. In the absence of any other apparent purpose to Goncharov's sub-novel we anticipate such an ironic relation between Raysky's work in progress and Goncharov's evolving novel, and there are some indications that this indeed is how we are meant to view *The Ravine*'s double perspective. Raysky believes that "life is a novel, and a novel is life," but the narrator intervenes to dissociate himself from his hero's literary efforts and to point out that "a novel is not reality. . . ."[48] Vera, upon occasion, like Pyotr Aduev before her, mocks him by transposing his self-consciously literary speech into a banal context. *The Ravine* also has its deflating characters—characters who, like Zakhar of *Oblomov*, exist on a lower plane of reality and comment upon or parody the protagonist. Raysky, in the throes of creative ecstasy, is observed through a peephole by uncomprehending peasants astonished at this "oddity." Vera, who is not only a woman, or even hardly a woman, for Raysky, but an ideal of art and beauty—"You are all poetry. . . . You are both the idea of beauty and the incarnation of that idea . . ."—has a comic counterpart in Polina, an aging and empty-headed coquette who pursues Raysky and tends to show up just at those moments when he is awaiting his ideal in passionate anticipation.[49]

But for the most part "life" (Goncharov's novel) fails to place Raysky's imagination and rhetoric into perspective as "the others" did

---

[47] *Sobr. soch.*, VIII, 87. [48] *Ibid.*, V, 43; VI, 41.
[49] *Ibid.*, V, 349; VI, 197, 155, 277-278; V, 303-304.

for Alexander Aduev and Oblomov. The comic deflations, when they do crop up, remain isolated exceptions, old and tired reflexes of writing that have lingered on. Turgid speech and exalted moods had always distinguished Goncharov's heroes, but, where in the previous fiction they had constituted a part of a total comic scheme, subject to incessant parody and irony, in *The Ravine* they largely stand alone, contributing to the overall pomposity and bombast of the novel.

In abandoning the rigorous irony and the comic view of experience that had served as the controlling intelligence of his previous fiction, Goncharov lost control of the character who he professed was his major interest. If we perceive fictional characters not as friends or relatives of the author who have inadvertently dropped in upon his pages, nor as spontaneously emitted projections of the self, but as artifacts to some degree controlled by the creative intelligence and designed to operate purposively within a meaningful structure, then Boris Raysky may not be a literary character at all and his novel may be something other than a literary convention. Besides acting as a mouthpiece for the author's views, he seems to have become his agent in another, extremely curious manner. The reader acquainted with the history of *The Ravine* comes away from the work with the uneasy feeling that Raysky's novel is merely a device employed by Goncharov to convey the doubts and hesitations he had about *his* novel. The sub-novel, instead of a *literary* convention intended to contribute to a total meaning, turns out to be *literally* the same novel Goncharov is writing. Thus we find Raysky making sketches of characters, collecting "material" and, like Goncharov at work on *The Ravine*, despairing at his inability "to group them harmoniously," to find "a tie between them." In the summer of 1860 Goncharov had decided to change his tactics and write slowly and methodically, a chapter at a time, and in Part Two, chapter thirteen, which was most likely written during that same summer, Raysky decides to write his novel "episodically, sketching a character who interests him, a scene that attracts or strikes him. . . ." *The Ravine* has the "pasted" quality Goncharov described: a number of scenes and characters are not related or related only incidentally to the plot. An apology or an expression of doubt by Raysky invariably accompanies their appearances. Thus, he finds a sketch of a Natasha "pale," but later decides to hold on to it until the " 'goal and necessity' of the creation appears . . ." —terms Goncharov often used in letters about his novel. "Why did he describe him? He doesn't fit in the novel; he has no role there," Raysky asks of an Openkin who has just had an entire chapter devoted to him, though he indeed has "no role." Goncharov vacillated about the subject of his novel, and we find Raysky turning first to Sofya and then to Marfenka to find the heroine of "the drama of passion," until he finally settles upon Vera.[50] As *The Ravine* shifts from a fictional biography to a drama of conflict interrupted by landscape scenes and "genre sketches" depicting the daily rounds of life upon the estate (justly cited by critics as the most praiseworthy moments of the novel), Raysky finds himself in a quandary over the kind of novel he is writing: he cannot decide whether his characters "are suitable . . . for a drama or only an idyll. . . ." At other times he is engaged in a novel of "psychological analysis drawing the data from himself."[51]

The expressions of doubt notably cease with Part Three, when the "drama of passion" takes hold. At the conclusion, however, several curious items appear that may also be disguised communications from the author concerning his work. Raysky suddenly discovers, while painting Vera, "that it was effrontery to draw her gaze in which her entire drama . . . resided," and proceeds to sketch her sleeping face, now with unusual facility, as "an image of somnolent peace. . . ." On the last pages of the novel he decides to abandon both painting and literature for sculpture. Sculpture (Raysky is inspired by classical Greek sculpture), though it can communicate a drama of its own, is by its nature the most stable of art forms, and it is somehow fitting that the last of Goncharov's heroes to seek a world of perfect stability should make it his final choice. Was Goncharov also acknowledging

---

[50] *Ibid.*, V, 112, 252-254, 124, 335, 154-155, 189-190. Raysky's novel eventually receives the title, *Vera: A Novel* (VI, 418), which was the title of Goncharov's work in progress after *Raysky, The Artist* was abandoned and until the summer of 1868.

[51] *Ibid.*, V, 165, 182, 307. Also see V, 156. "What kind of novel shall I find there in that remote corner, in the country! An idyll perhaps . . . or a novel . . . with fire, movement, passion!"

his failure to overcome the static forms of the previous fiction and to render more dynamic modes of experience?[52]

While completing *The Ravine*, Goncharov noted that ". . . the second half would probably constitute a separate novel."[53] The shift from Raysky's biography to Vera's drama effectively split the work in two, so that we have not only a novel with irrelevant scenes pasted in but two novels pasted together. An even more serious rupture of unity results from the chasm between Raysky and the fictional world in which he is located. Raysky writes a novel that illuminates neither his own personality nor those of the characters around him, and that in terms of the larger novel proves to be a redundancy. He indulges in weighty moral preachments and intense self-dramatizations that largely stand without commentary or response from his fictional community. Raysky views his situation as "a tragedy"—which may be how his author came to see it[54]—but he never finds a tragic action (or any other action) to participate in.

Earlier we saw that in Raysky (and several others, notably Vera) Goncharov was trying to create what was for him a new kind of character—a character who is not fixed in a single idea or aspect of the self but who retains the potentiality for alternative possibilities. But failing to locate an action through which the potentialities of his personality can achieve definition and clarity, Raysky remains located in a partial self as much as Alexander Aduev and Oblomov before him. To revert to Paul Goodman's terminology, he stays locked in his initial "sentimental disposition," his "changeability" as the novel defined it, and in the absence of any clarifying action "the emerging unity" of his attitudes, which Goodman calls "character," never appears.[55] As the novel progresses, Raysky's unresolved "changeability" becomes merely a chronic moodiness alternating between exaltation and depression, so that, for the lack of any unified image of a total

---

[52] *Ibid.*, VI, 371-372, 422-424.

[53] In a letter to S. A. Nikitenko, July 12, 1868. Cited in Tseytlin, *I. A. Goncharov*, p. 233.

[54] See below. For Raysky's view, see *Sobr. soch.*, VI, 291.

[55] See above, chap. five.

character, "changeability" must be described as his essence. Once again we have been returned to our starting point, as yet another Goncharov hero clings tenaciously to a dominant and single aspect of the self through the course of a novel. However, the difference between the previous situations and Raysky's is huge, for while Alexander Aduev and Oblomov experienced an external reality that commented upon and circumscribed their obsessions—and defined them for the reader—Raysky speaks to a world that has nothing to say to him in return.

With *The Ravine* Goncharov wrote the novel he said he would not write. He denied art the capacity to treat the "topical" and yet wrote a novel treating contemporary issues. His view of a literary type as stable and fixed, though consistent with his earlier comic and ironic approaches, seemed to preclude a "dramatic manner" of presentation. Nevertheless in *The Ravine* he strove to perceive character dynamically and situation dramatically. Several factors may have compelled Goncharov to abandon Raysky in midstream and to turn from the ironic fictional biographies he had written before (and may have originally intended in *The Ravine*) to a social drama. The poet Innokenty Annensky in a perceptive essay suggested that Raysky was too complex for Goncharov, and he also may have been too close: ". . . often I myself crawled into him and felt as if I were in a dressing gown sewn to fit perfectly."[56] Though the fit was good, the repressed and anxious Goncharov must have felt uneasy in Raysky's gown, for Raysky's fantasies are largely sexual in nature. Like Alexander Aduev and Ilya Oblomov, Raysky is a dreamer; like them he tries to realize his dreams in reality, but where Alexander and Ilya Ilich sought an ideal "poetic moment" of love that would transcend ordinary humdrum experience, Raysky seeks his ecstatic paradise—*ray* means "paradise"—in what Alexander had ignored and Oblomov had feared—ordinary sexual passion. In rejecting an idealized, esthetic version of love—". . . 'sacred, profound, elevated love' is a lie!" "No, I want ordinary, vital, animal passion . . ."—Raysky

---

[56] Annensky, in *Russkaya shkola*, No. 4 (April 1892), p. 75. Goncharov, in a letter to D. N. Tsertelev, September 16, 1885, *Sobr. soch.* (Pravda), VIII, 487.

instead idealizes passion. It becomes his transcendent moment: "Passion is constant intoxication, . . . eternal flowers beneath your feet, . . . an idol. . . . Anxieties, the petty troubles of life, everything disappears—infinite triumph alone suffuses you. . . ."[57] Though his rhetoric is as banal as always, there are interesting ideas at work in the character of Raysky, foremost of which is the relation of sexual sublimation to artistic creation. Raysky can never decide whether to direct his passion toward art or toward women, or indeed whether the objects of his passion are really women or only subjects for works of art. But Goncharov in this instance lacked the intellectual sophistication and the moral courage to face Raysky's, and perhaps his own, dilemma squarely. The melodrama his life had become—the paranoia that was in full swing when *The Ravine* was completed—enabled him to project his unacceptable emotions outward and upon another, the villainous Turgenev, and the melodrama of *The Ravine* serves a similar purpose. Instead of pursuing the implications of his hero's confusion of art and life, which is at the same time a confusion of esthetic feeling and sexual passion, he conveniently dropped the subject, projected animal passion upon an operatic villain, manufactured yet another passionless strong man to wed yet another feminine icon, and closed the doors of his idyllic estate to any emotions more intense than familial affection. Aduev and Oblomov had sought refuge from passion in similar idyllic landscapes, but while the locales of their retreat had been treated with critical irony—blended in *Oblomov* with great imaginative sympathy—*The Ravine*, following the urge of melodrama to maintain unequivocal distinctions of virtue and vice, turns Malinovka into an object lesson for those who would stray into the arena of passionate life.

Goncharov may have fallen from comedy into melodrama for another reason. He had apparently succumbed to that not infrequent temptation of comic artists—the ambition to write something "serious" and "important," as if comedy can only be trivial. In a letter to Sofya Nikitenko of August 21, 1866, he wrote that in the character of Boris Raysky he wanted to realize "the sole artistic ideal" of his career, "the portrayal of an honest, good, and sympathetic nature, an

---

[57] *Sobr. soch.*, VI, 57-58, 66-68.

idealist to the highest degree, who struggles all his life searching for the truth, encounters lies at every step, is deceived, and finally grows cool and falls into apathy and impotence out of a consciousness of his and others' weakness, that is, the general weakness of human nature." He attributed previous failures to realize his ideal to the dominance of the Gogolian "negative tendency" (*otritsatel'noe napravlenie*), which turned his attention to "partial types, . . . [their] grotesque and comical sides, . . . instead of a serious human figure."[58] Gogol also tried to be something other than a comic artist at the end of his career—and with similar disastrous results.

Finally, changing circumstances in the history of Russian literature undoubtedly had much to do with Goncharov's decision to write a social drama. Russian realism was born in the "physiological sketches" or "slices of life" popular in the forties—a form that continued beyond the decade and is reflected in the genre scenes of common life in Goncharov's novels. In the fifties there appeared a number of works centering upon the experiences of a single hero, frequently narrating his fictional life—e.g., Tolstoy's *Childhood* (1852), *Boyhood* (1854), *Youth* (1857); Sergey Aksakov's *Family Chronicle* (1856), *The Childhood of Bagrov the Grandson* (1858). Goncharov's first novel, though it proved too fragile to exert an influence, presaged the biographical fiction of the fifties, and *Oblomov*, for all its eccentricities, was representative of it. With the sixties Russian novelists began to concentrate their energies upon depicting the intricate fabric of social life; Turgenev, whose novels first appeared toward the end of the previous decade, anticipated the trend. As a result, the Russian novel became decentralized, shifting from a single dominant protagonist to a wide spectrum of characters representative of different social groups; we need only compare Tolstoy's earlier fiction and the large and complex worlds of *War and Peace* (1865-1869) and *Anna Karenina* (1875-1877). The more explicit social concerns of the novel were complemented by an increased dramatic emphasis, often expressive of social conflict. Interest in depth-psychology grew as the relations between society and the individual became a focus of interest. Dostoevsky's major novels, which com-

[58] *Ibid.*, VIII, 366.

mence in the sixties, provide the clearest examples of the increased dramatic and psychological emphasis of the Russian novel, and its growing complexity of plot.[59] Leon Stilman found in the introduction of the nihilist theme into *The Ravine* "a visible effort to bring the novel up to date"[60]—to give it contemporary political relevance (another aspect of the fiction of the sixties)—and we have witnessed an all-too-visible effort to bring the novel into conformity with current *formal*, as well as thematic, interests of the Russian novel. Goncharov's crisis in the sixties, though it had profound psychological causes, was also the crisis of an artist attempting to bend his distinctive personal vision to new literary trends.

[59] My argument here has been influenced by Prutskov, *Masterstvo*, pp. 129-138.

[60] *American Slavic and East European Review*, VII, 56.

CHAPTER IX

Goncharov and His Trilogy

THUS far we have concentrated the greater part of our attention upon the individual features of Goncharov's three novels. *A Common Story* resembled a classical comedy of manners; *Oblomov* was built upon a complex system of tensions between elements of romance and realistic irony; in *The Ravine* Goncharov attempted to write a novel intensely dramatic in manner and more firmly anchored in contemporary social reality than his previous novels had been, but the result was melodrama. For all their differences in scope and manner is there anything that unites the three novels? Does Goncharov's fictional corpus display a dominant attitude or approach to experience, so that we can speak of the world of the fiction as we have spoken of the worlds of the individual novels?

As might be expected, three works conceived within a five-year span of their author's life reveal a number of similar concerns and mannerisms, some at the level of minutiae, others more important. It seems profitable, however, to maintain our general approach and proceed from a fact of formal organization to interpretation. In all three novels experience tends to fall into a similar pattern. In *A Common Story* Alexander Aduev regularly turns from passivity to action and back to passivity, creating a rhythm of experience that remains subordinate to the controlling linear plot of the novel. In the absence of a strong plot line in *Oblomov* a similar curve of action provides the dominant pattern. In both novels love entanglements contribute the action at the top of the curve before a predictable decline. The pattern is obscured in *The Ravine*, where Goncharov abandoned his apparent protagonist in midstream, but the progress of Malinovka's social world describes a similar arc, from peace to the incursion of passion in summer to the final triumph of an autumnal peace without passion. Passion, often explicitly sexual, forms the problematical center of Goncharov's fiction.

It is problematical because it disrupts that rock-like stability Goncharov's characters seek, a stability that the novelist perceived as the true subject of literature. The entrance of passion into the fiction also marks the point where two irreconcilable attitudes toward experience collide. Through love of a woman Goncharov's heroes seek to escape their painful isolation and enter the world of "the others," but each is hindered by a conception of love as an ideal and transcendent condition. Instead, they meet obstinate women who refuse to share their idealized visions, or they are forced to confront the obligations, uncertainties, and imperfections of ordinary life. In either case they feel shattered.

The usual curve of action, then, rises to an attempt to capture the ideal in love and declines into failure, with the qualification that the story of Raysky's failure is subordinated to the tale of Malinovka's triumph. The pattern seems to suggest an interpretation of Goncharov's novels as repeating a story of systematic disillusionment, a fall from the ideal to the real. But we have also noticed a counter-tendency in the fiction: a raising of ideal conditions to replace those that have been rejected. As Oblomov and Raysky fail to find paradise in love, their novels postulate alternate versions of paradise, Arcadias where the turbulence of passion is either unknown or successfully resisted, idyllic gardens beyond history or barricaded against its incursions. In *A Common Story* this alternate vision of an ideal world remains undeveloped, though its outlines can already be perceived in the frame chapters depicting Alexander's native Grachi, the house he leaves and eventually returns to in the final chapter (before the epilogue) to recover the peace he could not find in the bustling competitive city. Goncharov's fiction confronts not only the ideal and the real but two versions of the ideal: the ecstasy of a moment that promises to but proves unable to transcend life, and an idyllic condition rooted in nature and the cycles of habit, impervious to change and empty of human passion. Two of the latter idylls are dominated by maternal figures, Alexander Aduev's mother and Boris Raysky's great aunt, the "grandmother"; Oblomov has a vision of his idyll in a dream that takes him back to childhood, and recovers it at the round, dimpled, nourishing elbows (breasts?) of Agafya Matveevna. It would seem that the major impulse of Goncharov's art—its longing for a world marked by perfect sympathy and untouched by the conflicts of adult sexuality or the demands of adult responsibility—is also a nostalgia for the mother-dominated condition of early childhood.

It is in their treatment of these three elements—idyllic love, the idyllic estate of childhood, and the "normal" world of maturity—that the three novels differ vastly. *A Common Story* concentrates its energies upon the downward turn of the curve, the ironic descent from ideal love (or an idealistic view of art) to the "common" life, treating the former as illusion and making comedy out of its loss. Alexander, unlike Ilya Ilich, rejects the gardens of childhood as a possible alternative, and the only other option presented in the novel is a sterile and empty maturity. *The Ravine* assumes an opposite attitude toward the declining curve of its pattern—from passion to peace. In the manner of melodrama it idealizes the conventional social world, the estate of Raysky's childhood, while projecting evil, i.e., passion, outward upon an alien villain. *Oblomov*, while rejecting, as all Goncharov's fiction does, the turbulence of passionate life and exposing the ecstatic transcendent moment of love as illusion, nevertheless maintains a delicate balance between the claims of the ideal and the real, the paradisiac memories of childhood and the claims of adult responsibility, imagination and necessity. It is in this refusal of the artist to commit himself to a single attitude toward experience that much of the success of that novel resides. While *A Common Story* is a bit too harsh and unyielding in its ironic stripping away of Alexander's illusions, and *The Ravine* is prudish and moralistic in its strainings to maintain unequivocal distinctions of virtue and vice, *Oblomov* displays that rare combination of critical detachment and sympathetic understanding that distinguishes great novels.

Finally, Alexander Aduev and Boris Raysky are artists, and Oblomov, though he lacks artistic as well as any other ambition, is also, as Stolz informs us, "a poet." But Goncharov's three protagonists are incomplete "artists," men endowed with artistic sensibility and imagination who are unable, because of a deficiency of discipline, persistence, and a sense of order, to objectify the promptings of their imagination into works of art. Instead they project the tendencies of their imaginations upon life itself and attempt to live in a world shaped by their private dreams.[1] The acknowledged theme of *The Ravine*—the confusion of art and life—is with different nuances the theme of Goncharov's major fiction. His three protagonists, as we have seen, direct their imaginations toward varying visions of the ideal. The collision of the ideal and the real was, of course, a great theme of nineteenth-century fiction. However, Goncharov's true interest lay not in an exposure of the illusoriness of the former—he formulated as many ideal possibilities as he derided—but in the exploration of a mind that refuses to distinguish the constructs of art and imagination from the actualities of existence.

The fears and confusion of Goncharov's heroes were also those of their creator. Like them he drew back from the uncertainties of passionate life and the demands of sexual involvement; like them he came to confuse the creations of his fancy with reality. But at its best Goncharov's work is something other than self-expression— indeed, it is at its worst when it is only self-expression, when the author speaks to us directly through Boris Raysky. Most often art served him as, in T. S. Eliot's words, "an escape from emotion" and "an escape from personality," though at one level it was an escape in a different sense from Eliot's. Not only has Goncharov evoked a series of Arcadias where passion is unknown and the conflicts of personality have disappeared, but one of his major efforts was to subdue the tensions between differing individuals in a total harmony of comic reconciliation. His prose, like the peaceful river of Oblomovka, flows smoothly, evenly, at times almost hypnotically, submerging in its indolent movement sharp emotion and even individual voices. Goncharov claimed to feel most alive while writing, and the life he sought in his art was one of profound, all-embracing peace. But as his fiction is not only self-expression, neither is it mere escapism. Goncharov

---

[1] When Stolz called Oblomov "a poet," Ilya replied, "Yes, I am a poet in life, because life is poetry," *Sobr. soch.*, IV, 184.

was able also to "escape" in Eliot's meaning—to make that leap that separates "the man who suffers and the mind which creates."[2] As he suffered with his heroes, as he postulated ideal alternatives to the fragmented and chaotic world of experience, his creative intelligence, before it failed him, weighed their longings against the limitations imposed upon men by human society and their own mortality. Among the most nostalgic of writers, he is also among the most civilized.

[2] "Tradition and Individual Talent," *Selected Essays: 1917-1932* (New York, 1932), pp. 7-11.

CHAPTER X

Last Works

THE attempt to adjust to the literary manner of the sixties had failed, and Goncharov did not again undertake a large-scale work. Despite his declared intention to retire completely from literature, he continued to write sporadically and at times well.

Much of the work of his last years was devoted to nonfiction and a good part of that to literary criticism. Goncharov's several attempts at self-criticism, the most important of which is the essay "Better Late Than Never" ("Luchshe pozdno, chem nikogda") (1879), are a valuable source for determining his views on art and the creative process.[1] Though they also include some helpful suggestions for interpreting the novels, as criticism they are too defensive and apologetic and at times merely repeat the standard arguments critics had employed for his work—it was Dobrolyubov, he suggests, who taught him to understand *Oblomov* correctly![2]

Goncharov's critical writings on the work of others also repeat the conventional generalities of the time, though upon occasion he breaks through with genuine insights of his own. I have already mentioned a piece celebrating Karamzin's contribution to the moral enlightenment of Russians.[3] Another, on *Hamlet*, written in 1875, follows Belinsky in viewing Shakespeare's hero as a strong and ex-

---

[1] "Luchshe pozdno, chem nikogda," begun as an introduction to *The Ravine* in 1870 (see *Sobr. soch.*, VIII, 66), was published in *Russkaya rech'*, No. 6 (1879). Also, "Predislovie k romanu Obryv," written in 1869 and first published in 1938, in *Literaturno-kriticheskie stat'i*, and "Namereniya, zadachi i idei romana Obryv," written in 1871-1872 and published posthumously, in *Russkoe obozrenie*, No. 1 (1895). Unless stated otherwise, works discussed in this chapter are cited according to *Sobr. soch.*, Vols. VII and VIII.

[2] *Sobr. soch.*, VIII, 71.   [3] See above, chap. one.

ceptional individual crushed by circumstances.[4] Goncharov's attitude toward Belinsky is conveyed in a penetrating profile, "Remarks on Belinsky's Personality" ("Zametki o lichnosti Belinskogo") (1881).[5] He approved of Belinsky's passionate responsiveness to works of literature—a critic must first "feel"; cooler, more rigorous minds could never have influenced the course of almost an entire literature—but finds that the same passionate intensity led to intolerance, fanaticism, and a disregard for historical perspective that turned Belinsky into a literary "Don Juan," pursuing every new fashion in thought or literature as if nothing had existed before. An essay on Ostrovsky calls the dramatist "unquestionably the greatest talent in contemporary literature!"—a judgment that is certainly questionable since at the time (1874) both Dostoevsky and Tolstoy were alive and well.[6] Goncharov saw in Ostrovsky an indication of the waning of the predominance of the aristocracy in Russian letters and the ascendancy of the more national "middle class"—the "class" to which Goncharov himself more or less belonged—and praised him for his rendering of everyday life and manners (*byt, nravy*), the very things critics chose to praise in Goncharov.

Much of Russian criticism in the sixties and seventies described literary works, whenever possible, as portraits of social mores and extolled the mode of social satire above all others. It is the merit of Goncharov's most ambitious critical undertaking, an essay on Griboedov's *Woe from Wit* entitled after a phrase from the play, "A Million Torments" ("Mil'yon terzaniy") (1872), that it tries to approach Griboedov's great play as something more than a static repre-

[4] "Opyat' *Gamlet* na russkoy stsene," first published in part, in *Tragediya o Gamlete, printse Datskom,* Vol. II, trans. K. R. [Grand Prince Konstantin Konstantinovich] (St. Petersburg, 1900); in entirety in 1952, in *Sobr. soch.* (Pravda), VIII, 197-205. Also, in *Sobr. soch.,* VIII, 197-207. Cf. Belinsky's "*Gamlet,* drama Shekspira," *Sobr. soch.,* I, 336-340.

[5] Written in 1873-1875 and published in *Chetyre ocherki* (St. Petersburg, 1881).

[6] "Materialy, zagotovlyaemye dlya kriticheskoy stat'i ob Ostrovskom," *Sobr. soch.,* VIII, 176. First published in the collection, *Pamyati A. N. Ostrovskogo* (Petrograd, 1923). An earlier "Otzyv o drame *Groza* Ostrovskogo" was published in *Otchot o chetvyortom prisuzhdenii nagrad gr. Uvarova 25 sentyabrya 1860* (St. Petersburg, 1860).

sentation of a particular milieu—an effort that gives the essay some historical importance. *Woe from Wit* is, as everyone says, "a portrait of manners, and a gallery of living types, and an always sharp, scathing satire," but it is also a comedy—"above all, a comedy." Its comic nature lies in its "action," its "movement."[7] Unfortunately Goncharov lacked the critical equipment to develop his insight into a description of the structural unity of the play, and his demonstration breaks down into an itemization of moments of dramatic confrontation. In line with his argument that *Woe from Wit* is a fully realized comedy and not just "a gallery of types," he pointed to a degree of complexity in the character of Sofya Pavlovna (he was the first to do so) and placed larger emphasis upon Chatsky's personal drama than was customary at the time.[8]

Goncharov did not devote separate essays to his fellow-novelists but mentioned them in passing. He gave no indication that he had grasped Dostoevsky's significance, had little to say about Gogol, whom he resembles in his use of caricature and parody, and expressed tremendous admiration for Tolstoy, whom he little resembles.[9] We have already seen what he thought of Turgenev.

A good share of the writing of Goncharov's last years consists of reminiscences, most of which resemble works of fiction in their use of fictional names, scenic representation, and other narrative techniques. The personal reminiscences, "At Home" ("Na rodine") and "At the University" ("V universitete") (1887-1888), reveal very little that is truly personal. Instead, they give an interesting picture of life in a provincial Russian town (Simbirsk) of the early nineteenth century and at Moscow University of the thirties. Goncharov never tired of telling the story of the journey of the frigate *Pallas* and "After Twenty Years" ("Cherez dvadtsat' let") (1874) and "Through Eastern Siberia" ("Po vostochnoy Sibiri") (1891),

---

[7] *Sobr. soch.*, VIII, 10-13. First published in *Vestnik Evropy*, No. 3 (1872).

[8] See Tseytlin, *I. A. Goncharov*, pp. 290-291. In addition to the critical essays mentioned above Goncharov wrote an essay, "Khristos v pustyne," in 1874 on the Russian painter Ivan Kramskoy (1837-1887). First published in *Nachala*, No. 1 (1921).

[9] See three letters to Tolstoy of 1887-1888, in *Sobr. soch.*, VIII, 494-499.

like the earlier "Two Incidents from Life at Sea" ("Dva sluchaya iz morskoy zhizni") (1858), continue the tale. The uncompleted "A Trip Along the Volga" ("Poezdka po Volge") written in 1873-1874, recounts one of his infrequent visits home, in 1862, to Simbirsk. Its interest lies in an entertaining characterization of a traveling companion who bears some resemblance to Boris Raysky, except that Ivan Ivanych Khotkov is treated comically and without portentousness. Khotkov is an artist who seldom finishes what he sets out to do, a man of talent and little depth, of charm without character. Though an eccentric and a failure, as men usually define those terms, he manages to touch everyone about him with his openness and generosity of spirit. He is a kind of character who often caught Goncharov's eye.[10]

The best of these fictionalized reminiscences and one of the finer pieces of writing of Goncharov's career is "Servants of Old Times" ("Slugi starogo veka") (1888).[11] In it the novelist pays a literary debt of gratitude to the several servants who, like Oblomov's Zakhar, cared for him through the years, cheered him in the loneliness of his bachelor existence—and maddened him with their incorrigible bad habits. To his continuing consternation most turn out to be drunkards or desert their hapless master to pursue the neighbors' servant girls. Out of either class prejudice or a literary manner, Goncharov had always treated the lower social orders with comic and yet affectionate condescension. The combination is not lacking in "Servants," as an amusing gallery of Dickensian curios from the lower classes fills its

[10] "Na rodine," written in 1887, was published in *Vestnik Evropy*, Nos. 1-2 (1888). "V universitete," published under the title "Iz universitetskikh vospominaniy," in *ibid.*, No. 4 (1887), was begun much earlier, in 1862-1863, and later reworked. "Cherez dvadtsat' let" appeared in part under the title "Iz vospominaniy i rasskazov o morskom plavanii," in the collection *Skladchina* (St. Petersburg, 1874); Goncharov later added it to *The Frigate Pallas*, and it is now included with it. "Po vostochnoy Sibiri," a manuscript of which was ready in 1889, was published in *Russkoe obozrenie*, No. 1 (1891); "Dva sluchaya iz morskoy zhizni," in a children's magazine, *Podsnezhnik*, Nos. 2-3 (1858). "Poezdka po Volge" was first published in *Zvezda*, No. 2 (1940).

[11] Completed in 1887 from notes collected over a period of time (it is subtitled *iz domashnego arkhiva*) and published in *Niva*, Nos. 1-3, 18 (1888) as "Slugi."

pages[12]—the funniest is the fifty-year-old fop Valentin, who apes the manners of the gentry and expresses his literary pretensions in recitations of Zhukovsky's poetry (of which he doesn't understand a line) or in love letters to a local laundress that mix lofty clichés with the rudest colloquialisms. This sort of "genre humor" had become Goncharov's trademark—it was already evident in the early "Podzhabrin"—but something else makes its way into "Servants": a perception of dark shadows behind the comic habits of these "simple folk," of suppressed longings and unspoken miseries that establish their humanity. Valentin's exaggerated sense of honor is ludicrous but it is also real; another servant, Stepan, is too violent in his drunkenness, his wife too wretched in her poverty to be simply quaint. However, it is the serf Matvey who more than any of the others frees himself from the straitjacket of comic caricature and becomes something other than a piece of exotica from "the people." He is a memorable character.

Matvey is a find—a servant who does not drink. He does not do anything right either. Like Zakhar before him, Matvey is a model of ineptitude, stemming from the contradictory urges to please and to do everything his own way: he works in a frenzy, so that no dish or cup remains safe in his hands; he keeps an elaborate account of the household's expenditures, including losses incurred by himself, but in an orthography of his own devising that the harried master must decipher; he has his own system, based on rank, for admitting or refusing visitors. Neither curses nor entreaties avail. Matvey persists.

Matvey also looks odd. Nature has placed incongruously long arms and stiff wooden legs on a terribly thin body, so that he reminds everyone of a monkey. Men have not been kinder: his owner, who has hired him out, was less patient with his stubbornness than the author and beat him mercilessly. Life has given him a bedraggled, defeated look. People laugh at him.

Matvey also has a dream—to be free. His dream causes as much trouble for his master as his peculiar systems of work. Money must be saved to buy his freedom, and he will not eat enough to stay healthy or dress himself appropriately. He engages in illicit money-

---

[12] Goncharov admired Dickens immensely. See *Sobr. soch.*, VIII, 110-111.

lending schemes into which he tries to draw the author. He proves as inept at caring for his savings as for the master's dishes, and, whenever he comes close to the required sum, he manages to dissipate it. However, he persists, and in the end, somehow, he scrapes up enough and is free.

Goncharov, as we have seen a number of times, was a writer under a compulsion to pin characters down, to see them in the "stable and fixed" forms of a single trait. He makes the attempt once again with Matvey—"He became for me an extremely complex and curious character study. I strained to find a predominant trait in him, so that I might subsume him under some category of human types." But it won't work. Like Oblomov before him, Matvey refuses to remain tied to a single defining characteristic. At first the author agrees with the general report that finds him "comical." Later he decides that Matvey is not funny but "pitiable"; then, both pitiable and funny. To this the author must add "nasty" when it turns out that the major entertainment in life of this longsuffering "living corpse" is, besides watching parades, the pursuit of thieves with a gang of fellow-servants in order to delight in beating them cruelly. Matvey is also honest, devoted, and of course stubborn, "incurably" so.[13]

His elusiveness, his refusal to be caught in a category, is a function of his humanity. Goncharov had recognized before (especially in *Oblomov*) the elusiveness of human personality, its "incompleteness" and resistance to final definition, but he also feared it, because it meant that men were unpredictable and could not be contained in fixed and stable forms. Matvey is also a serf, a man of "the people," and if any predominant trait exists in that bizarre mixture of comic pedantry and abject suffering, awkwardness and indefatigable industry, cruelty and gentle devotion, it is his stubborn persistence in doing things his own way. Matvey survives—"He bore everything: the beatings of his master, constant hunger; he lost his strength from work, but he did not lose his spirit."[14] It is only right that Matvey gains his freedom in the end, for he had always held tenaciously to a small area of freedom even in his slavery. Goncharov's contemporaries often criticized him for ignoring the common people in his fiction and not

[13] *Ibid.*, VII, 367, 380.   [14] *Ibid.*, p. 369.

understanding them ("Servants" opens with an apology), and, though there is truth to the charge, he may have understood them better than those who wished only to glorify them.

Goncharov's reminiscences revert to the style of "the natural school" of the forties in their static representations of characters and scenes from everyday life—a manner found not only in that lone "physiological sketch," "Ivan Savich Podzhabrin," but also in the novels (Part One of *Oblomov*, most of which was written in the forties, echoes the natural school in its portrayal of a typical day in Oblomov's life and, in the "Dream," of the typical days of life in Oblomovka). "A Christmas Tree" ("Rozhdestvenskaya yolka") written in 1875, is a journalistic piece discussing the joys and discomforts of the Christmas season (gifts cost money; trees litter one's apartment, etc.); it includes a scene very much in the style of the natural school, as it evokes a bustling Petersburg of the holiday season through descriptions of the activities of representative citizens. "May in Petersburg" ("May mesyats v Peterburge") (1892) marks a complete reversion.[15] It *is* a physiological sketch. The sketch portrays the habits and foibles of Goncharov's neighbors as evinced on a characteristic day in May in the house on Mokhovaya Street where the novelist had spent almost half his life. The cast ranges from a pretentious countess through the petty bureaucrats or *chinovniki* who were almost obligatory for this sort of thing to the predictably comic workmen of the courtyard. It is old stuff, but the easily colloquial and relaxed manner of a writer who has mastered the genre gives it appeal. It also has a certain poignancy. Near the end Goncharov asks "What conclusion can one draw from all this?" and answers "None at all. A May passed, another, and a third—the heat of summers replaced them, then the foul weather of autumns, and so on. The house still stands on the same place. One must begin again from the beginning. . . ." It is the limitation of the genre that it can only present "stable and

---

[15] "Rozhdestvenskaya yolka" was first published in 1952, in *Sobr. soch.* (Pravda), VII, 459-463; a corrected version may be found in *Literaturnyy arkhiv*, IV (1953), 99-106. "May mesyats v Peterburge" was prepared for publication by Goncharov in 1891 but printed after his death, in *Sbornik Nivy*, No. 2 (1892).

fixed" forms in the eternal returns of daily life. Nevertheless, the writer proceeds to itemize changes in the lives of his characters. The tone is elegiac: "Life, always life, it keeps moving little by little, always forward and forward, like everything in the world, and on heaven and earth."[16] But if we look closely, we note that nothing essential has changed. As so often in Goncharov's fiction, the external situations of his people may have become different, but their characters and manners remain the same. Something is changing, though —life "keeps moving" the narrator laments, as Oblomov had before him—and "May in Petersburg," written in the year of Goncharov's death, conveys on its last pages a sense of a world slipping away from the novelist, that world of small domestic pleasures and consolations he loved and had portrayed so well.

Goncharov also wrote several short stories in the last two decades of his life. "A Literary Evening" ("Literaturnyy vecher") (1880) resembles the sketches (as the sketches and the reminiscences resemble each other).[17] Though it tells a story, the story does not lead any place and remains a static portrayal of an evening's discussion of literature by a group consisting of a reactionary, a nihilist, and representatives of every shade of opinion between. As a story it is wordy and deadly; as a literary discussion it indicates that Goncharov, contrary to those critics who called him naive or ignorant of contemporary issues, possessed a fairly intelligent understanding of the arguments of his age. His views, however, are more accessible in his letters and essays (in "A Literary Evening" they are distributed over the middle range of characters between the nihilist and the reactionary), and the story has little, if any, interest.

"The Vicissitudes of Fate" ("Prevratnost' sud'by"), written with "May in Petersburg" in 1891, is like it subtitled "a sketch," but it has a central hero and tells a story.[18] The narrative follows a straight and simple line, presenting a progression of events in the life of the ex-

---

[16] *Sobr. soch.*, VII, 423-426.

[17] Written in 1877, published in *Russkaya rech'*, No. 1 (1880).

[18] Goncharov's last composition, it was written several weeks before his death and published posthumously, in *Sbornik Nivy*, No. 1 (1893). It may be found in *Sobr. soch.* (Pravda), VII, 480-489.

officer Leonty Khabarov and, quite uncharacteristically of Goncharov, without halting upon accumulations of realistic detail or delving into the psychology of the hero. The manner is somewhat reminiscent of Tolstoy's post-1880 popular tales, except that the point is anything but Tolstoyan. Khabarov, an honest and industrious man living in the age of Alexander I, comes to ruin because he lives in a world where men are less than industrious and not altogether honest. "I know that you are not to blame," one of the several employers who feels compelled to fire him exclaims, ". . . [that] you are an industrious and honest man. . . . Such a man is not needed here. . . ."[19] At the brink of suicide, from which he is restrained only by his Christian faith, Khabarov wanders in distraction into the Tsar's garden at Tsarskoe Selo (he is admitted because he still wears his officer's uniform), runs into Alexander I, the Tsar befriends him, and everything is put well. As in the early tale "A Happy Error," Khabarov's story turns upon "a vicissitude of fate" and thereby loses any moral edge it might have acquired.

"Fish Soup" ("Ukha") (date unknown, but late) is in its narrow limits a completely successful story.[20] Like "The Vicissitudes of Fate" it evolved from an incident the writer had heard in his youth in Simbirsk. Three couples of the town's lower middle class set out in two carts for a picnic in the country. The giggling wives tease their driver, a simple-minded and mutely suffering church sexton called Erema. They poke their umbrellas into his ribs, while the husbands goad them on from the adjacent cart. Erema remains silent and only bares his teeth slightly at every renewal of his torments. Devout and humble, he crosses himself at each church the party passes and, as is the custom, beseeches the saint or divinity after whom the church has been named to "pity us sinners." But the simple Erema, as it turns out, possesses a secret talent of which his tormentors are unaware. Come to their destination, the men go off to catch fish for the soup,

---

[19] *Ibid.*, p. 484.

[20] The handwriting of the manuscript has caused the editor (Tseytlin) of *Sobr. soch.* (Pravda) to assign it to the last years of Goncharov's life. See VII, 490-495, 502. It was first published with errors in 1923, in *Goncharov i Turgenev.*

leaving the wives to tend to the campsite and keep their eyes on Erema, for Erema, besides being humble and devout, is lazy. In turn, each wife dutifully goes to check whether he is performing his duty and tending the horses; each discovers his mysterious talent; each spends an hour with the gentle sexton and returns in "an excited condition," straightening her clothes and somewhat abstracted. The trip home repeats the trip out—the same goading on the part of the husbands, the same churches, the same "pity us sinners"—except that the women, fallen strangely silent, no longer poke their umbrellas at Erema, while he, as quiet and self-effacing as always, no longer bares his teeth. "The fish soup was glorious," the narrator informs us.

"Fish Soup" is a charming, unassuming piece and we regret that Goncharov didn't attempt more like it. As the sketches hark back to the natural school of the forties, the playful anecdotal quality of "Fish Soup," though also subtitled "a sketch," recalls the first stories of the thirties, especially "A Happy Error." Like it (and like *A Common Story*) "Fish Soup" depends for its effect upon a pattern of symmetrical and ironic returns. However, it is less elaborate and contrived, more relaxed and laconic than the stories of the thirties. Goncharov concentrates on the anecdote itself and tells it with little embellishment and, once again, without extended use of realistic detail. As the style, though not the moral range, of "The Vicissitudes of Fate" suggested late Tolstoy, "Fish Soup" echoes the early, humorous Chekhov of 1879-1886, which is about the time when Tolstoy's new manner was emerging. The description of the march of the picnickers with its blending of terse perceptions and repeated fragments of speech into a total impression—Erema's "pity us sinners," his white teeth, the husbands' "Give it to him good, give it to him good," the refrains of a song started by one, then picked up by another—is very Chekhovian.

The slender corpus and small range of Goncharov's late work can undoubtedly be explained by the devastating effect of the failure of *The Ravine*. Having failed at his attempt to create a novel of complicated plot and dramatic entanglement, he returned to the less demanding playful anecdotes and genre sketches of his early years. Goncharov had come full circle, but so had Russian literature. By

1880 the era of the Russian realistic novel was largely over. The causes for its demise were many, but, among other reasons, it collapsed under the weight of its own esthetic. The commonly held goal of the realists to offer "the objective representation of contemporary social reality"[21] returned much of Russian realism to the sketches of social manners that had marked its beginnings. The great masters of the Russian novel, and the author of *Oblomov* is among them, had placed their representations of the social texture of contemporary life into complex imaginative structures controlled by profoundly personal visions of experience. An impending decline of the Russian realistic novel can already be discerned at the moment of its greatest triumph —the sixties and seventies. Most of the important fiction of those decades was produced by men who more or less belonged to Goncharov's generation: Dostoevsky, Saltykov-Shchedrin, Tolstoy, Turgenev. The work of the second generation of realists who appear at the time is, except for Leskov, of the second rank. Much of it is either unabashedly tendentious like Chernyshevsky's *What Is to Be Done?*, or in the manner of Gleb Uspensky tends to break down into ethnographical sketches of the daily lives of ordinary Russians, lacking the imaginative scope that has insured the survival and universal appeal of the older realists. In the end, to cite a brilliant exponent of Russian modernism surveying the achievements of the Russian novel from the vantage point of the 1920's, ". . . everything turned into painting."[22] Goncharov, in returning to the genre sketch of his youth, was again following a current trend in the cycles of literary change.

If the Russian realistic novel had seen its day, Russian literature was anything but dead. Goncharov's fiction begins, prior to his interest in the physiological sketch, in the light unassuming play of the stories of the thirties and ends in the similar play of a story like "Fish Soup." The two periods are analogous, for the thirties also

---

[21] See Wellek, *Concepts of Criticism*, pp. 252-253.

[22] Evgeny Zamyatin, "Novaya russkaya proza," *Litsa* (New York, 1955), p. 199. Tschiżewski [Chizhevsky], in *Russische Literaturgeschichte des 19. Jahrhunderts*, II: *Der Realismus* (Munich, 1967), pp. 65, 163, notes a return to the style of the natural school and the physiological sketch in the writings of Uspensky and the radical and populist writers of the sixties and seventies.

witnessed the exhaustion of a genre (the lyric) and of a style (romanticism). Art as play unsettles people who look to it for ultimate significance. Artists, however, seek in play a release from stale forms and the possibilities of new combinations. It was too late for Goncharov, but a similar kind of play led in the hands of Chekhov to a vital body of literature, though one much different from what had come before. As for Goncharov, though he had kept relatively aloof from literary circles and isolated himself in the latter half of his life, he had managed over the course of his career to reflect almost every literary current of prose fiction in his age: the whimsically romantic story of the thirties, the physiological sketch of the forties, the biographical novel of the fifties, the novel of social conflict of the sixties, and a return in the last two decades of his life to the sketch and anecdote, which in several instances exhibited a new emerging style—more terse and spare than that of the realistic manner. His career, whatever else we can learn from it, testifies to the force of tradition in shaping works of art.

A Selected Bibliography

A. D. Alekseev's *Bibliografiya I. A. Goncharova: 1832-1964* (Leningrad, 1968), and *Letopis' zhizni i tvorchestva I. A. Goncharova* (Moscow-Leningrad, 1960) have made an extensive bibliography unnecessary. The list below does not include all works consulted or referred to in this study, but is limited to accessible and important texts of Goncharov's writings, and scholarly and critical works concerned in part or entirely with Goncharov and of historical or intrinsic interest.

By Goncharov

IN RUSSIAN

Literaturno-kriticheskie stat'i i pis'ma, ed. A. P. Rybasov. Leningrad, 1938.

"Neizdannye stikhi," *Zvezda*, No. 5 (1938), pp. 243-246.

Neizvestnye glavy "Obryva," ed. V. F. Pereverzev. Moscow, 1926.

"Neobyknovennaya istoriya." Neizdannaya rukopis' I. A. Goncharova. *Sbornik Rossiskoy Publichnoy biblioteki.* II, No. 1: *Materialy i issledovaniya,* 7-189. Petrograd, 1924.

Povesti i ocherki, ed. B. M. Engel'gardt. Leningrad, 1937.

Sobranie sochineniy. 8 vols. Moscow: Pravda, Biblioteka Ogonyok, 1952.

Sobranie sochineniy. 8 vols. Moscow: Goslitizdat, 1952-1955.

ENGLISH TRANSLATIONS

A Common Story, trans. Constance Garnett. London-New York, 1894.

Oblomov, trans. Natalie Duddington. London-New York, 1929.

Oblomov, trans. Ann Dunnigan. New York, 1963. Probably the best.

Oblomov, trans. David Magarshack. Harmondsworth, Eng., 1954.

The Precipice, trans. M. Bryant. New York, 1916. Abridged beyond recognition.

The Same Old Story, trans. Ivy Litvinov. Moscow, 1957. Includes excerpts from "Better Late Than Never."

The Voyage of the Frigate Pallada, ed. and trans. N. W. Wilson. London, 1965.

ABOUT GONCHAROV

Annensky, I. "Goncharov i ego *Oblomov,*" *Russkaya shkola,* No. 4 (April 1892), pp. 71-95.

Aykhenval'd, Yu. *Siluety russkikh pisateley.* 2d edn. Moscow, 1908.

Baring, Maurice. *An Outline of Russian Literature.* New York, 1944.

Belinsky, V. G. "Vzglyad na russkuyu literaturu 1847 goda," in *Sobranie sochineniy,* ed. F. M. Golovenchenko, III, 802-821. Moscow, 1948.

Beysov, P. S. *Goncharov i rodnoy kray.* 2d edn. Kuybyshev, 1960.

Beysov, P. S., ed. *Materialy yubileynoy Goncharovskoy konferentsii.* Ul'yanovsk, 1963.

Brodskaya, V. B. "Yazyk i stil' romana I. A. Goncharova *Obykno-*

vennaya istoriya," *Voprosy slavyanskogo yazykoznaniya,* No. 3 (1953), pp. 129-154, No. 4 (1955), pp. 203-230.

Chemena, O. *Sozdanie dvukh romanov.* Moscow, 1966.

Demikhovskaya, O. "Neizvestnaya povest' I. A. Goncharova 'Nimfodora Ivanovna,'" *Russkaya literatura,* No. 1 (1960), pp. 139-144.

Desnitsky, V. "Trilogiya Goncharova," in *Izbrannye stat'i po russkoy literature XVIII-XIX vekov.* Moscow-Leningrad, 1958.

Dobrolyubov, N. A. "Chto takoe oblomovshchina," in *Izbrannye sochineniya,* ed. A. Lavretsky. Moscow-Leningrad, 1947.

[Druzhinin, A. V.] Review of *Russkie v Yaponii v nachale 1853 i v kontse 1854 godov, Sovremennik,* No. 1 (1856), Part III, pp. 1-25.

Efremov, A. G. "Yazyk i stil' IX glavy romana I. A. Goncharova *Oblomov,"* *Russkiy yazyk v shkole,* No. 2 (March-April 1962), pp. 27-34.

Engel'gardt, B. M. Introduction to *I. A. Goncharov i I. S. Turgenev po neizdannym materialam Pushkinskogo doma,* ed. B. M. Engel'gardt. Petersburg, 1923.

———. Introduction to "Putevye pis'ma I. A. Goncharova iz krugosvetnogo plavaniya," *Literaturnoe nasledstvo,* Nos. 22-24 (1935), pp. 309-343.

Evgen'ev-Maksimov, V. E. *I. A. Goncharov.* Moscow, 1925.

Favorin, V. K. "O vzaimodeystvii avtorskoy rechi i rechi personazhey v yazyke trilogii Goncharova," *Izvestiya Akademii nauk SSSR: otdelenie literatury i yazyka,* IX, No. 5 (1950), 351-361.

Freeborn, Richard. *The Rise of the Russian Novel: Studies in the Russian Novel from Eugene Onegin to War and Peace.* Cambridge, England, 1973.

Gančikov, Leonida. "In tema di 'Oblomovismo,'" *Ricerche slavistiche,* IV (1955-1956), 169-175.

Gifford, Henry. *The Hero of His Time.* London, 1950.

———. *The Novel in Russia: From Pushkin to Pasternak.* New York, 1965.

Grigor'ev, Apollon. "Russkaya literatura v 1851 godu," and "I. S. Turgenev i ego deyatel'nost' (po povodu romana *Dvoryan-*

skoe gnezdo)," in *Sochineniya*, I, 31-32, 414-424, 446-447. St. Petersburg, 1876.

Harrison, Jane Ellen. *Aspects, Aorists and the Classical Tripos*. Cambridge, 1919.

Krasnoshchekova, E. *"Oblomov" I. A. Goncharova*. Moscow, 1970.

Kropotkin, P. *Ideals and Realities in Russian Literature*. New York, 1915.

Labriolle, François de. "Oblomov n'est-il qu'un paresseux?" *Cahiers du monde russe et soviétique*, x, No. 1 (January-March 1969), 38-51.

Lavretsky, A. *Esteticheskie vzglyady russkikh pisateley: sbornik statey*. Moscow, 1963.

Lavrin, Janko. *Goncharov*. New Haven, 1954.

Likhachev, D. S. *Poetika drevnerusskoy literatury*. Leningrad, 1967.

Louria, Yvette, and Seiden, Morton I. "Ivan Goncharov's Oblomov: The Anti-Faust as Christian Hero," *Canadian Slavic Studies*, III, No. 1 (Spring 1969), 39-68.

Lukács, Georg. *The Theory of the Novel*, trans. Anna Bostock. Cambridge, Mass., 1971.

Lyatsky, E. *Goncharov: zhizn', lichnost', tvorchestvo, kritiko-biograficheskie ocherki*. 3d edn. Stockholm, 1920.

———. *Roman i zhizn': razvitie tvorcheskoy lichnosti I. A. Goncharova*. Prague, 1925.

Lyngstad, Alexandra and Sverre. *Ivan Goncharov*. New York, 1971.

Macauley, Robie. "The Superfluous Man," *Partisan Review*, XIX, No. 2 (March-April 1952), 169-182.

Manning, Clarence A. "Ivan Aleksandrovich Goncharov," *The South Atlantic Quarterly*, XXVI (1927), 63-75.

———. "The Neglect of Time in the Russian Novel," in *Slavic Studies*, ed. Alexander Kaun and Ernest J. Simmons. Ithaca, N. Y., 1943.

Masaryk, Thomas G. *The Spirit of Russia*, ed. George Gibian; trans. Robert Bass. Vol. III. New York, 1967.

Matlaw, Ralph E., ed. *Belinsky, Chernyshevsky, and Dobrolyubov: Selected Criticism*. New York, 1962.

Mays, Milton A. "Oblomov as Anti-Faust," *Western Humanities Review,* XXI, No. 2 (Spring 1967), 141-152.

Mazon, André. *Ivan Gontcharov: un maître du roman russe.* Paris, 1914.

Merezhkovsky, D. S. *Polnoe sobranie sochineniy.* Vol. XVIII: *Vechnye sputniki.* Moscow, 1914.

Mikhel'son, V. A. *Gumanizm I. A. Goncharova i kolonial'nyy vopros.* Krasnodar, 1965.

Miliukov, Paul. *Outlines of Russian Culture,* ed. Michael Karpovich; trans. Valentine Ughet and Eleanor Davis. Vol. II: *Literature.* New York, 1942.

Miller, Orest. *Russkie pisateli posle Gogolya.* Vol. II. Moscow-St. Petersburg, 1907.

Mirsky, D. S. *A History of Russian Literature: From Its Beginnings to 1900.* Rev. edn., ed. Francis J. Whitfield. New York, 1949.

Moser, Charles A. *Antinihilism in the Russian Novel of the 1860's.* The Hague, 1964.

Narokov, N. "Opravdanie Oblomova," *Novyy zhurnal,* LIX (1960), 95-108.

Neumann, B. "Die Gončarov-Forschung, 1918-1928," *Zeitschrift für slavische Philologie,* VII (1930), 153-178.

Ostrogorsky, V. *Etyudy o russkikh pisatelyakh.* Vol. I. Moscow, 1888.

Ovsyaniko-Kulikovsky, D. "I. A. Goncharov," *Vestnik Evropy,* No. 6 (1912), pp. 193-210.

Ovsyaniko-Kulikovsky, D., ed. *Istoriya russkoy literatury XIX veka.* Vol. III. Moscow, 1910.

Pereverzev, V. F. "K voprosu o monisticheskom ponimanii tvorchestva Goncharova," *Literaturovedenie,* ed. V. F. Pereverzev, pp. 201-229. Moscow, 1928.

———. "K voprosu o sotsial'nom genezise tvorchestva Goncharova," *Pechat' i revolyutsiya,* No. 1 (January 1923), pp. 32-45, No. 2 (February-March 1923), pp. 34-47.

———. "Sotsial'nyy genezis oblomovshchiny," *Pechat' i revolyutsiya,* No. 2 (March-April 1925), pp. 61-78.

————. "Tragediya khudozhestvennogo tvorchestva u Goncharova," *Vestnik Sotsialisticheskoy akademii*, No. 5 (August-September 1923), pp. 164-177.

Piksanov, N. K. *Roman Goncharova "Obryv" v svete sotsial'noy istorii*. Leningrad, 1968.

Piksanov, N. K., ed. *I. A. Goncharov v vospominaniyakh sovremennikov*. Leningrad, 1969.

Poggioli, Renato. "On Goncharov and His *Oblomov*," in *The Phoenix and the Spider*. Cambridge, Mass., 1957.

Pokrovsky, V. I., ed. *I. A. Goncharov, ego zhizn' i sochineniya: sbornik istoriko-literaturnykh statey*. Moscow, 1905.

Polityko, D. A. *Roman I. A. Goncharova "Obryv."* Minsk, 1962.

Polyakov, M. Ya., ed. *I. A. Goncharov v russkoy kritike: sbornik statey*. Moscow, 1958. Includes essays by Belinsky (abridged), Dobrolyubov, Pisarev, Druzhinin, Mikhaylovsky, Saltykov-Shchedrin, and others.

Pritchett, V. S. *The Living Novel*. London, 1946.

Protopopov, M. A. "Goncharov," *Russkaya mysl'* (November 1891), pp. 107-131.

Prutskov, N. I. *Masterstvo Goncharova-romanista*. Moscow-Leningrad, 1962.

————. "Romany Goncharova," in *Istoriya russkogo romana*, ed. G. M. Fridlender, I, 514-559. Moscow-Leningrad, 1962.

Prutskov, N. I., and Malakhov, S. A. "Poslednie romany Turgeneva i Goncharova," in *Istoriya russkogo romana*, ed. G. M. Fridlender, II, 149-192. Moscow-Leningrad, 1964.

Rapp, Helen. "The Art of Ivan Goncharov," *The Slavonic and East European Review*, XXXVI (1957-1958), 370-395.

Raynov, T. "*Obryv* Goncharova, kak khudozhestvennoe tseloe," *Voprosy teorii i psikhologii tvorchestva*, VII (1916), 32-75.

Reeve, F. D. "Oblomovka Revisited," *The American Slavic and East European Review*, XV (1956), 112-118.

————. *The Russian Novel*. New York, 1966.

Rehm, Walter. "Gontscharow und die Langeweile," in *Experimentum medietatis*. Munich, 1947.

Rybasov, A. *I. A. Goncharov*. Moscow, 1962.

Setchkarev, V. "Andrej Štolc in Gončarov's *Oblomov*: An Attempted Reinterpretation," *To Honor Roman Jakobson: Essays on the Occasion of His Seventieth Birthday*, III, 1799-1805. Janua linguarum. Series maior, vol. XXXIII. The Hague-Paris, 1967.

Shklovsky, Viktor. *Zametki o proze russkikh klassikov*. Moscow, 1955.

Slonim, Marc. *The Epic of Russian Literature: From Its Origins through Tolstoy*. New York, 1950.

Solov'ev, A. *I. A. Goncharov*. St. Petersburg, 1910.

Stender-Petersen, Adolf. *Geschichte der russischen Literatur*. Munich, 1957.

Stilman, Leon. "Oblomovka Revisited," *The American Slavic and East European Review*, VII (1948), 45-77.

Superansky, M. "Vospitanie I. A. Goncharova," *Russkaya shkola*, Nos. 5-6 (May-June 1912), pp. 1-19.

Ter-Mikel'yan, S. G. "Bol'naya dusha Goncharova," *Russkiy filologicheskiy vestnik*, Nos. 1-2 (1917), pp. 20-46.

Tschižewskij, Dmitrij. *Russische Literaturgeschichte des 19. Jahrhunderts*. Vol. II: *Der Realismus*. Munich, 1967.

Tseytlin, A. G. "Goncharov-kritik," in *Istoriya russkoy kritiki*, ed. B. P. Gorodetsky, II, 288-302. Moscow-Leningrad, 1958.

―――. *I. A. Goncharov*. Moscow, 1950.

―――. " 'Schastlivaya oshibka' Goncharova kak ranniy etyud *Obyknovennoy istorii*," in *Tvorcheskaya istoriya*, ed. N. K. Piksanov, pp. 124-153. Moscow, 1927.

―――. *Stanovlenie realizma v russkoy literature: russkiy fiziologicheskiy ocherk*. Moscow, 1965.

Utevsky, L. S. "Vokrug *Obryva*," *Literaturnoe nasledstvo*, Nos. 22-24 (1935), pp. 755-764.

―――. *Zhizn' Goncharova*. Moscow, 1931.

Vengerov, S. A. "Druzhinin, Goncharov, Pisemsky," in *Sobranie sochineniy*, V, 61-96. St. Petersburg, 1911.

Woodhouse, C. M. "The Two Russians," *Essays by Divers Hands: Being the Transactions of the Royal Society of Literature*, XXIX, 18-36. London, 1958.

Zakharkin, A. F. *Roman I. A. Goncharova, "Oblomov."* Moscow, 1963.

Index of Proper Names and Titles

STUDIES OF THE RUSSIAN INSTITUTE

PUBLISHED BY COLUMBIA UNIVERSITY PRESS

THAD PAUL ALTON, *Polish Postwar Economy*

JOHN A. ARMSTRONG, *Ukrainian Nationalism*

ABRAM BERGSON, *Soviet National Income and Product in 1937*

HARVEY L. DYCK, *Weimar Germany and Soviet Russia, 1926-1933: A Study in Diplomatic Instability*

RALPH TALCOTT FISHER, JR., *Pattern for Soviet Youth: A Study of the Congresses of the Komsomol, 1918-1954*

MAURICE FRIEDBERG, *Russian Classics in Soviet Jackets*

ELLIOT R. GOODMAN, *The Soviet Design for a World State*

DAVID GRANICK, *Management of the Industrial Firm in the USSR: A Study in Soviet Economic Planning*

THOMAS TAYLOR HAMMOND, *Lenin on Trade Unions and Revolution, 1893-1917*

JOHN N. HAZARD, *Settling Disputes in Soviet Society: The Formative Years of Legal Institutions*

DAVID JORAVSKY, *Soviet Marxism and Natural Science, 1917-1932*

DAVID MARSHALL LANG, *The Last Years of the Georgian Monarchy, 1658-1832*

GEORGE S.N. LUCKYJ, *Literary Politics in the Soviet Ukraine, 1917-1934*

HERBERT MARCUSE, *Soviet Marxism: A Critical Analysis*

KERMIT E. MC KENZIE, *Comintern and World Revolution, 1928-1943: The Shaping of Doctrine*

CHARLES B. MC LANE, *Soviet Policy and the Chinese Communists, 1931-1946*

JAMES WILLIAM MORLEY, *The Japanese Thrust into Siberia, 1918*

ALEXANDER G. PARK, *Bolshevism in Turkestan, 1917-1927*

MICHAEL BORO PETROVICH, *The Emergence of Russian Panslavism, 1856-1870*

OLIVER H. RADKEY, *The Agrarian Foes of Bolshevism: Promise and Default of the Russian Socialist Revolutionaries, February to October, 1917*

OLIVER H. RADKEY, *The Sickle Under the Hammer: The Russian Socialist Revolutionaries in the Early Months of Soviet Rule*

ALFRED J. RIEBER, *Stalin and the French Communist Party, 1941-1947*

ALFRED ERICH SENN, *The Emergence of Modern Lithuania*

ERNEST J. SIMMONS, editor, *Through the Glass of Soviet Literature: Views of Russian Society*

THEODORE K. VON LAUE, *Sergei Witte and the Industrialization of Russia*

ALLEN S. WHITING, *Soviet Policies in China, 1917-1924*

Published by Teachers College Press

HAROLD J. NOAH, *Financing Soviet Schools*

Published by Princeton University Press

PAUL AVRICH, *The Russian Anarchists*
PAUL AVRICH, *Kronstadt 1921*
EDWARD J. BROWN, *Mayakovsky: A Poet in the Revolution*
LOREN R. GRAHAM, *The Soviet Academy of Sciences and the Communist Party, 1927-1932*
PATRICIA K. GRIMSTED, *Archives and Manuscript Repositories in the USSR: Moscow and Leningrad*
ROBERT A. MAGUIRE, *Red Virgin Soil: Soviet Literature in the 1920's*
T. H. RIGBY, *Communist Party Membership in the U.S.S.R., 1917-1967*
RONALD G. SUNY, *The Baku Commune, 1917-1918*
JOHN M. THOMPSON, *Russia, Bolshevism, and the Versailles Peace*
WILLIAM ZIMMERMAN, *Soviet Perspectives on International Relations, 1956-1967*

Published by Cambridge University Press

JONATHAN FRANKEL, *Vladimir Akimov on the Dilemmas of Russian Marxism, 1895-1903*
EZRA MENDELSOHN, *Class Struggle in the Pale: The Formative Years of the Jewish Workers' Movement in Tsarist Russia*

Published by the University of Michigan Press

RICHARD T. DE GEORGE, *Soviet Ethics and Morality*

Library of Congress Cataloging in Publication Data

Ehre, Milton, 1933-
    Oblomov and his creator.
    (Studies of the Russian Institute, Columbia
University)
    Bibliography: p.
    1. Goncharov, Ivan Aleksandrovich, 1812-1891.
I. Title. II. Series: Columbia University.
Russian Institute. Studies.
PG3337.G6Z633   891.7′3′3   72-5378
ISBN 0-691-06245-5